Sex and Money

Behind the Scenes with
the Big-Time Brokers

JOHN D. SPOONER

1985

HOUGHTON MIFFLIN COMPANY ∽ BOSTON

Library of Congress Cataloging in Publication Data

Spooner, John D.
  Sex and money.

  1. Brokers.   2. Stocks.   I. Title.
HG4621.S745   1985   332.6'2 [B]   84-22570
ISBN 0-395-35408-0

Printed in the United States of America

V 10 9 8 7 6 5 4 3 2 1

For my family, all the Spooners
and the Fines in their various disguises.
And for Katy, who knows that
"God is good and Jack is fishin'."

Money, which represents the prose of life, and which
is hardly spoken of in parlors without an apology,
is, in its effects and laws, as beautiful as roses.

— *Ralph Waldo Emerson*

The omnipresent process of sex, as it is woven
into the whole texture of our man's or woman's body,
is the pattern of all the process of our life.

— *Havelock Ellis*

Contents

SEX AND MONEY

1

Some of the Players and Some of the Rules

You think the investment business is stuffy? You think people sit around brokerage offices making important decisions involving millions of dollars with cold rational judgment? I work in a carnival, in a carnival atmosphere, and so does every stockbroker and money manager in America. When Wall Street went down the drain in 1970 and hundreds of respected firms disappeared, my company (or what was left of it) was swallowed by a survivor, and I was told to report to a new office in a different part of the city. I had lost all of my capital in the old firm; clients were shocked and bleeding with the collapse of prices. I carried my books of customer records to my new job feeling very much like Nicholas Nickleby, buffeted by ill fortune, with a family to support, an orphan of the Wall Street wars.

Remember starting in a new school? The stares, the real and imagined whispers of strangers, the anxieties? I carried my account books through the new board room on the fortieth floor of a new building. The conference room had been converted for my use as a private office, and I heard people yelling as I approached. "You bastard," I heard someone screaming. "You son-of-a-bitch," someone else called. I heard clapping and whistles. In front of my office door two men were rolling over on the floor, pummeling each other, cursing. Several other people reached in and pulled them apart, holding on tightly, preventing them from reaching each other.

Tempers cooled and I was introduced. The battlers were Tony Corvo, the head of the back office, the bookkeeping department, and David Ward, a broker in a three-piece suit who had gone to Princeton and hunted ducks. The back office is where the accounting is done in a stockbroker's office. Tony's job was to supervise all figuring of debits and credits, hire and fire secretaries, and, on this day, clean out the conference room for my use. David Ward had been storing his prior years' tax returns in a file drawer there. Tony had emptied all the drawers into a huge trash bin. David's tax returns lay among Chinese take-out lunches, butts from a hundred ashtrays, and all the dirty paper towels from ladies' and men's rooms. David Ward had exploded when he learned of this and tried to stuff Tony into the bin on top of uneaten egg rolls and duck sauce.

"I'm sorry to be the cause of all that," I said to Tony later.

"Not to worry," he said. "The preppie needed a lesson." Tony was in his office, folding up very carefully a New York *Daily News.* He was folding the paper into a shape that made it very hard, a weapon. "This is a Brooklyn war club," he said. "It can kill a man, see?" Tony whacked it against his desk. It made tiny marks in the metal. "We don't get mad," he said; "we get *even* in Brooklyn."

Later I apologized to David Ward, wanting to cover all bases.

"Can you imagine that ginzo throwing out my old tax

records?" he said. "I just saw red. One reason I went so crazy is that my father was an investment banker and he served eleven months in jail for not filing tax returns for *ten years*. Do you believe it? He advised other people on tax implications in their business decisions and he just never filed. Claimed he was too busy for several years, missed deadlines, and forgot. After that he was frozen at the switch, couldn't do it at all. I think the thought of my not having proof that *I* filed drove me temporarily nuts.

"But that's why we're in this business," he said. "You've got to be a little crazy to handle it. For years I couldn't talk about my father's serving time in jail. But I've been seeing a psychiatrist. He got me shaken loose. So now I tell everyone."

I settled into my office and determined to keep all my tax records at home. That was my introduction to the new firm — a fist fight on the floor, with the other employees cheering on the fighters. That night I told a client about the incident. He was a seventy-year-old corporate lawyer who had seen it all. "That's a wonderful spot to work," he told me. "A place of emotion is a great place to make a lot of money. A place of emotion is the best of all places to spend your days. But it's a *terrible* place for your nights."

* * *

January 1983. That was ten years ago, and he was right. We're still on the fortieth floor: fifty-five stockbrokers, twenty-seven secretaries, ten back-office and support personnel, one office manager, an eight-person institutional department dealing with banks, insurance companies, and mutual funds. And we have Sebastian, the messenger, an elderly fascist who pinches women in elevators, cafeteria lines, and while waiting to drop packages at the post office. His job is to sort and deliver the mail and run legal documents from building to building in the financial district. We put up with his being a fascist because he comes in every day on time, never wants a vacation, and works for virtually the minimum wage. We would hire Hitler if he worked for the minimum wage.

There are two ways to really know people. One is to live with them; the other is to handle their money. Fear and greed dictate the fluctuations of the stock market; it is emotion that makes the game, just as it rules our lives. I should know. I handle and manage money for over thirty-five hundred clients, male and female, all over the world. They want to talk about more than their money; they want to talk about their lives.

We are in the midst of a wonderful time now in financial markets: greed is rampant. Stockbrokers who were taking second jobs bartending a year ago are now talking about second *homes* and six-figure incomes. "Ronald Reagan wants a healthy, booming stock market," a client recently told me. "I'm informed that his blind trusts are loaded with Dow Jones companies. The average (now at almost eleven hundred) is headed for fifteen hundred, an all-time high. The boom is on." In the winter in the East it is popular to talk about where in the world you are going for vacations: Florida, Arizona, the Caribbean Islands. No one is talking about vacations this winter. Everyone in the investment business is too busy making money.

There are many new names for stockbrokers in the modern investment business. Some firms call them registered representatives, some financial consultants, some others investment executives. I am concentrating on the action of the Street in this book, not on tax shelters, not on insurance or annuities, not on mortgages. This book is for the people who are hoping to see a dollar grow into four or five dollars. For that we have stockbrokers, and the new titles obscure what most of us like to do best. (The Street, of course, is Wall Street, but wherever the action of the stock market is, the people involved refer to themselves as being "in the Street," that is, in the investment business. We may be in Little Rock or Kansas City, but a little piece of us always knows that the heart of the beast is in lower Manhattan.)

4

Every office is a family; every office has its rituals. Big Jimmy Minot blows his whistle each morning at 10:00 A.M. to signal the beginning of trading. He blows a regulation U.S. Army brass whistle that he wears around his neck to ward off potential muggers and to use as exclamation point at the end of important sentences. Big Jimmy Minot has the office next to mine. He makes a good living as a trustee. A trustee usually watches the investments, or directs the investments, of large pools of capital. Jimmy, though, makes no decisions. He places the money with investment advisers who, when they buy and sell, put all the trades through Big Jimmy. He pockets the commissions.

Jimmy is one of the most honest people I know. After he blows his whistle every morning, he yells out, "Do I know anything? If I knew anything, I wouldn't be in this business." Not exactly an inspiration to the young brokers. But Big Jimmy must blow his whistle and tell his truth. And wait by his phone to take the orders.

After the whistle is blown in the morning, a cowbell is rung by Mad Mark the Institutional Salesman. Mad Mark keeps a cowbell on his desk because he is superstitious. All people in the money business are superstitious. One broker I know will never buy a stock beginning with the letter c; another will never buy a computer company; one friend of mine who left the business to make cheese in Vermont would never buy a company whose home office was in Dallas. All of these superstitions arose because these people got burned in companies that had the characteristics they will forever avoid.

Mad Mark the Institutional Salesman is an intellectual. One of the few in his end of the business who has ever read a Russian novel. Mark was given the cowbell by an oil-exploration company in which he had invested as a tax shelter. "Every time we hit a gut buster [a producing well]," he was told, "the news will be on the Dow Jones ticker. You ring that bell, Mr. Mark; you'll be getting rich." All the Dow Jones announcements sub-

5

sequently were about dry holes, more assessments (extra payments) for Mark, and empty dreams. Mark rings the bell at every sad announcement, hoping reverse psychology will work. Big Jimmy tells him, "You can ring that bell till the cows come home, before that outfit will find oil. That's why it's a cowbell." Jimmy's whistle drowns out Mark's bell; the market opens at ten o'clock in the morning; the prices are off and running.

Our offices take an entire floor of a midtown bank building. There is a small reception area with a switchboard and operator and various green plants that fight a losing battle with the surrounding high-rise buildings. From this area, subdued and quiet, you enter the main board room, bursting with the clatter of the ticker, teletype machines, newsprinters' Dow Jones and Reuters, phones, and constant chatter. Private offices run the length of the rear wall, the bigger producers (brokers generating more than a quarter-million in gross commissions a year, of which their share is roughly 40 percent before taxes) occupying the most space.

The office manager is tucked in the midst of these prima donnas in an office of his own, with a couch, a quotation machine, family pictures, and recruiting posters from the U.S. Marine Corps ("a few good men"). The manager is Elliot Smith, ex-Marine, ex–college jock. He squeezes a squash ball most of the day, alternating hands. He also pushes against his desk drawers for isometric exercise. It's no fun to shake hands with Elliot. He has a three-word motto, done in needlepoint above his quote machine. *Up your gross* is his motto. This means that he is solely dedicated to improving all of his salesmen's gross commission figures. We call him "Up-Your-Gross" Smith, and he considers it a compliment. An ell off the main board room houses Mad Mark and the institutional section. The private offices along that wall contain Big Jimmy Minot; next to him, in the corner, looking over the city, is me.

You must know that under the tumult in brokerage offices

lies the truth. And the truth is this: What are your numbers? How much business do you do? I have a corner office and no delusions. I have bookshelves, an Oriental on the floor, mementos of past victories on the walls, framed book jackets, the photos of the best-looking members of my family, a small ice chest, ficus trees, flowering plants, and no delusions. The day my numbers stop, I know very well that out will go the bookshelves, the photos into a box. The ice chest will be sold at a discount to the new occupant. Stockbrokers lease their space from their employers. We create a commission dollar. The firm takes from this dollar *roughly* 60 percent. For the 60 percent they provide you with a desk, quotation machines, phones, a secretary, and more sales help in terms of product and research than you ever thought possible.

* * *

This is a good place to explore and expose a myth. I plan to discuss several myths in this book. This myth involves the money that stockbrokers make; it is called the Myth of the Customers' Yachts.

You know the story of the stockbroker showing off his new yacht to a friend and the friend says, "Yes, but where are the customers' yachts?" A man I play squash with said to me last week, "You must have made enough in the last three months to retire." I always nod in agreement or smile slightly when anyone says this to me. The truth is that no broker I know or have heard of has made enough to retire in the last three months. Or indeed in any three months.

In this period the stock market, measured by the Dow Jones average, has advanced some 300 points. The trading volume has broken all records, with 100-million-share days the norm and not the exception. But the truth is that relatively few customers of brokers have participated in this record advance. Why is that? Fear dominated financial markets for almost fourteen months, from March 1981 until the summer of 1982. Since then the explosion upward has been characterized mostly by investors fighting to break even or fearful until very recently to participate at all. The public is never early in the game. Most of the record volume has been caused by institutions moving in and out of large positions, hundreds of thousands of shares at a whack.

Stockbrokers themselves generally own very little stock. Ask your stockbroker what he owns; if he puts his own money into what he recommends to you. Clients never ask this question, and yet it seems obvious. Why should you own what your adviser doesn't touch himself? Most stockbrokers have not participated in this historic rally in prices. For a long time no one in the industry trusted the advance to last. Now, at almost 1100 on the Dow, there is universal feeling that it's too late to jump in. If my squash-playing friend meant that commissions for the last three months have been enough on which to retire, well, no one has ever earned enough commissions in three months to take a walk. Even salesmen of jet aircraft to Middle Eastern oil sheiks. And it's all ordinary income anyway, taxed at the highest rates. Forget the myth of the brokers' yachts. In bear markets they all get repossessed. And no stockbroker worth his salt pays cash for anything.

* * *

January 15. The market is strong today, and I am wandering about the board room, searching for ideas. This is the business of brainpicking. We are always on the hunt for the magical *they* who know all, see all. The phones are constantly in use. The brokers cannot create commissions without making the clients hungry for the product. There is Up-Your-Gross Smith, the manager, peering out from his glass-enclosed office to make sure the phones are not being used for personal reasons. And he can tell. "When the brokers' expressions are relaxed," he says, "I know they're not talking to customers. They're talking to travel agents, they're talking to relatives. We want a high level of intensity in this office, productionwise."

8

The private offices hold people with specialties and with relatively big production numbers. The people who hold down desks in the main board room are either old-timers playing the game out of years of habit, or the youngbloods, brokers on their way up, itching to push the current private-office occupants out into the cold. The youngbloods also push the clients, and they push themselves.

Jane Kaplan is a youngblood. She pushed one husband out into the cold and was lucky enough, in her words, "not to be stuck with a kid." Jane had been trained by Merrill Lynch. Merrill has one of the best training programs in the industry, and most other investment houses can't wait for Merrill's trainees to graduate. They know that many of these young brokers are ripe for the plucking, ripe to be stolen away, leaving the cost of their training to be absorbed by the people who are Bullish on America. When Jane Kaplan first came into our office, she came around to introduce herself. "John," she said, "I won't beat around the bush. What does it take to do a million [in commissions] a year? Frankly," she said, "you don't look so hot to me. What's your gimmick?"

You all know people like Jane. They are known as "room-clearers." The room-clearers have a comment to offend everyone, and they use it in tones that do not allow compromise. Jane Kaplan prospects the way most youngbloods in the securities industry prospect for new business. She cold-calls. This means using the Yellow Pages' listings for doctors and lawyers. It also means using mailing lists specially targeted for professionals or for residents of wealthy suburban towns. Jane worries her prospects like a terrier. I overheard one of her conversations. "Dr. Peters," she said, "you don't know me, but this is Jane Kaplan and this could be one of the lucky days of your life."

Jane is allowed to plow ahead because she *makes people curious*. Seldom do cold-called prospects want to talk with, much less see, the calling brokers. Almost everyone wants to see Jane Kaplan. She is coy on the phone; she teases. "It's so tough to make people greedy for my merchandise over the phone," she says. "So I'm going to make them greedy for *me*." Jane Kaplan is skinny and nervous and wears tailored suits to the office. The male brokers, particularly the youngbloods, dislike her "pushiness." But they're pushy, too. What they really dislike is her success with cold-calling. Last year Jane did $150,000 in gross commissions, which netted her approximately $60,000. She wants a private office.

"Hey, Jane," one of the other youngbloods calls to her. "You see the *Journal* today? You see that a lady Hutton [E. F. Hutton] broker posed nude for *Playboy*? That's a better door-opener than you got."

Jane, on the phone waiting, puts her hand over the speaker. "Up yours, Marvin," she says. And then into the phone, "What is the nature of my call?" she says. "It's about the doctor's emotional future." She gets through to the doctor immediately and launches into her pitch. The youngbloods make faces and know that she'll probably get an order. They call her Jane the Impaler, only in part because she has an old-fashioned spike on her desk, on which she slaps her successful leads.

There are several things you must understand early about the investment business. One of them is that there are a lot of nicknames for the people in the game. This is because nearly all of them believe they are individual entrepreneurs; that they carry their business in their hip pockets. The sky is the limit in any commission business. You can make whatever you can produce. The company takes a slice; you take a slice. In an industry given to large egos, the participants think of themselves as knights errant, killing the dragons of high interest rates, fighting the black knights of lousy research, saving the endangered maidens and the widows at the mercy of the evil lawyers and of even crueler inflation. Stockbrokers like nicknames the way defensive front fours in the National Football League like nicknames.

Another element of the investment business you should

understand is that it is still overwhelmingly a male domain. If sexual harassment in the office were ever pursued by female employees, half the stockbrokers in America would be in jail. Stockbrokers tend to have traditional marriages, wives at home in traditional roles. Or else stockbrokers get divorced. Blurring of roles is a difficult concept for people in the investment world, because it is so easy to keep score in the stock market. You buy a stock at 10. It goes to 11, you have a profit; it goes to 9, you have a loss. That is an easy concept to grasp. So is this. Husband goes to an office. He is the breadwinner. Wife stays at home with the kids in the kitchen. This is one reason women are notably absent from Wall Street board rooms and another reason that secretaries who make waves about their "rights" don't last very long in their jobs.

We have two secretaries in our office who are officially designated "floaters." That is, they work for no specific brokers. They go where they are needed: on the switchboard, filling in for other absent employees, reordering the stockroom. They float. Our floaters, Lisa and Jill, are called the Gold Dust Twins. They are both blond; they both wear sweaters and jeans or tight-fitting slacks to work. They go to dating bars and new wave rock and roll clubs. Last year they went together to Club Med Trinidad and the year before to Paradise Island, where each won something under $50 at roulette. Lisa and Jill also are frequently requested to go out with clients visiting from other cities, with supervisors and auditors from headquarters in New York, and with securities analysts in town to do research on local companies. Lisa and Jill always go on these dates. They are not paid to do so, but the evenings are always on the expense account of the firm.

"Will you date a client of mine coming in from Saint Louis?" Big Jimmy Minot asked Lisa recently.

"What's he like? Is he married?" she asked suspiciously.

"He's a big client," Jimmy said. "His company makes beer in the Midwest is all you need to know, and he loves to spend money."

Lisa shrugged her approval. "I never met anyone who makes beer. Just people who drink it. Why shouldn't I go on an expense account date? What I do is less dangerous than being a stewardess, right?" The floaters can always find a silver lining.

There are 146,000 registered stockbrokers in America. Less than ten percent of them are women. And of those, a significant number are so-called investment assistants; that is, secretaries who are authorized to place orders for their bosses' clients. Jane the Impaler Kaplan is a bona fide stockbroker. As I pause by her desk, she covers up the screen of her Quotron, the computer quote machine that monitors the market. Every broker has his favorite companies constantly updated on the bottom of the screen, a permanent reminder of the state of his personal little empire. Jane was covering the screen with her hand so that I wouldn't see her current selections. "For Christ's sake, Jane," I said, "you think I'm going to steal your stocks?"

"I know you're not, Spooner," she said, "because you're not going to see what they are."

"Jane," I responded, "come *on*. We're all on the same team."

"I'll be on the same team," she said, "when I'm in your office and you're out on the floor. What do you think this is, a game? This is my *life*. Hey, Jill" — she turned away from me and signaled to one of the Gold Dust Twins — "would you and Lisa be free tonight maybe for dinner with a couple of corporate lawyers?"

"Gee, I'm sorry, Jane," Jill said. "We promised a long time ago to do something with Smitty [Up-Your-Gross Smith]. Besides, lawyers never talk to *us*. They just talk to each other." Jill moved away to the Xerox machine. Jane the Impaler fumed. "You see what women have to put up with?" she said. "It isn't enough we have to dig in twice as hard; we have to stand in line for the goddamned floaters."

* * *

January 27. There is an item in the *Wall Street Journal* today that will teach you one of the most important of all lessons about the stock market. Here it is. "Purcell, Graham and Company, a New York Stock Exchange member firm, sends clients a report updating the Super Bowl stock market predictor theory. The bottom line: it will be bearish if the Dolphins win Sunday, bullish if the Redskins win." The Redskins won, 27 to 17. Superstitions abound in stock market analysis, as they do among brokers. And that's natural, because it is a business of fear and greed, of emotion. The market is an Alice-in-Wonderland business. It really has nothing at all to do with housing starts, money supply, auto sales, or interest rates. It has to do with emotions. The people who are the most successful investors are the people who are good at predicting human behavior patterns. Remember this when you wonder why the market is going up when everyone in your industry says that business is terrible. Remember this when your company cuts a dividend and the stock goes *up*; remember this when you buy the stock market on wonderful news like the end of a war or the end of a long strike, and you wonder why prices suddenly head *down*. *The stock market is a state of mind.* Resisting your natural impulses to be euphoric or full of panic when the media demand these reactions will be your first step toward profit.

Jane the Impaler had asked me what my gimmick was. Anyone who has been a successful investor has developed formulae that have served him well over the years. Some successful investors or money managers buy emerging technologies and concentrate on firms in high-growth areas, companies like Digital Computer, Wang, and Apple. Others use fundamental analysis, approaching companies by combing their balance sheets and income statements, looking for hidden meanings that can lead to turnarounds in basic business and profits. There are technical analysts also, who plot price history and trading-volume history for companies and markets and claim to see patterns on their graphs and charts. If you play tennis or golf and find success with highly unorthodox swings, it doesn't matter whether you have classic form. The payoff is a drive down the middle or a passing shot that wins a point. The result is what counts. The same thing is true in the investment world. If you deal with a broker who has a rundown office over a candy store and the candy store owner has to call him to the phone *and he makes you money*, that's all that counts. Chic stands for nothing in the investment business. Does he make you money is all that counts.

We Americans have always needed diversion in our lives, national pastimes and crazes that lift us outside our particular daily routines. Gold rushes and frontiers have vanished. Mahjong and canasta are replaced by Monopoly and Scrabble, then video games, then Trivial Pursuit. But in this century, periods of underlying personal anxiety have been characterized by concentration on speculation, gambling, the desire to make and accumulate money. In the 1920s the stock market raged with action as fortunes were won and lost, and everyone traded on margin (credit) — until the fever burst in the Great Depression. In the 1960s, during Vietnam, there were fears that our society was being torn apart. At the same time, millions of people thronged to the stock market to enjoy the action, which took them away from their larger fears. The more anxiety we have, the more we try to drown it in money. There is a record divorce rate in America; there are record numbers of single-parent families with record numbers of children in broken homes. Men do not know what to expect from relationships. Women know better what they expect but are bitterly disappointed that what they expect is not available. What a perfect era for wild stock markets, everyone playing a hand, everyone in the pool for profit!

* * *

More people are applying for jobs in the investment industry than at any other time in history. The prudent and the patient and the people who truly want to take advantage of the frenzy will find that there is a sure way to make money in the stock market . . . if they are mature enough to handle it.

14

Most huge profits in the market in the last ten years have been in companies that the average person of substance has never heard of, or in companies that seem so boring that no one would buy them if you called him and solicited his order. I call the use of this phenomenon the *Hart, Schaffner & Marx Gambit*. The Hart, Schaffner & Marx Gambit is too boring for ordinary investors or speculators. You have to want seriously to make money to follow it. It takes time. It doesn't happen in a month or two. Here's how the Hart, Schaffner & Marx Gambit works. First, we approach it from the conventional brokerage point of view:

December 7, 1978:

BROKER: Manny, I've got a great cheap stock for you. They're giving it away.

MANNY, THE CUSTOMER: Are you gonna keep me in suspense until the last act? What is it, and how much?

BROKER: It's Hart, Schaffner and Marx, and it's nine and a half.

MANNY: (Silence.)

BROKER: Are you there, Manny?

MANNY: For recommendations on Hart, Schaffner and Marx, I have to go to my broker? I could go to my tailor. I like things that are *hot*. Is this high technology? Is this energy?

BROKER: If I told you that within two years you can sell this stock for better than two times what you paid for it . . . plus an eight percent dividend, what would you say?

MANNY: I'd say, How do I know I'm gonna live that long?

This is the key to the Hart, Schaffner & Marx Gambit: most people with money in the stock market care more about action than they do about capital gains. The average customer would be so annoyed watching Hart, Schaffner & Marx trade for fourteen months between 9½ and 11 that he would call in disgust to say "I don't care what it's selling for. It's boring. You're boring. Sell it and send me the check."

Hart, Schaffner & Marx was an undervalued asset when I

first bought it at 9½ in July of 1979. It paid an eighty-cent dividend, 8 percent. Not much by recent memory's inflated return standards, but I believe in getting something while you wait. You are nothing but lucky if you buy at the low or sell at the high. Play the game between the extremes; you will always make money. Finding value and realizing its potential takes time. It usually takes years for an artist or a sculptor to realize the potential *you* may have recognized years ago. The land you bought on the marsh awaiting the shopping centers could sit there sucking up interest charges for decades before the developers see what you saw. The trouble with the stock market is that you can see prices *every day*, every hour if you choose.

Hart, Schaffner & Marx has been a better investment over a two-year period than any artist, any development, any coin, any antique. But because it was not as interesting, because the price could be seen each day, emotion entered the equation. And most people, after months of watching the stock do nothing, ran like thieves with a net profit of a point. *Action* in the stock market is more important to almost everyone than capital gains. Do you really want to make money? I sold Hart, Schaffner & Marx for a small account at 23. It was August 12, 1981, and the market, based on the Dow Jones average, had gone *down* almost a hundred points in the previous nine weeks. The Hart, Schaffner & Marx Gambit is impervious to stock market disasters. Such companies have a rhythm all their own. They are boring. But they don't collapse in bear markets; they seldom rise in the frenzy of greedy bull modes. In time, though, they will outperform anything you can do with your money. More important, in the latter years of the 1980s, they will become the vehicles to make you rich. (For you purists, yes I know that Hart, Schaffner & Marx has changed its name to Hartmarx. Standard Oil of New Jersey is also now Exxon. But it doesn't mean that I approve.)

Americans love the fad of the moment; we are a nation that loves to pay for status. And no place on earth is more trend-conscious than Wall Street, a shepherd's delight. You want to get rich, you have to concentrate on *value*. This is where the explosion in prices is going to come, and this, if you have the patience, is where you should be. Let me illustrate the boring fundamental approach to getting rich on value. The following table illustrates examples of buying value when it is out of favor and ignored. The companies are those I recommended in a cover story in *New York* magazine in January 1975. They were the only companies I mentioned.

SECURITY	1/75	8/1/78	8/5/81
Gerber Products	9	31	(offer at 38) 31
Hershey Foods Corp.	9	22	33
Papercraft Corp.	7	21½	33
Coke of Los Angeles	8½	40	40 (takeover)
General Cinema Corp.	6	42	70 (figuring splits)
Keyes Fibre Co.	12	35	35 (takeover)
Triangle Pacific Corp.	5	44	37

See how long it took for value to appear? Two years, three years, five years. But the choices beat the hell out of the inflation rate during that time, beat the hell out of real estate, gold, precious metals, or whatever else you could name. And your investment was liquid; you could get out when you wanted, with your money in your hands in five business days. While you waited, the companies paid dividends averaging 10 percent at a time when the prime rate fluctuated between 6 and 8 percent. The point of this illustration is that the same value in American companies exists today, waiting to be recognized, to be realized. It's a matter of choosing the areas of value, or of having them chosen for you.

* * *

"I couldn't make a living from your stocks," Paul Bennett said when I wandered into his office and asked him what was hot. Stockbrokers all bird-dog ideas from each other. We are all looking for our heroes in an industry where heroes become bums, and vice versa, with each tick of interest rates, with every notch of inflation. "Your stocks are too boring," he added. "Whenever I've bought your stocks, my clients after seven months all threaten to move their accounts to Paine Webber. Then I sell them out, they lose half a point, and I have to beg them to stay and promise them winners. It isn't easy."

"Then my stocks double a year after your clients sell." I grinned.

"Who can wait that long?" Paul Bennett asked, chewing on a jelly doughnut and sipping hot chocolate, which he claims gives him energy in the morning.

Paul Bennett is a reluctant bachelor with all the trappings of the swinger: a condominium apartment on the waterfront, a Mercedes 300D, a $75,000 income, and a penchant for generosity. But for Paul the glass is always half empty, and "it isn't easy" is the phrase that finishes most of his sentences. He works what I call "the sympathy routine" in life and in business. The sympathy routine involves pouring out your troubles, your failures, your heartaches, to all who will listen.

Paul starts with the women he dates. Tall, dark-haired, and attractive in a vulnerable way, Paul approaches women any-where — bus stops, elevators, bars, restaurants — and hands them his business card with handwritten messages on them. The messages say things like "I don't need your commissions, I need your love." Or "Be honest, you've never had dinner with a wonderful stockbroker." Or "Can we have a drink? I'm not Jewish but I'm terribly sensitive." After making the connection, Paul pours out his first tales of woe: his bad back, his aunt's nursing-home treatment, the sick alternator on his Mercedes. But after one date Paul says to the lady, "Do you have an IRA [an Individual Retirement Plan]? One of the benefits of dating me is that I not only can tell you about my screwed-up family life; I can tell you about investments. I'm very good at invest-ments," he adds, "because it takes my mind off my troubles." Usually after two dates Paul comes into my office and tells me,

"I'm in love with this woman Paula, this new woman. But I know it's not going to be a long-term thing. We watched the cable in my apartment last night, I sent out for Chinese — a very classy evening."

"How do you know it won't last long?"

"I opened up an IRA for her. I bought two hundred Champion Spark Plugs in the account, and they promptly cut the dividend. It dropped a point overnight. It's a bad sign."

"One day doesn't make an investment."

"I'm sure the woman Paula and I are doomed. She's a lovely woman and she's introducing me to her parents tomorrow. It isn't easy." Within an hour, everyone in the office knows about Paul's date and his investment in Champion. They also learn that he had shrimp and lobster sauce for dinner, because he points out the stain on his tie. Two weeks later I see a middle-aged couple sitting in Paul's customers' chairs next to his desk. Wandering by, I hear the man say to Paul, "We feel so bad about the way things worked with Paula."

"She's a lovely woman," Paul says. "But I'm wrong for her."

"We feel so bad," the man continues, "we want to open a joint account and deposit a hundred thousand to start. We appreciate how conservative you are."

"Sometimes too conservative," Paul says, reaching for an order ticket.

"It's not easy raising a daughter," they say in sympathy. Paul is counting commissions in his head. Solemnly, he agrees.

"It's not easy in general," he says. "It's not easy at all." The sound of a ringing cowbell is drowned out by the scream of an Army whistle. Another dry hole for Mad Mark; a positive earnings report for Big Jimmy Minot. We all have our totems, and we clutch at whatever seems to be working.

* * *

One snowy morning, the last week in January, Sardonic Sandra walked in and handed me my mail. Sardonic Sandra, my assistant, treats the world with disdain, which, when dealing with me,

19

she insists is love. Sandra has been with me for six years and is registered to do business as a stockbroker. This allows her to earn commissions in addition to her clerical salary, an incentive for her to stay with me forever.

"He's doing it again," she said. "I suspect Sebastian is copying your correspondence and keeping a file to send to the Internal Revenue."

A rule of the office was that all incoming mail was to be slit open as received. There were two reasons for this. One, so that checks could be immediately recorded and no chances taken that brokers might divert customers' funds into strange places like their own personal accounts. Two, so that any letters of complaint would be seen by Up-Your-Gross Smith first and not be destroyed by stockbrokers wanting to slip malfeasance under the rug or into the trash. As a senior officer of the firm, I felt that all my mail marked "Personal" should be delivered intact. Smith, the manager, agreed to this, but Sebastian, the messenger, reveled in ignoring the instructions. Three envelopes, each with "Personal" typed or handwritten on the front, had been sliced open.

Sebastian was reading the *National Enquirer* when I confronted him. "How many times do you have to be told personal is personal?" I asked.

"Look," he answered, not looking at me. "We get five hundred pieces of mail a day. Do I have time to make exceptions? You're supposed to be a liberal, right? Doesn't that mean everyone is treated the same? You swallow that tripe, all I want to give you is what you believe."

"I believe in personal liberty and the right to privacy."

"I believe in liberty too; that's why I open your stuff, same like everyone else's." He smiled. "I see by the checks you're still buying the same boring stocks. Don't you know that Reagan is going to give us the biggest bull market in history? You've got to go with growth until you liberals get him out. Then buy gold, because it's all over for America."

20

There is no winning an argument with Sebastian. He went on underlining the *Enquirer* in yellow marker pen. We all have our totems, and we clutch at whatever seems to be working. Outside my windows the snowfall increased in intensity and cars seemed stalled all along the highways. Mussolini made the trains run on time; Sebastian arrived every day, rain or snow, sick or well. You could count on him.

2

Heroes and Heroines

Valentine's Day, February 14. The market has been strong, which more than makes up for the two feet of snow on the ground. Cars spin out on the highway. Accidents slow traffic into town enough so that commuters can read newspapers propped against their steering wheels as they wait to ease forward, inches at a time. My newspaper is tucked in my briefcase in the trunk of my car. So I crawl into town and think about heroes. In the investment business, a hero is easy to identify: he's anyone who gives us a winner.

Remember Deep Throat, the secret informant in *All the President's Men* who would meet Woodward and Bernstein in a Washington garage? One of my heroes is also a man of shadows. I too meet him in a garage, where he passes wisdom along to me. I call him the Leprechaun. Last June, on a sunny morning that promised good things, I drove into town and did the mindless circle up the ramps of my parking building to the seventh floor. The stock market had been so bad for so long that coming to work was an effort of will. And it was the kind of day that reminded you of the end of school, freedom for the summer. Just the kind of day to watch people lose more money and complain more about the economy, their jobs, the problems with their children. "Psychiatrists get paid by the hour," I mused; "they don't have to wait for a commission." Feeling sorry for myself, I never noticed the car pulling into the next space till it almost tore off my driver's door. A little man emerged from the car, a black Mercedes sedan at least ten years old. He nervously apologized for the near miss.

"Not your fault," I said. "I wasn't paying attention." The little man kept apologizing, using his hands for emphasis, fluttering them up and down as if hoping that if he flapped hard enough, he would fly away. I recognized him as a money manager for one of the most successful private pools of capital in America. The fund, which he personally ran, had assets of over $700 million and had never had a down year.

I came around to his side of the car. He could not easily walk away. "I'm Spooner," I said. "I know your reputation. Are we really going down the drain? I find it difficult to get perspective anymore. Is it all over?"

The legend says that if you can capture a leprechaun by the coattails, he has to do your bidding until you let him go. I was not going to let this leprechaun escape. The Dow Jones stood at 844 and I needed a miracle. He wore a wool three-piece navy suit, warm for June, a white shirt, and a blue tie with tiny red bulls on it. He was very slight, about five feet four. Through the driver's window of his Mercedes I could see a foam rubber cushion lying on his seat. His way blocked, my leprechaun decided that his coattails were grabbed and the only way he could get free was to spill his story.

"Two days ago," he said, "we went long the market. We bought up to, or were planning to buy up to, ninety percent of our reserve cash, which is sizable. IBM, Wang, Digital, General Motors, Hewlett-Packard. That's it, and good morning to you."

He scuttled away, his head bobbing downward, as if he were trying to hide it under his arm.

"Don't you want to know what *I'm* buying?" I called to him. "I'll return the favor."

The Leprechaun snorted. "Other opinions are irrelevant. They anger the blood," he said and picked up his pace, wanting to avoid being caught with me on the elevator.

I came into the office ecstatic: a legend had given me a buy signal in the midst of a market that had been a bloodbath for months. I passed on the Leprechaun's message to Mad Mark the Institutional Salesman. "He was probably lying to you," Mark said. "Anyone can say buy IBM. But it's nice to hear that there's hope somewhere. I've got to listen to the squawk box, excuse me."

The squawk box is Mad Mark's idol. He believes what it tells him; he follows its orders explicitly. Every major investment house has its squawk boxes, black amplifiers of phone hookups that are directly wired to the firm's main offices. Information comes over the boxes all day: recommendations on stocks and bonds and special products; speeches by different sales coordinators about market conditions and contests and items of interest geared to increase productivity. The institutional hookup tells of research on specific companies and what mutual funds, banks, and insurance companies should be contacted to buy our wares, that is, what we are recommending. Mad Mark loves to pretend that the Wizard of Oz is on the other end of his squawk box. If the box doesn't say buy IBM, then he would be damned if he'd recommend it. "You work for a company," Mark says, "then you play the company game."

"That's what I like about institutional salesmen," I said. "You can always say it was someone else's fault." Mad Mark smiled and turned up his amplifier. I went into my office, believing in my leprechaun, and began to buy Wang Labs at 30.

Today, eight months later, on Valentine's Day, the stock sells at 33½ after a recent two-for-one split. Better money than candy.

24

I finally make it through the snowy streets to my parking garage. "Jesus," I think, "prices are the same in the marketplace in Palm Springs, in Scottsdale. I could ride a *bike* to work." In bear markets, bad weather adds insult to injury. In bull markets it is a pain in the butt. It makes you late; it keeps you from entering orders. Thinking about lost commissions in the snow, I hurry to the elevator in the parking garage.

While I'm walking there, the Leprechaun in his black Mercedes flashes by on his way to an upper level. I run up two flights of stairs and catch him emerging from the car. "You're my hero," I yell to him. "How does it feel to have caught the market on the lows?"

Immediately he begins flapping his hands. The Leprechaun would make a lousy spy. Some people just cannot stand being confronted.

"I'm late for a meeting," he says. "But I *will* give you another story. I believe that the energy stock crunch is way overdone. I do not think that the price of oil will collapse, as many analysts are saying. I am beginning as of now to buy domestic energy companies: Standard of Ohio, Indiana, California, Arco, Phillips, and Union Oil."

"What about the internationals?" I plead. "Exxon, Texaco, Mobil, Gulf."

"Aah," he answers, shuffling away, "that's enough for now."

"I'm going to wait for you every day," I say to the Leprechaun.

He shakes his head. "Information you get every day is worthless. The best information comes only *once in a while.*"

I have already begun buying the energy stocks, but the investment business is a neurotic one. You can doubt your own judgments when for months you watch the stocks you pick go sideways, when for months the financial press comments negatively on the energy area. Getting confirmation from a hero is a wonderful tonic. You love to walk into the office every day with "an idea." Something you can get your teeth into, something you can sell to the clients.

The board room is already crowded when I enter. All the

25

brokers are in, and most of their customers' chairs are occupied. There is a row of seats along the front of most investment house board rooms. The seats are reserved for customers who spend the day watching the ticker tape, trading stocks, keeping warm. For the rest of the 1980s, board room seats will take the place of temples, park benches, cafeterias, where the elderly go to reminisce and seek companionship. The ticker tape will be their companion in the 1980s. There the action does not depend on strong limbs or well-tuned libidos. All you need there is the ability to write a check and cross your fingers. Regulars appear in board rooms the way regulars call in to certain talk shows on the radio. One of our regulars stops me on the way to my office.

"John," he says, "can I ask you a question?" It is Teddy Loveman, the shoe dog. He is my client. He ran shoe factories for over fifty years and was finally forced to retire by a son-in-law whom Teddy made the mistake of putting in his business. "In the retail trade," Teddy would say, "you start the son-in-law in handbags, where they can do the least damage. I put mine on the road and in six months the schmuck comes in and says, 'Dad, I can see how we gotta change things!' What can you do if you have an only daughter?" Teddy sits in his chair looking up at the ticker and turns his portfolio over several times a month. He always starts his conversations with the same words: "Can I ask you a question?"

"Don't ask whether you can ask me a question," I say. "Just ask me the question. What am I going to say, no?" This may sound harsh, but it's the way you must talk to old shoe dogs. If you don't, they will tromp all over you.

"Okay." Teddy smiles. "You know what I'm going to ask. When are you going to give me a winner?" We have this conversation every day, but it never fails to annoy. Teddy does it on purpose. "I've given you a thousand winners over the years, Teddy. But you never stay in them long enough to do yourself any good."

"Name one," Teddy challenges.

"Jesus, it's first thing in the morning, Teddy. I've got fifty people to talk with."

"You see!" he cries to the board room, triumphant. "He's never made me a nickel. He gives me discounts like Hitler would give me discounts, and on top of it all I got to pay ten dollars to a parking lot just to come in town and be humiliated."

"Here, Teddy," I say, giving him a parking coupon from the booklet of twenty I buy each month. It saves me fifty cents a day.

"Wouldn't take it," he says, but he does, and settles down into his chair for the morning. The ritual is over; he has won a victory over the system, however small, and he has caused my stomach to start churning. Teddy is happy and holds the parking coupon aloft for the customer next to him to see. "My big-deal broker pays for my parking. That's because I buy thousands of shares a year."

"You're a schmuck, Teddy," his neighbor says. "My son picks me up every day, and I get a much bigger discount than you."

"If you weren't a woman," Teddy says, "I'd take you in the shoe business." His neighbor is Norma the Duchess, a woman as big as all outdoors, with three strands of pearls. She has out-lived two husbands, buys stocks based on how the corporation president's picture looks in the annual reports, and backed *Hello, Dolly, Mame,* and *My Fair Lady.* She sings to herself the songs from these shows as the prices flash by on the ticker.

In the midst of a chorus of "I'm Getting Married in the Morning," Harry the Cloud slouches by with a paper cup of black coffee. Harry the Cloud is another board room regular, one of the chorus of customers who fills the seats in the front of the room. Harry the Cloud is a lounge piano player, which gives him his days free to sit around our board room and complain. For Harry the end is always near. His health is awful and get-ting worse, his stocks are rotten, his unflagging belief is that America and the market are just around the corner from col-lapse. Harry the Cloud is bearish on himself, bearish on the world.

"Don't sit next to me, Harry," says the Duchess. "You sit a seat away."

"Are you too stuck up for some good advice?" the Cloud asks, spilling coffee on his shirt.

"Whatever you got, you keep to yourself. I feel too good to be depressed. And it's Valentine's Day."

Harry slumps in his chair. "Valentine's Day only means a massacre," he says. "They'll kill the market today. It's overheated, overvalued. When the brokers throw darts and prices go up, it's time to sell short."

"Why don't you move *two* seats away," says the Duchess. I leave the chorus and go to my office. Teddy Loveman has left a present on my desk, a commission schedule from a discount brokerage firm. Attached is a note from Teddy: "Shoe people fight each other all day and then fight for the check at night. When are you going to fight for the check?"

Since May Day, 1973, stock commissions have been competitive, no longer fixed by the New York Stock Exchange, as they had been for so many years. Customers can compete for service, execution of orders, and price. Most institutions (banks, mutual funds, insurance companies) that deal in thousands of shares at a time get giant discounts. These institutions can do business for as little as two or three cents per share. Money managers, advisory companies, many trust departments of law firms, get 20 to 50 percent discounts on trades. These discounts are from the old posted fixed commission rates that brokerage firms still charge their average customers. Typically, these rates represent approximately 1½ to 2 percent of the dollar amount traded. If you buy a hundred shares of a $20 stock, the commission is $53.50. A thousand shares of a $20 stock, the commission is $378.

Should you use a discount brokerage firm, where discounts can range from 50 percent to 80 percent of listed prices? If you do your own trading, manage your own money, and know exactly what you want to buy and sell, you would be foolish not to use a discounter. Of the approximately thirty-five hundred clients on my books, every single one needs and wants his or her hand held during transactions. This is not to knock my clients. We all need reassurance; we all want a human reaction to our life experiences, whether they're medical, legal, or only social. We need reinforcement.

"I want to buy Cetus," a client with very positive feelings recently said. Cetus is an over-the-counter company, selling at around 14, that does research in genetic engineering. It has over $90 million in cash and almost no long-term debt. I liked the idea.

"Buy me a thousand shares," the client said, "but before you do it, what do you think?" *What do you think?* is the motto of the investment business, the single most asked question. Discount brokers don't give opinions; they don't give therapy. They are merely order-takers. All of our time is valuable. I am selling a service that includes reason and experience. In general I will not discount my services the way J. C. Penney discounts merchandise. What I do for all my clients is give a modest discount on transactions. This means 5 to 15 percent off the listed fee structure. I do this without being asked, and it shows on customers' buy and sell confirmations as "preferential rates."

I see Teddy Loveman standing at the door to my office. He grins at me. "Well, genius," he says, "you see what discounts I can get down the street?"

"You get no conversation down the street, Teddy," I tell him. "You get no free coffee and a place to sit. You get no reassurance and no ear to listen about your sons and your factories and your gall bladder. Do you ask your doctor, your accountant, your lawyer, for discounts? Do you break *their* balls every day of the week?"

"Hey," Teddy says, "it's a big difference. *They're* not in a whore's business. You're in a whore's business. What have you done for me lately?"

* * *

Today, after the close of the market, we're having a Valentine's Day party. We have lots of parties in our office: for holidays, when an employee leaves, for record trading volume, for big Dow Jones average days. We even have parties when the markets are horrible, parties to drown out sorrow and to compare horror stories. This is a party for a bull market.

Do bull markets make everyone feel wonderful? That myth will be exposed in this chapter. The truth is that rampant bull markets with high volume and everyone in the pool are much more difficult to deal with than bear markets. The reasons for this phenomenon are psychological. Most of us find success harder to handle than failure. The inherited money or the lottery payoff or the sudden rise to fame that changes the recipient often leads to disaster.

When the stock market is low, when fortunes ebb, when recession surrounds us, we are all in the same boat. We can swap our stories of disaster and failure. Having company makes us feel better. Last fall a client in the home furnishings business said to me, "Things are so bad, even the liars are complaining." It was okay to be suffering, because everyone else was suffering. It became chic at cocktail parties and dinners to compare how bad one's business was, how disastrously one's stocks were performing. The complaints were the same in neighborhood bars in Detroit and Pittsburgh. Men drinking Iron City beer bitched about the auto and steel industry and about unemployment. You could feel guilty in these bars if you had a job. But when markets boom and people go back to work and orders come in to factories, we focus again on our essential goal: beat the hell out of the other guy. Bull markets produce scenes like this:

"John, got anything hot?" asks Paul Bennett the Bachelor. "Can you believe my clients are killing me?"

"What's the trouble?" I ask.

"They want to know why I didn't buy them Analogic or American Express or Federal Express or Commodore, all doubles or triples in the last six months. I've only got them up twenty or thirty percent and they tell me they all want to pull their accounts."

In bull markets someone *always* has a hotter stock than you. It can drive you crazy. And when it drives you crazy, you make sure that your stockbroker feels the heat. Teddy's question, "What have you done for me lately?" is a constant theme in a bull market. You are always trying to top your previous capital gains advice. And money never lies fallow in the hands of stockbrokers; we never run out of inventory. The pressure to outperform your neighbor becomes intense in a greedy, upward market. In many ways it is a time of unhappiness, producing the kind of mental exhaustion that tells you that, sooner or later, you are doomed to fail.

The Valentine's Day party gives some evidence of this malaise. Like the Boston Celtics of the 1960s, we have nowhere to go but down. Jug wine and cheese and crackers are the party fare. Tony Corvo, the head of our back office, is also in charge of ordering the goodies. He lets two of his clerks off from their duties at three o'clock and sends them to a package store that kicks back free wine to Tony in return for the business.

Tony always has at least one sideline operation going that brings him cash. His clerks operate as his runners, offering us specials on fruit and nuts at Christmas, baskets of candy at Easter, personalized golf balls, and, this week, heart-shaped chocolates with Italian liqueur centers. Most of the time we buy, because back-office problems that are not solved immediately turn into nightmares for both customers and brokers. People who don't buy the special offerings from Tony find their problems at the bottom of the pile. We all wonder when he is going to announce that he's branching out to laundry or linen supplies and providing us with escort service to our cars because the streets are full of dangerous characters.

I'm talking with several of the youngbloods from the board room. One of them is telling me about a problem. "What would you do?" he asks. "I speak to this guy every day. He buys stocks.

I give him great information and service. I mail him stuff every day, research notes, clippings on his companies. So he calls me and asks to be sent twenty-five thousand from his daily interest account."

Daily interest is our name for money market funds, one of the results of high prime rates, the easy-access funds that have attracted billions of dollars in recent years.

"What are you doing with the money?" the broker asked his client, a reasonable question, since we're always worried that someone else may get control of our customers' assets.

The broker continues, "The guy tells me that he has just bought a hundred-thousand-dollar annuity and he needs the extra dough from me to pay for it." The broker begins to yell. "I told him that *I* sold annuities also. Why didn't he ask *me*? I service him daily and he buys a hundred-thousand-dollar policy somewhere else."

He grabs me by the lapel. "Should I tell him to take the rest of his account and shove it? Christ, a hundred-thousand-dollar annuity. That's a gross commission of four thousand dollars. Is that borscht?"

He calms down somewhat. "Should I tell him to take a hike?"

I hand him a plastic glass of wine, but a voice behind me says, "Sure, get drunk in the office. What do you care? You guys get it coming and going. We get it in the ear." I turn and see a middle-aged man in a topcoat and tweed cap. He is talking to another young broker, recently married, a hard-scrabbling serious type who makes a hundred phone calls a day and works late.

"I'm driving home," the man in the tweed cap says. "And the radio says that the market hit a record high. Up ten points. Almost eleven hundred on the Dow Jones. You bought me Frank B. Hall [an insurance agency stock] nine months ago. It's up a lousy ten percent and *today it went down*. A record day on Wall Street" — he is now purple in the face — "and my stock goes down. I had to come back in town and let you have it." The young broker is calm.

"Actually, Mr. Wheelock," he says, "you paid twenty-six and a half for the stock. It's up, based on the closing price today, sixteen percent so far."

"That stinks!" yells the customer. "It isn't in health care, it isn't in computers, it isn't even in telecommunications." He grabs a glass of red wine and tosses it all over the young broker. Before any of us can react, Tweed Cap turns and walks away, yelling as he leaves, "Sell it and send me a check. A record high, and I'm sucking hind tit."

Tony Corvo is livid. "I can catch him in the elevator with a Brooklyn war club," he says.

"No, no," says Up-Your-Gross Smith. "Just submit the bill for cleaning and we'll pay for it out of petty cash. Or I'll journal some commissions to you to cover it. [The manager has business at his discretion to pass out to brokers, a slush fund, really, to cover mistakes or reward special efforts.] But let this be a lesson. You're in a business where you're damned if you do and damned if you don't. People can't stand sitting in stagnant situations. They want action; give them action. Just looking at that guy, topcoat, cap; he's a player. He should be in options, commodities, at least a high-technology stock. Step up to the plate, kid. They want action; it's your job to give 'em action. I got twenty applicants for your desk and phone. Never forget it."

The young broker looks to be in shock. He dabs at his shirt front with paper napkins. Heroes and bums.

Mad Mark the Institutional Salesman slaps me on the back. "I've got a real treat for you. Call this number." He hands me a slip of paper with the New York City area code. I take my wine into my office and dial the number. Busy. I dial again with the same result.

Mad Mark has come in. He is joined by the young broker with the red stains on his shirt. "I acted in the best interests of my client," the broker says. "Long-term capital gains are everyone's best tax shelter. Frank B. Hall is a cheap asset. It's going to sell much higher someday."

We are silent. Mad Mark slaps the broker on the back. Mark

33

is physical. Always slapping backs, pinching cheeks, giving high fives like a basketball player who has completed a slam dunk. "If you can't stand the heat, kid, move to the institutional side. You ever see me down, discouraged? That's because I don't make decisions. I just take orders. If you're an order-taker, the crazies don't throw wine in your face. On our side of the biz, all they do is make sure they drink every drop. And that there are cigars passed with the brandy. Call the number, John."

I dial the New York number again and put the call on my speaker phone so that it can be broadcast. It rings and is picked up. A female voice answers, dripping with promises for the lonely and the curious. "Hello," the voice says, "I'm Belinda, your centerfold for February. Ooh, is that for me, so big and red? I just love all-day suckers. Mmm, I can hold it in both hands and I can almost put the whole thing in my mouth." The message dissolves into noises and ecstasy and finally finishes. "Now that's what I call a Valentine's treat, sugar. I can handle you any time."

"Every day there's a new number," says Mad Mark. "It beats Dial-A-Prayer." The young broker is embarrassed.

"Let me tell you something," I say to him. "Whatever you learned in business school has nothing to do with the stock market. It has nothing to do with the kicks people seek from phone calls like that or what people really want from their money. Bernard Baruch, one of the geniuses of Wall Street, gave some money to a young broker to invest years ago, and the young broker, wanting to impress Baruch, pressed a little too hard and lost the money. Almost in tears he went to the wizard and apologized. "This is a lesson, son," Baruch said, "to remember always. You can't be God for a commission."

Our young broker still looks crestfallen. It takes years to build up scar tissue in the market. Lisa, one of the floaters, comes into my office. "We thought we'd take you out for a Valentine's drink," she says to the young broker. "You need some cheering up."

34

"I've already had some drinks," he replies, refusing to brighten.

"We mean a *real* drink," she says, pressing him. "Not some jug wine. A real drink, like a Marguerita." That's what's great about the investment business. Everyone's an expert.

We tend to believe the words of unknown people, people who manipulate our tastes, our opinions: the advertising agencies, the news media. In money matters stockbrokers traditionally seek scapegoats for their mistakes: the research department, other brokers, the unnamed sources of their friends. You know the saying "What's an expert? Someone from sixty miles outside of town." The unseen expert is much more glamorous, mysterious, and therefore, we think, much more likely to be right.

Conversely, we tend to believe that anyone we know personally who has achieved great success in any field must have achieved that success totally through accident. We tend to diminish the accomplishments of people we know well, especially people we have known from childhood. We remember their complexion problems from adolescence. And we do not like to admit that the classmate who was a klutz in high school has done better than we. Heroes and heroines we have never met can always remain heroes and heroines. But once we realize that Robert Redford is shorter than we are, that Faye Dunaway in the flesh is quite plain, it is the beginning of the end. In the money business, our heroes are expected to provide the answer to our dream: the perfect stock. I tell clients who seem never satisfied, "Right, all you want is a stock that doubles in a year, pays a ten percent dividend, and is guaranteed never to go down even an eighth of a point after you buy it."

"Of course," they say. "Isn't that why we pay you commissions?" What's frightening is that they are serious.

* * *

We all have people we look to for inspiration or example. And I am always on the lookout for what is truly happening in

America. Not what the newspapers or the television news offers. But what the people think. I have said before that you never can know about people until you deal with their money. This is another reason that understanding Wall Street can help you understand society at large. Whenever I doubt my own ability to assess trends in the marketplace, one of the people I call on is Herbert the Big Hitter.

Herbert the Big Hitter is one of the biggest producers of stock brokerage commissions in America. For the seven-figure commissions he produces, his firm has built him a throne room for an office. Herbert looks fine in a throne room. He has a working fireplace, an eight-by-ten Karastan, wall hangings by an up-and-coming local artist who lives with a decorator who found the Karastan, and birch logs for the fireplace at $250 a cord. Herbert has the secret for getting rich in this decade, and I believe him.

"Why complicate your life?" he says. "It's simple. You can get rich in the stock market in the next five years. That's where the value is, and money is going to go to value. You wanta know what I mean by cheap? In nineteen sixty-five American Telephone and Telegraph sold at seventy-five dollars a share. Today it's fifty-five . . . *twenty points lower*. Their business has expanded enormously and the dividend has been raised countless times in this period. Yet it's still twenty points lower than it was *sixteen years ago*. Name me another commodity in the world that has gone down over sixteen years other than my pecker.

"U.S. companies are the cheapest commodities in the world. If you wanta make money, you will buy American companies: common stocks. If you don't wanta just make money but you wanta be *rich*, you will play Herbert the Big Hitter's Concentration Game."

He continues, "That means buy the hell out of one company, add to it on dips, accumulate it, and don't sell until your score is made."

Herbert has done this for himself several times in the past five years. This is how it's done.

"First rule in working a stock," Herbert says, "you must never have to call anyone to ask their permission to buy or sell. You gotta have a pool of capital, partly yours, mostly not yours. Anyone in the investment business who is a big producer handles only discretionary accounts. [A big producer is generally considered to be anyone who generates over $500,000 a year in gross commissions. A Super-broker is anyone who generates over a million.] This means when you wanta spend the money, you spend the money.

"Now I got a family to feed," Herbert says, "and I particularly got two unmarried daughters with a big sickness. They need to go to Lord and Taylor's and spend twelve hundred dollars on a dress. Now this is not unusual, but they need to do it every week. So I'm not shy about pushing the chips on the red or the black. First thing I always tell people is that I got a ton of money on the stock myself. Most of the time I do. Then I say, 'Not only do I want you to buy this stock, I want you to do yourself a favor, buy some for your mother, buy some for your retirement fund.' These two are clinchers: I got *my* dough in it; I want you to put your *mother* in it. That's like waving the flag on July Fourth.

"Now I got my company, then I line up the orders, making sure everyone is nice and greedy, which they always are. Then I have all the clients sign a margin agreement that allows them to buy twice as much as they ordinarily could."

Margin is credit. You put up $1000. You borrow $1000 from the brokerage firm. You pay interest on the borrowed $1000 and hope that the leverage works in your favor.

We sit in a restaurant while Herbert explains his techniques. He has ordered a Manhattan with four cherries: "With a lot of fruit I can gag it down." Herbert is not a promoter. He believes in what he buys and sells the way Billy Graham believes in Jesus. He does his own research, saying, "Wall Street research is bullshit. The people who are Wall Street analysts are people who failed in the professions they analyze and needed a job."

Here is an example of how Herbert picks a stock. In 1977

37

his daughters' high school, in a cost-cutting move, eliminated the budget for band uniforms. Herbert's daughters play the saxophone, and Herbert will do anything to keep up his daughters' interest in anything other than clothes and eating hot fudge sundaes and anchovy pizzas. "They look unbelievably horrible in a uniform," he says. "But that's not the point. In their uniforms they felt *pride*."

Herbert wakes up at three-thirty in the morning, every morning, and does his best thinking. The band uniform situation obsessed him. "The government is going broke," he determined. "The cities, the towns are going broke. What are the local municipalities going to do?" He jumped up in his bed and screamed out loud, "They're going to legalize gambling! That's what they're going to do." Herbert's wife had long since got beyond waking up over his discoveries. She dreamed peacefully of shoes from Geller; suits from Bill Blass.

Convinced that the United States was going broke and needed to approve fund-raising from any new sources, Herbert began to buy Resorts International stock at prices ranging from 8½ to 15. This was in 1976, before gambling was legalized in New Jersey for Atlantic City. He rode the stock for almost two years, selling out at between 80 and 95. He made over $700,000 for his own account, millions for his clients, and established his daughters in the Pantheon of heroines at Bonwit's and Bloomingdale's.

In the good old days of stock promotion before the Securities and Exchange Commission and the National Association of Securities Dealers, there existed a stock-fraud technique that involved a group of promoters taking a position (buying) in an obscure listed company whose shares could be violently affected by limited buying or selling. The promoters would buy carefully and quietly for themselves over a period of months. When they had their own investments in place, they would call a number of brokerage firms and mailing-list names and extol the virtues of their company.

The word of the promotion would spread; the investment

community could watch the daily trading increase from hundreds of shares to thousands of shares. They could watch the stock move from 5½ to 8 on action that could only mean something big was happening. The promoters would place orders in fairly large amounts with enough different brokers to show significant volume and price action. This would lend credibility to the stories of improving conditions at the company.

The volume and activity caused by the promoters was called "painting the ticker tape" or "painting the tape." It was a creative enterprise. As more amateurs were sucked into the company on increased volume, the promoters would continue the hype, slowly easing completely out of the stock at higher and higher prices. When they were totally out, the stories stopped, the amateur investors were bagged, the stock usually collapsed, and the painters of the tape moved on to different canvasses.

After the killing in Resorts International, Herbert sent out five thousand mailing pieces to his clients, selected country club membership lists, and three temple brotherhood rosters that he got from a client who was a funeral director. The mailing piece was a typewritten message: "I bought Resorts International at 7½ and sold it at 80. Did you?" He stamped his name, address, and telephone number beneath it. A typical caller to Herbert after this would ask two questions: "What are you buying now?" and "What do you think of Polaroid? I've had it for eleven years. Now it's twenty, and I'm croaking with it at sixty-five."

Here's where Herbert sucked them in. "Look," he'd say. "You do business with me, we're in it to make money, not to play guessing games. I get involved with three or four companies at a time, tops. I know all about them. I speak to management. I speak to the specialist on the floor. I don't have time to know about Polaroid or Mobil or Telephone or whatever tips you get on the golf course. I'm paid to make you rich. You don't get rich on companies you never heard of. Send in your money and we'll get to work. I even got a stock you should buy for your mother."

Herbert buys and he calls; he buys and he talks. He buys ten thousand shares of a new favorite, and he talks about it wherever he goes to anyone who will listen. And everyone listens, because everyone wants to double his money. Here are the steps usually followed by a big hitter in working a stock.

1. *Dipping In.* A big hitter buys for himself and his family. Herbert goes to New York to visit the specialists and to entertain the floor traders of his own firm who will execute his orders. When he visits the specialist on the floor of the Exchange, he asks personal questions about the specialist's hobbies. If he plays tennis, Herbert sends him a graphite racquet. If he plays golf, he sends him a set of Ping irons. People in the money business always accept gratuities. They believe they deserve them.

2. *Discovery.* Herbert finds the stock he wants to buy. It will always have a New York Stock Exchange or American Exchange listing and have a large capitalization so that institutions (banks, insurance companies, pension funds, and so on) can become involved. Herbert *must* buy shares in a company where there can be large activity and where he can eventually unload a big position to buyers who can generate the cash.

3. *Validating the Claim.* Herbert says, "People who are going to invest big dough want to hear you say, 'I just talked to the chairman of the board and he tells me that things are going gangbusters.' People want you to be Big Daddy; they want you to tell them that everything is going to be all right. I always go to meet management of the companies I buy. I let them entertain me. You'd be amazed what corporate officers tell me. Usually I open them up as accounts. After I've met management, I find some brokerage house research report that recommends the stock. You can always find some firm somewhere that recommends something you're interested in. Then I make thousands of copies of the report, stamp my name and number on it, and send it out. This makes me official in the eyes of my clients. I know the management on a first-name basis. And I get a black and white endorsement from another authority source."

At this point Herbert goes into

4. *The Attack.* The Big Hitter buys almost indiscriminately here, accumulating a position that can run up to a million shares of a major company, such as ITT, which has over a hundred million shares outstanding. During the day he is all business — buying in the morning, going to lunch with institutional buyers. ("It's easy to spend millions of other people's money," Herbert says. "Institutions are worse with billions than you are with a thousand bucks. And they can be suckered into buying huge amounts faster than you can hustle a dentist into a penny uranium stock.")

All afternoon he will also buy five thousand shares here, a thousand shares there, trying to attract attention by keeping up the volume, trying to attract other brokers around the country by his activity, which shows up on the ticker tape. Technicians or chartists, people who plot the movement of prices on graphs, pay a lot of attention to trading volume at different prices. Herbert knows that if he helps increase volume in his favorites as they hit new high points, it will attract new buyers, who think something special may be happening. And every day, at the close of trading, Herbert throws in an order to buy a hundred shares of his favorite "at the market," that is, at the best price currently available. "I do it," he says, "so that it'll show in the newspapers the next day as an uptick, as a plus finish for my stock."

The Big Hitter naturally believes in leverage. If you do business with him, you do it on margin. Every time your stock increases by a certain amount (if you trade on margin), it increases your *buying power*; your ability to develop extra money to purchase more stock. If your buying power allows you to buy ten more shares or fifty or a hundred or a thousand on the way up, you *will* own more stock. The Big Hitter will always push you and push his buying power to the limit when he works a stock. Herbert always wins. If he's right, he's a hero. If he's wrong, being a great salesman he goes on to another company and promises the moon.

5. *Pulling the Plug.* Buying is easy in the stock market. Selling

is the difficult part, the key to making money. Herbert the Big Hitter may play a stock from 25 to 40 in a year and decide that it's time to roll into something else. The customer is never allowed to sit with cash after a sale; there is always something new to buy.

Very quietly, Herbert comes in early one day and goes to the institutional trading desk, where blocks of stock in excess of five thousand shares are traded. "Work on a hundred thousand Mee Too Chemicals," he instructs the trader. "Sell it at thirty-eight or better (or higher) and sell it today." All week he may work on his position, still exuding confidence in the stock to all he sees, to everyone he speaks with.

For a week or so after he has sold his position, he still sings the praises of the company. Then, suddenly, a new company is all he speaks of. "Metabolic Engineering," he will say. "Now this is the stock for the next five years. This company will be able to reproduce crude oil growth in the laboratory equal to half of Libya's output. Do yourself a favor, buy some for your mother."

"Fine," says another stockbroker, "but what about my Me Too Chemicals? You said it should be good for sixty."

"Oh, Jesus!" says Herbert. "I've been out of that for months." The message here is the message Herbert the Big Hitter believes in: "Maintain no personal relationships." Herbert explains it by saying, "You're either a hero or a bum in the investment business. Sometimes you're only a bum. A stock goes up, you sell it, it doubles after you sell it, the client is pissed. A stock goes up, you look for more, you don't sell it, it goes down, the client is pissed. So they don't want me for love; I don't want them for love. Let me work for dough; let me take the commissions. No client is ever satisfied and they'll always stick it in your ear if they get a chance. So don't give me fairy tales. With Herbert you get a one-way street, a run for your money. Not many people in life give you that."

"What about love and romance in the money business?"

"You only get it from the hustlers. The *real* people care about giving you a run for your money. But I'll give you an example of romance, and it involves what I always say: Never try to kid a kidder. Now, when I work a stock, I'm in control. But people are always trying to sell me on their stock, to get me in and help try to run it up. I'll listen to anybody as long as they know that you can't kid a kidder.

"One day a surgeon calls me," Herbert says. "He's just back from what they call 'giving a paper' in Munich. 'Giving a paper' is doctor talk for a free vacation at somebody else's expense. It's a racket where the doctors go to Acapulco or wherever to pat themselves on the back and have their wives bitch about the jewelry on other doctors' wives. If the doctors go alone, it's an excuse for them to get laid out of town. Hey, I don't care. Every step I take is tax deductible, and everybody I meet is a potential client and if you knew how many times I took my in-laws out to dinner last year and said they were different corporations, you'd want to turn me in for a piece of the action. Anyway, the surgeon says he wants to know about Tantalum.

" 'Tantalum,' I say. 'You tell *me*. It's a drug, right?'

" 'No,' the doctor says, 'it's a strategic metal.' "

(A strategic metal is a material, like vanadium or chromium or manganese, in relatively short supply and of prime importance to defense work. Many of our strategic metals we import from politically sensitive places, like South Africa, the Soviet Union, Cambodia, and the Middle East.)

" 'Well,' I tell the doctor, 'you got me. If I thought it was a drug, I guess I don't know too much about tantalum. But I thought you said Trimantin, that antiulcer drug.'

" 'You mean Tagamet.'

" 'Right, Tagamet,' says I." (A good stockbroker never admits he doesn't know.)

The surgeon is a top account of Herbert's and operated on Herbert's cousin for polyps in the uterus. Herbert violates his basic formula of even talking about stocks other than his own, and is not happy about it. "I asked the other brokers in the office about tantalum, and I shoulda known, no one had ever heard of it. So I call the surgeon and I give him the classic broker routine: 'I called the research department in New York. We've got a guy specializes in defense. He said, "Tantalum, very interesting, very short supply, prices could explode. If you've got a pure play on it we'd be interested." So now, Doc, that you've got me all hot and bothered, what have you got, and you better buy twenty-five thousand shares for all the time I spent on this.'

" 'I want to buy a stock, over the counter, called Doomsday Materials.'

"Naturally over the counter," Herbert the Big Hitter says to me. "Has a doctor ever volunteered to buy a listed stock?"

The doctor buys ten thousand shares at 2½. On his way home from Munich he had met a man on the plane who was one of the largest stockholders in Doomsday Materials and urged the doctor to buy some. It was "going to be *the* stock of the nineteen eighties."

"If I had a dime for every time someone called me with a story that such and such was going to be the stock of the decade or the next Xerox," says Herbert, "I wouldn't need to talk to anybody anymore."

The doctor buys the stock and insists that the man he met on the plane from Munich was the richest, most charming, intelligent person he had ever met and that he lived in a suite in the Beverly Wilshire Hotel, right down the hall from Warren Beatty. "Furthermore, Herb," said the doctor, "I told him what a hitter you were, and he's going to call you and tell you about tantalum."

"Beware when someone you've never met calls you from the Beverly Wilshire Hotel," I say to Herbert.

"Well," Herbert says, "you've gotta stay on your toes. I did get a call. The man's name was Darrin Black, N. Darrin Black, and I never ever got along with anyone who uses an initial and a middle name to go by.

44

" 'I've got a small network,' Black says, 'of special brokers who want to make a lot of money for themselves and their clients and they're smart enough to recognize an opportunity.'

"I told him," Herbert said, "I don't need anyone else's ideas."

N. Darrin Black ignored Herbert's response. " 'I'm inviting these special sophisticated brokers to a three-day seminar on tantalum and on Doomsday Materials at Dorado Beach, Puerto Rico. Do you play golf?'

" 'I play golf,' I say.

" 'Do you visit casinos?'

" 'I roll the dice.'

" 'Can you make it for three days on Columbus Day weekend, all your expenses paid by me?' says Black.

" 'First class?' I ask. 'No groups with chickens, goats, and nuns?'

"Black laughs. 'This is a first-cabin presentation for first-cabin people.'

" 'Send me a ticket,' I say.

"Since I do roll the dice," Herbert tells me, "and since I see nothing wrong with listening to a story, I figured that if this guy was picking up the tab for maybe twenty people for three days, and Dorado being no fleabag, he's talking minimum fifteen hundred dollars per guest, probably almost fifty grand for a dog and pony show in the sun. One thing is sure, I tell myself, I better buy some of this Doomsday Materials before the meeting. Sure as hell they'll run the stock afterward. The right promotion can move up a doggie poop company. The important thing is getting the clue when to bail out.

"I buy ten thousand for myself and, sure enough, I pay as high as three for it. I also buy stock for my best customers without telling them what it was, maybe as much as seventy-five thousand shares. Before I get on the plane for San Juan, I call the office. The stock is three and a half. The doctor's already up ten grand and I don't know tantalum from lead balloons.

"A limo meets me at the airport, which is always a good sign, and I shut my eyes on the way to Dorado because I hate to look at how most of the poor bastards in the world live. I check into the hotel," Herbert goes on, "and I'm directed to a reception table, where they give me a room key, three new Maxfli black Dot golf balls, a can of Wilson tennis balls, a paperback book of casino odds in Puerto Rico, and a printed schedule of events. As soon as I hit the room, I call the office to buy another ten thousand Doomsday Materials, because now I know these bastards are organized and they're going to promote the shit out of the stock. I talk to the office for an hour, because I'd rather hear the prices than nap any day. Naps take dough out of my pocket.

"Luckily, the first event we have is cocktails," Herbert tells me. "And I get my first glimpse of N. Darrin Black. He's wearing a white Italian suit, white shirt, silk tie the color of a thousand-dollar bill. He's also the tannest white man I've ever seen, with blond wavy hair that reminds me of how people used to look in high school. If you happened to go to high school in Beverly Hills.

" 'Herbert the Big Hitter,' he greets me, and I'm impressed that he knows me but I'm not embarrassed, because I can usually buy and sell anyone I see in a room ten times, and I happen to be in a white suit also. We get introduced around the terrace, and every guy there, all brokers, produces business better than half a million in commissions a year. We're all drinking rum drinks with fruit, and feeling no pain, when N. Darrin Black gives his first speech after rapping on his glass with a spoon.

" 'Dorado Beach,' Darrin starts off, 'El Dorado, legendary land of gold. Today it is real, no legend, and this terrace is where the tall dogs pee.

" 'You see this nugget?' Darrin asks, holding up a piece of rock. 'This is pure tantalum. No aircraft, no bomb, no nuclear reactor, no tank shell, no radar, no sonar or electronic instrument, can be manufactured without this material. And where does most of it come from? From southern Africa, from the Soviet Union. Is Ronald Reagan committed to a stronger

46

America? An America that can no longer be pushed around? Well, if military spending is being beefed up to forty billion a year and we get supplies of tantalum cut off, what's going to happen to the price? What I'm holding here is a key to America in the eighties, a strong America with flexing muscles. What I'm holding is a piece of tantalum from what we think is the largest domestic supplier of the mineral, Doomsday Materials' number one mine in Helena, Montana.

" 'Tantalum in nineteen forty-five sold at four hundred dollars a ton. Now it's *seventeen* dollars a ton, and escalating by the week. The U.S. government is starting to stockpile tantalum. We're in on the ground floor with this company, gentlemen. You movers and groovers are going to make your clients rich. And yourselves rich, also. Let me introduce my assistant, Gaelen Fisk. She's the most beautiful mining engineer in America. She'll give you a taste of tantalum you won't forget. Then let's get on with the cocktails.' "

Herbert tells me that Ms. Gaelen Fisk looked as much like a mining engineer as he did the Easter Bunny but that "they both paid heavy attention to me at cocktails, during dinner, and later in the casino. She's next to me at the crap table," Herbert tells me, "and she's rubbing right into my arm, so it's difficult to throw the dice. I like to twist them coming out, turn my hand over to give a little extra flick. 'Let's go out for a drink, Herb,' she says to me after she rubs so hard on my arm that I throw a seven and crap out.

" 'What about Darrin?' I say, being polite, since he was paying.

" 'We're going to do what we came down here for,' says she.

"So into the bar we go," says Herbert, "and by now, since it's too late to call the office, I'm ready to find out why we came down here. Hey, life isn't all money after ten P.M."

In the bar they each order J & B with soda. "She stirs it with her finger," says Herbert. "And I never saw a woman do that before and she looks at me and says, 'Are you going to help us, Herb?' Well, Gaelen Fisk had my two favorite things, long dark

47

hair and a big bottom lip, and I reach out and grab her hand, the one with the finger that stirred the drink, and I say, 'My name is Herbert the Big Hitter and I earned my name the hard way. Some people think I'm a prick. I say that I pay attention to what's important. If we're going to play muftie puftie, let's go back to my room. If we're going to gamble, let's gamble. But making money, I don't need to go to Puerto Rico and look at brochures or listen to a hustle with fat stockbrokers from Fort Lauderdale. Which is it?' Gaelen Fisk sticks her tongue into her drink as she sips her drink, and I'm hoping she'll go for the room.

" 'Let's talk about making money,' she says. And for the next half-hour she gives me chapter and verse about strategic metals in general and Doomsday Materials in particular: the acquisitions they had in mind, the richness of their ore, the potential European buyers, the earnings, which could be over ten dollars a share in two years. 'We expect Doomsday to be a hundred dollars a share *minimum* in two years,' she says.

"Then she says, 'It could even be as much as a *thousand* dollars a share.'

"I signed for the drinks and went back to the casino," Herbert tells me, "thanked N. Darrin Black for the hospitality, put a hundred on red for one spin of the wheel, won, and went to bed.

"You gotta keep things separated in your life," Herbert the Big Hitter says. "Don't talk to your wife during the business day. Don't fall in love for a piece of ass. Keep your eye on the apple, which is getting rich enough to tell anyone to kiss off.

"I come back to my office, count up my holdings in Doomsday Materials. I have a total of seventy-five thousand shares, twenty thousand for me, ten for the surgeon, the rest scattered in other accounts. The stock's moved up to six and a half, seven, mainly, I knew, on the brokers from Puerto Rico buying heavily. Darrin Black keeps calling me to update me on their plans and I ride with the stock. Two weeks after I'm back, Gaelen Fisk calls me

48

and says, 'Darrin's gone to Germany, two banks have promised to buy up to two hundred and fifty thousand shares, and we're looking at a company that processes chromium. Which is even in shorter supply than tantalum.'

"I punch my machine," Herbert goes on. "Doomsday is eight and a quarter.

" 'I'll tell you, Herbert,' she says. 'I met Darrin on March nineteenth. We want the stock to be nineteen by the nineteenth.'

" 'On the way to a thousand a share, right?' Herbert says.

" 'Right,' says Gaelen Fisk, the most beautiful mining engineer in America.

"I get off the phone," the Big Hitter says, "and instantly begin selling all of my Doomsday. It takes three days, with Darrin Black promoting elsewhere and me hitting the bids. I sell it all between eight and eight and a half, generally a minimum hundred percent profit. The only client who doesn't sell is the surgeon, who says that short-term profits kill him. So an asshole is an asshole. The day after I sell, Gaelen Fisk calls me.

" 'You double-crossed us,' she yells into the phone. 'We take you to Puerto Rico, you hold my hand, drink our drinks. You said you'd help us. *You've* been doing all the selling.' "

Herbert tells her, "Don't confuse free drinks with real life, sweetheart," and hangs up. "I learned a lesson years ago," Herbert says to me, "and it's become Herbert's market rule number one. When anyone calls and tells me a six-dollar stock is going to a hundred, I immediately become a seller."

Doomsday Materials currently sells at thirty cents. N. Darrin Black and Gaelen Fisk are working a company in DNA research, and Herbert the Big Hitter had a pillow made for the eight-piece couch in his office. On the pillow is embroidered *Never kid a kidder*. With his profits from Doomsday he invested in a tax shelter, a government-subsidized housing project outside San Juan, Puerto Rico. The tax writeoffs will total a little better than three to one on his investment.

3

New York: Ring Around Rosie

It is the end of March, the time of slushy streets and gray flannel skies and the time to make my quarterly visit to New York. I have a lot of clients in New York City. Like clients everywhere, they like to see you; they like to have their hands held. Most customers forgive you for losing them money. What they do not forgive is your giving the impression that you are ignoring them. New Yorkers, being more neurotic than most Americans, need the reassurance that you are there, paying attention to them. I go to New York every three months to hold hands, touch base, pick up gossip, and let the patients know that they are loved.

One of my New York clients is Henry the Red. I always see him on my trips there, because he likes to put the work, and particularly New York, into perspective for me.

"New York is a hick town," Henry the Red has often said to me. Henry the Red is a philosopher who spends his days making maternity dresses. The motto of his manufacturing company is *You knock 'em, we frock 'em*. Henry the Red lives in a two-bedroom apartment on Park Avenue and Sixtieth Street with his second wife, whom Henry calls the Widow Fryberg.

"New York is a hick town," he repeats, "because it can never concentrate on anything for more than six months. We are like little metal balls in a pinball machine, smashing around in vain, looking for a free game. But all most of us really get in New York is 'tilt.'

"This is the town of the emperor's new clothes," he goes on, warming to his subject. "Everyone's afraid to admit we're spiritually naked. New York reminds me of the old Speedy Gonzales joke with the punch line 'This won't hurt, did it?' People are constantly out to screw you, afraid in turn of being screwed. We whip ourselves into a frenzy every day; we get violently excited about trivial things. Fads come and go faster than we change styles in sportswear. And on weekends everyone you know races to get as far away from the city as possible. They wouldn't be caught dead in the city on weekends."

"Why don't you move, if you've put up with this for too long?"

"Hey," Henry the Red says, "you've got to complain about it; you've got to get it off your chest. If we moved, where would the Widow Fryberg get egg creams? There would be no Caviarteria. Where else could we stand in line for two hours on Third Avenue in the rain to see a movie I know I'm going to hate but we're told we should like? So we stand in line. I'm right! New York *is* the ultimate hick town. But it's also the only town."

Henry the Red sits in cafés opposite Lincoln Center on weekends in the spring. He has a masseur come to his apartment three afternoons a week. "Conversation is my first love," he says. "But to be a philosopher on weekends, you have to make garments during the week. Otherwise, in New York you have no legitimacy."

If you're a visitor to New York, on business or pleasure, maintaining control is the key to your trip. You cannot panic when confronting New York. The way an animal senses that you are afraid, New York can also smell that fear. You're dead in New York if she smells that fear. This is the edge that New York has: she gives you doubts that perhaps you're not good enough, perhaps you don't have it. There are only two ways to operate successfully in the city: either with a great deal of money, or without any money at all. I have been in New York under both conditions. Now, flying down on a gusty March day, I condition myself for the city the way an athlete warms up for a game. I try to remember the past, the rules for making it in New York.

I trained on Wall Street in the early 1960s, making $75 a week and living in a resident hotel that cost me a third of that. I shared a toilet with someone I never saw. The toilet compartment connected our two rooms. My room looked over an airshaft. It had a sink in one corner, a bed, and a small bureau. If I stretched out on the floor, I could touch the opposite wall. The cockroach population ensured that I would never stretch out on the floor. There was a communal kitchen in the hallway with an ancient refrigerator in which I was allowed some small space. I kept one item there, a bottle of Frascati wine that cost ninety-nine cents. I would drink that alone or with a guest in one sitting and replace it the next day, hoping that I was in time to preserve my little piece of the grimy icebox. My guests in those days were always dates who were too drunk, too foolish, or too romantic to mind the squalor.

I did not see myself then as a mover in high finance. My adventures were not in the office. They were elsewhere, as I tried to see whether I could make it through the month on my salary. I was a scrounge in a three-piece suit. Sex was relatively easy to obtain; it was money that was hard. And I assumed, at age twenty-three, that those conditions were more or less permanent. I would meet friends of mine in various bars, such as the

Cattleman at Grand Central Station. We'd nurse draft beers for fifty cents and eat free chicken wings until dinner was no longer necessary. Young lawyers were paid $7500 to start at that time; medical students and interns were paid virtually nothing. We were all broke. New York is wonderful if you are broke or have $5 million. Anyone in between those figures seems permanently squeezed, always playing catch-up.

After my training period, I left the city. As I was carrying suitcases down my dingy hallway, I bumped into a young lady opening the room next to mine. She was lovely. This was the person who had shared my toilet, whom I had never met in six months. Six months of hearing flushing sounds. She smiled at me. "Ships that pass in the night," she said. I left her my last bottle of Frascati.

When I next returned to New York it was on my honeymoon. The first thing I did on entering our hotel room was lie on the floor. "What are you doing?" my wife asked.

"It would take ten of me to touch the other wall," I answered. "And no roaches." We had a suite at the Plaza. After that, each time my wife and I came to New York we booked a room at the Plaza, and each time we checked in we were told, "We're terribly sorry, Mr. Spooner, but all our rooms are gone. We're going to have to give you a suite, if you don't mind. Of course the rate will be that of a double room."

"Of course," I answered, and after the second time this happened I accepted the procedure as our just due.

An investment banker friend of mine has told me that no one likes to make a deal unless it is consummated in New York. As if being there somehow makes it bigger; as if being there makes it official. New York really is Oz, and we all treat it the way Dorothy and her companions did that kingdom: with anxiety. Getting suites at the Plaza for the price of a room became part of the ritual I needed to feel up to the situation, up to the challenge of New York meetings and New York clients.

On the second of our Plaza suite trips, I learned to develop the routines for impressing New Yorkers. One routine is this: if you're given a suite at the Plaza for the price of a room, invite lots of people to visit and never tell them your good fortune. Let them all think you naturally need a suite for the high-rolling that brought you to the city in the first place.

"Come up to our suite," we told Michael and Emily Pinata, friends who had invited us to a cocktail party. "To your *suite?*" they said. "We'll bring champagne." We were in our late twenties then, saving to buy a house and wondering whether I would ever have clients who would buy more than a hundred shares at a time. The Pinatas brought a bottle of Piper Heidsieck and couldn't believe the size of the rooms, the bath, the closets, the bed. "Wait until you meet these people tonight," Emily promised. "The movers and shakers in the city; they'll *love* you." Michael Pinata was a corporate attorney, just starting to develop a feel for his profession. Emily was from Santa Barbara and treated New York as her college, always signing up for classes at Hunter and the New School in Chaucer, ballet, bookbinding. Her latest class was in karate. "Look at this," she announced, kicking a small vase halfway across our suite's living room. It bounced on the thick carpeting and did not break. "The thing is," she said, "it's spiritual. One workout, and my mind is cleansed for days." She took a swipe at a lamp with an elbow. "Everyone in my class is getting ready for the revolution, and I want all my options open."

Bobby Kennedy had recently been killed. All our New York friends were constantly shoving clenched fists into the air and greeting each other with "Power to the people." But we went to the party in a decidedly uptown frame of mind, the champagne having prepared us for meeting strangers and the surprises that faces from the past may bring. The party was in a brownstone in the East Eighties. No one drank wine then unless it accompanied the meal. Gin and Scotch and bourbon poured with a heavy hand were the normal cocktails. Parties called from six to eight ended at ten-thirty, with the guests going on somewhere else, more to sop up the booze than to dine.

54

The party was my first introduction to Tommy (the Boomer) Hancock, the kind of money manager who becomes legendary in New York. For if New York is Oz, the Boomer was one of her special Munchkins. It was his party, in his brownstone apartment. Michael Pinata was one of his lawyers.

The Boomer never had only one of anything. He had two automobiles: one new Thunderbird, one antique Mercedes. He had two televisions, two bartenders, two rental houses: one in Southampton for weekends, one in Brittany for six weeks in the summer. He had two women at the party: one, a junior editor at Random House; one, his recently divorced wife, who flew small planes and waited for her trust check every quarter.

Boomer Hancock attacked life. His party was full of people he thought he should have: brokers, bankers, lawyers, art dealers, publishers, models, several New York Giants, two New York Rangers, and assorted Europeans who either had titles or were about to inherit them. The Boomer moved about his party, introducing people, pushing them to the bars for more drinks. He did not merely introduce you by name; he gave you a handle. "John, meet Tolly Levine," he would say. "She was on the cover of *Vogue* last year; lousy tits, great skin. John is a stockbroker, Tolly. One of the best, got the bridal suite at the Plaza. His wife, Susan, the long blonde with the pearls, will probably inherit fifteen million." The Boomer made most of it up as he went along. And he did the inexcusable: he said what was on his mind. By ten-fifteen he had pulled the left breast out of the dress of Tolly Levine, called the New York Rangers "Canadian toothless assholes," fired two of his lawyers, promised to buy an Andy Warhol for $23,000, lent a woman photographer his Diner's Club card, and made a lunch date with me for the next day at our suite.

The Boomer and Emily Pinata then gave a brief karate exhibition, in which Emily broke a tray full of glasses with a turnaround kick and the Boomer fell completely down his flight of stairs to the front door. Susan and I left. Two cabs refused to pick us up and the third drove us twenty blocks in the wrong direction, taking advantage of our condition. The desk clerk at the Plaza demanded identification before he gave us our key. I couldn't pronounce our room number without getting hysterical.

Susan woke up at five in the morning in our giant bed. "Darling," she said, "I feel sick."

"Umm," I said.

"I feel sick," she repeated. "And I can't move my legs." I woke up; she sounded panicky. "God!" she cried out. "I can't get my legs apart!" I dived under the covers, feeling ill and also frightened. I saw why she couldn't get her legs apart. She had passed out with her underpants around her ankles.

When the Boomer arrived for lunch, Susan was wandering the galleries of Madison Avenue and I was numb. He walked in wearing a gray, pinstriped, double-breasted suit over black cowboy boots. His dark hair was receding rapidly, but the dome that shone down from his six-five frame made him appear even taller. "I'm here to simplify your life," said the Boomer, scaling his wide-brimmed Dobbs hat onto a couch. "How about a Bloody?" Boomer Hancock managed people's money for a fee. He was thirty-one years old. "Twenty-Four Dollar Management" was the name of his company. The name came from the price supposedly paid the Indians for the island of Manhattan. He controlled assets of approximately $70 million.

"How are you going to simplify my life?" I asked him.

"Because I'm going to turn your business into a no-brainer," he said. "You're going to send clients to me. You're going to be a bird dog for Twenty-Four Dollar Management. You send me clients. I manage their dough. When I make buy-and-sell decisions, we give you the orders. Your customers thrive, you get the credit and the commissions, and the only thinking you do is about thanking me for making your life so easy."

"What if you *lose* my clients' money?" I asked.

He laughed and swallowed three quarters of his drink in one gulp. "I don't lose money. I have the best formula on the

56

Street. I play concepts; I play fads like you'd play catch with a tennis ball on the beach."

The Boomer told me how he had grown up poor in Providence, Rhode Island, his father a foreman in a textile mill, his Hancocks no kin to the Revolutionary autograph king, his name an accident. He was an all-state high school fullback, went to Yale after a postgraduate year at Andover, and then discovered two secrets that forged his adult life: bombast would intimidate people into giving in to him, and dreams would sell better than anything tangible. He was aggressive by nature, and in college he began running numbers for several New Haven low-level racketeers. The Yale students took chances, particularly the fancy set from New York, who always seemed to have money and cars and invitations to parties. They were the boys who never went to class but played bridge in the afternoons and poker at night.

"I started work in Boston," the Boomer told me, "in a brokerage firm run by an old Blue who had seen me play football. I stayed two years, until I realized that New York was the only place for me. You couldn't sell dreams in Boston; New York was 'concept city,' and that's where I had to make a stand. I had visited New York and seen the anxieties, seen people join El Morocco and pay five hundred dollars a year to say 'Hi, man,' to some asshole from television; seen people hang out at the bar at the Brook to say that they'd caught a glimpse of Harold Geneen. I wanted this town where people reward inadequacies and walk dogs while they hold paper napkins in their hand and pick up the crap. How can you not make a million in a city like that with an attitude like mine and a name like Hancock?"

* * *

I want to tell you about money managers, or investment advisers, as they are usually called. How do they differ from stockbrokers? I invest your money and charge you a commission

every time you buy or sell. I (atypically) keep 45 percent of each
commission dollar; the other 55 percent goes to the firm that
employs me. An investment adviser puts your money to work
for a fee, generally ranging from half of 1 percent to 2 percent
of your assets. Under this arrangement, you also pay commis-
sions to the brokers who execute the orders directed by the
adviser, but these commissions are usually at deep discounts,
even pennies per share. A particularly aggressive investment
adviser can run what is called a hedge fund. This is a pool of
capital whose participants pay no fee. But the adviser keeps 20
percent of all profits. The investment adviser in many cases is a
former stockbroker who resented giving pieces of the com-
missions to his firm. The hedge fund manager is even greedier
than the adviser — greedier and more egocentric — for if you
don't make money, neither does he.

There are several ingredients necessary for the investment
adviser. The first is the entrepreneurial spirit: you must want
to work for yourself. The second is an angel, someone who
either believes in your ability and wants to provide you with
the first large piece of business (money) to get started or is a
rich relative who has no choice.

* * *

In Boomer Hancock's case, his first wife's family kicked in $1
million. "Then it was easy," the Boomer told me. "You mention to prospective investors, 'Hey, the Barbarossa Company
pension fund just put in a million. I'm putting a ceiling on
what I'll invest the first year and I am taking *no* account under
two hundred and fifty thousand.'

"This does several things," the Boomer continued. "Of
course you never mention that the Barbarossas are your in-laws.
But my line to investors is key. First, they hear the word 'pension.' This makes everyone breathe a sigh of relief, because
somehow 'pension money' is a very responsible phrase. Pension
means retirement to people, and no one can fuck around with

retirement. Would anyone trust his retirement money to a weirdo, a flake? The last element that is needed is a gimmick, something different. 'Why should we give our money to you?' people will ask. 'What's your track record?' "

The Boomer paced my Plaza suite and told me why his management methods were unique. "This is the greatest town for fads in America," he said. "Luckily, the investment business is the greatest *business* for fads in America. Every year on Wall Street there is a new word, you know what I mean? 'Bowling' in the early sixties, 'electronics' in the middle sixties, now 'computers.'

"What I do is this: I've got a guy in Providence. I went to high school with him and he was going to be a priest until he made twenty thousand in Syntex and discovered his real religion: stocks. I call him 'the Monk.' He lives above a bowling alley and he reads every single magazine published, including *Soldier of Fortune* and *Teen*. He reads every regional newspaper, which he drives to Cambridge, Massachusetts, to buy, and he has made a young fortune for himself by discovering what Americans are thinking about before they even know themselves. He idolized me when I played football and he wrote my application essay for Yale and half of my high school themes. I send him tickets to every Yale-Harvard game, and on January first each year I call him and he says to me 'drugs' or 'retail' or 'mobile homes' or 'pollution,' and that's the fad I buy.

"Wall Street chases the big companies first in the field. Then every little piss-ant company that remotely resembles anything to do with the fad is bid up. When the Monk calls me and gives me the word, I buy every company I can grab in the field with sales over a hundred million. If I'm buying drug companies, for instance, I just ride them up as the fad develops. Perhaps this takes six months to a year. In this business you hear stories all the time. But as the fad matures, the first time someone tells me that a little company in La Jolla is coming up soon with a drug that cures liver cancer, et cetera, and it's selling for three and a half dollars a share, I sell every drug stock I own. Out. No waiting, no hedging. You know why? Because at or near the end of every fad in the market someone hypes a stock located in California that sells for under five dollars a share. It's always the kiss of death. Investment fads begin in New York and are killed in California.

"But I've got another wrinkle on this idea," the Boomer went on. "*One month* after I've sold all my drug stocks, I then sell them all *short*."

When you sell a stock long, *you are merely disposing of it, getting rid of it. When you sell a stock* short, *you hope that it will decline. Selling short allows you to profit from this decline; the more the stock drops, the more you make.*

"Why do I wait a month?" asked the Boomer rhetorically. "Because fads *always* go farther up than you think they will go. The reverse is true in the stock market. On the way down, the once-popular stocks go much lower than anyone thinks they'll sink. As long as I have the Monk," Boomer finished his pitch, "this town is mine. How much money can you drop in the pot? How simple can I make your life?"

I told the Boomer I appreciated his visit but that making my life simpler did not include giving control of it to other people. "I can't depend on one source for investment advice," I told him. "What if something happens to the Monk?"

"Nothing's going to happen to the Monk," he said. "I still send him tickets to Yale games. I buy him his subscriptions to *Barron's* and *Business Week*. What if you step off a curb and a taxi runs you over tomorrow? What if the ground opens up and swallows you?"

"I'm sorry, Boomer. I can't send you any business right now."

"Then what the hell did you come to New York for?"

"I came to take something *away*, not to leave it here."

He grabbed his trenchcoat and jammed his wide-brimmed hat on his head. "Well," he said, sticking out his hand. "You'll need the Boomer someday. I'm going over to the Racquet and Tennis Club and sit in the locker room. You can always pick up a few hundred thou from the guys with trust funds. The trust fund guys you can always sell dreams. They're afraid to say no to the Boomer. I *breathe* on them."

Not long after this, the inevitable. I booked a room at the Plaza for a New York visit and they gave me a room, not a suite. I was furious, like the man who for years had been cashing Social Security checks to which he was not entitled. He had done it for so long, he felt they were actually his. This marked the end of my scrounging days in New York and the beginning of my systematic trips to the city to gather assets. I began to develop what I call "Spooner's rules for making it in New York when you don't live there." Some of these rules are:

1. Never stay with friends; always stay in a hotel and give a frivolous reason, like "I just adore the terry-cloth robes at the Ritz-Carlton" or "the room service French toast at the Regency," or "Serge Semenenko used to give me stock tips at the Pierre." This makes New York friends think that you have important things to do with other people and also makes them think you have more money than you actually have. This independence will also make your friends much more likely to have a dinner party for you. Your host and hostess would never give a dinner party for anyone they *really* understood.

2. Has it ever struck you that New Yorkers always argue about where to go to dinner? When in the city, always insist on going to the restaurant of *your* choice. It is easy to develop favorites of your own and important to go there on a regular basis during your trips. Two visits are enough to get you recognition. New Yorkers go wild when an out-of-towner is welcomed and known in one of their restaurants. Have your own favorite piano bar for afterdinner drinks and always say, on the way there, "I used to love Bobby Short at the Carlyle. But we never go there anymore since the night he refused to sing 'A Shooting Box in Scotland.'" The more specific you are

about New York trivia, the more successful your raiding party will be.

3. Take a squash racquet with you to New York and carry it to meetings. The racquet serves two purposes. At the meeting you inevitably will be asked about it. "I have a game after lunch at the University Club." This assures New Yorkers that your time is rationed and that you are a man of decision. If there is time pressure and they think they are holding you from a sporting event, New Yorkers will say yes faster than people anywhere else.

The second purpose of the racquet is for use in walking the streets. Carry it over one shoulder at a jaunty angle. No one will ever mug you if you carry a squash racquet, a handy, portable, legal weapon.

4. When gathering assets in New York, that is, taking money out of the city to manage, I use the carrot and stick method. Give them the compliment, lead them on. "You know," I will say, "this city has more good information, more good sources and ideas, than any city in the world."

"Sure, that's why you come to New York," the client says.

"But the pace is such, no one ever gets a chance to put it together and see what it means."

"I know," the client says with a sigh. "There's so much happening, I can't even run my own business, much less pay attention to my money and my investments."

"That's where I get perspective," I tell him. "I come in fresh, pick the best brains, fly out in peace, and think about it. I have time to think about it and time to concentrate on what sounds right. Then I can invest without confusion, according to my own timetable. With no confusion or pressure, especially the pressure for lunches, drinks, and dinners, my time goes into your portfolio, not into war stories at P. J. Clarke's."

"Where do I sign?" asks the client. Clients know New York is the center of everything. But since it is also the center of confusion, they want their affairs maintained in what they believe is an atmosphere of calm. The Indians are still ready to give away Manhattan. But now the Indians are called New Yorkers.

Remembering the past, I would get off the plane, quicken my pace up to New York level, and shift my routines into high gear. I would need this energy to convince my clients again that I was indeed the expert from sixty miles outside of town whom they desperately needed.

There are times of the year when hotel rooms in New York are at a premium. Heavy convention and sales meeting seasons, fall and spring, can be difficult if you want one of the best hotels. Everyone reading this book has a friend who is in New York often on business. Salesmen on the road always make it a point to know hotel managers, maître d's, waiters, ticket reservation people at airlines. This is their edge, their way of getting to an order early. Have these friends make hotel reservations for you if you visit New York infrequently. It will usually ensure you a good room at the best hotel during difficult seasons.

Teddy Loveman, who sits in our board room watching the ticker tape, makes our reservations in New York. Even though he's retired, after forty years of shoe shows in Manhattan he has a well-established network. His routine with support people has always been the same. If he required reservations from a woman, he would say, "Can I ask you a question? What shoe size are you, darling?" (If it was a man, "What shoe size is your wife?") Since Teddy could get designer shoes at cost, or even (from friends) for nothing, on his next trip he would deliver high-fashion shoes that retail for over a hundred dollars a pair. This trip, Teddy booked me into the Park Lane on Central Park South near Fifth Avenue.

After meeting with clients in the morning, at lunch, and during cocktails, I decided to call Zan Furnace, an old friend who handled New York the way you might handle modeling clay. Zan was married to an art dealer who was never home. She was a magnificent hostess who shamelessly lied about everyone to make her guests sound fascinating.

"Come for dinner, darling," she said. "I'll increase your business dramatically so that you'll owe me one. You don't mind being descended from Russian royalty for the evening, do you?"

I didn't mind being anything for that evening, and by eight-thirty I was in Zan's living room, which was full of people drinking champagne and about to munch on cheeseburgers grilled over mesquite.

"Why do you care if I make a hit in New York or not?" I asked Zan.

She looked at me. "The truth? I could say it's because I like your wife. But actually I care only because of how it makes me look. You come in, you're descended from a Russian princess, but you also manage money, make a splash, everyone remembers the almost-prince. That's good for a week's, maybe two weeks' gossip at Mortimer's, the Club, the Colony. For us, it's good for a month of invitations. As soon as this is over I have to try to top it. Do you know that most of the important women in New York have press agents? My husband makes only two hundred thousand a year, so I have to make splashes by being inventive."

"Like allowing me to be the catch of the evening."

"Exactly."

Zan circulated, hugging bodies, kissing cheeks, sipping champagne. She was almost six feet tall, with hair as black as if it belonged to Diana Ross. There are people in every crowd who claim they drink only champagne, and Zan was one of them. She wandered about the room, spreading compliments. Then she returned to me. I was watching the lights outside the apartment window, wondering whether the party would actually bring me business or only a free dinner.

"I run in the Park, you know," Zan said. "Most of my friends run in the Park, hoping to see Al Pacino or Robert Redford when he's in town. Men call me all the time for running dates. It used to be that they'd call for lunch or drinks. Now it's running dates. There's a man in this room, married to my fifth best friend. He's after me all the time. The trouble is in New York that the successful men work for years to make their wives submissive. Then when they succeed at that, they don't want the wives anymore. I'm always getting asked to bed by married men because they think I'm slick."

"What do you do about it?"

"Well," she said, "I do go jogging with them and I do have lunches and drinks. But I never take an affair all the way. I can't do that to my family, and it's just too time-consuming."

"But you're flirtatious; you advertise."

"I suppose I do," Zan said. "That's why I do *something* about it."

"What do you do about it?" I asked. She threw down another tulip glass of the champagne. "I give hand jobs," she said.

"You do what?"

"You heard me right," she said. "I give hand jobs. Men in New York are satisfied with that."

"That answers the question," I said, "as to whether there's life after high school."

Zan laughed. "A woman has to do something that makes her unique in New York. Women here are so vulnerable. All my married friends entertain and worry about having people who haven't met each other. I mean, it's important to have people no one has met. My friends are bitter that their husbands have made it big but spend no time with them. You have to make an effort to survive here. I was on the cover of *Town and Country*, but it's old news now. You have to make an effort. No one will notice if you sink."

"The little lady has been monopolizing you all," one of the guests said. Zan introduced us for the second time and hugged him. "James Lee Pyle is from Dallas," she said. "Don't you know that Texans are trying to take over New York? That's why we're having mesquite cheeseburgers. They muscle their way onto the charity boards. To do that you either have to give big money or raise it. James Lee gives it. I raise it."

"You raise it, all right, sugar," he said, trying to kiss her neck. James Lee was a small Texan. Even with his three-inch boot heels, he had to stand on tiptoe to reach her.

"John is the best stock picker in the East," Zan said. "And he can fit into his grandfather's uniform from the czar's guard."

"Is that right? What do you like in the market?"

"Well, I've been buying an undervalued forest products' company," I said. "Southwest Forest, a lot of value, big board, and eleven and a half."

"Don't give me a song and dance. Zan likes you, you eat cheeseburgers, buy me ten thousand shares." Zan moved away, smiling. She took her empty champagne glass and rapped on it for silence with a shrimp fork. "I have only a few things to say. First, thanks to the out-of-towners for showing us a few tricks. Second, if you have friends moving to New York, Eighteenth and Second is the wrong place to live. Third, I had my eyes done, but why not? Fourth and most important: remember; I want to lead a white linen life." Everyone applauded. James Lee Pyle laughed louder than anyone. "You know," he whispered to me, "she cheats on her husband."

I said nothing.

"She gives hand jobs," he said. He put on an overcoat. Before heading out, James Lee reminded me, "Don't forget that ten thousand shares. Buy them and ship them on out." He handed me his card, and added, "One of Zan's friends told me that they play a game at dinner parties in New York. During coffee and brandy they go around the table and everyone has to name the one word that most characterizes their life. Zan's friend told me that Zan always says 'Perplexed.'"

When I said good night, I told Zan the story.

"I may say 'Perplexed,'" she said. "But remember, you got

a ten-thousand-share order and I'm holding your marker." The winds blew at gale force and I walked back to my hotel, knowing that in New York, more than in any other American city, women held the aces.

The next morning Joey the Trader picked me up at the Park Lane in a limousine. Joey used to work in my office and switched firms for a bigger piece of the action. We had run into each other at lunch the previous day, and I told him I was going to Wall Street the next morning to see an attorney client. "Hey," he said. "I'm at the Plaza and I'm going downtown too. I'll pick you up. No sense leaving anything on the New Yorkers' plate that ain't necessary. Why pay for a cab when you got Joey?"

Everyone wants to beat New York. My friend Joey the Trader has put many small nicks in her sides, raiding New York from afar, coming away with small prizes and retreating back into safe harbor. Nicking New York is a game for many people. For Joey the Trader it has been a crusade.

In business you don't have to search for the truth; it is continuously coming after you. In the money business it is more important to know the players than to understand most of the rules.

There is a fraternity of traders in the investment business. They deal strictly with institutions: banks, mutual funds, insurance companies, enormous pools of capital. The traders deal in big blocks of stock — hundreds of thousands of shares at a time — selling to the institutions, buying from them. Traders generally are paid salaries plus bonuses. They are not on commission, the way stockbrokers are. They live in big cities and are mostly Irish or Italian. They are street-smart, cynical, and know where to get tickets to any sold-out sporting event, musical comedy, or celebrity concert. They entertain their institutional clients three or four nights a week. A lot of entertainment is required to get orders for twenty thousand, fifty thousand, hundreds of thousands of shares.

There is not a national event of any importance for which traders do not instantly have jokes. The traders' network operates instantly, cross-country, on the trading desks of America, consoles of up to thirty lines apiece. Traders are the sergeants of the investment business, wiseass people with all the answers.

Joey says to me, "If sex is number one and money is number two, what are three and four?"

"Health and good weather," I say.

"No, dummy," says Joey. "Three and four are seven."

But actually only one and two exist for him — sex and money — the latter being the most important route to the former. Joey is twenty-nine years old. He is like a lot of people in America. He will put some money in the poor box on Sundays. But taking care of his family comes first. Taking care of his family does not leave a lot of time for dwelling on whether the whale survives or public broadcasting makes it. Joey works at having Joey and his family make it. Whatever is left over goes on the Steelers with six points or toward the quinella at various tracks.

But while Joey struggles for the perks that surround his eighty thousand a year, he moves billions of dollars around for the largest banks, mutual funds, and insurance companies in America. Joey is a conduit for money, with tremendous power to force millions of dollars in commissions to be channeled through his brokerage firm. How does he do it?

While we were having cocktails one evening a few months ago, Joey told me how. "Basically, romance is the key. But you gotta understand. There's all sorts of romance. There's lunch romance and dinner romance and romance at neutral sites."

"What's the difference?" I asked.

"Lunch romance is relatively easy," Joey told me. "It takes from one and a half to three hours and is done either head to head or group. Head to head is done fancy, the most expensive restaurants, the most expensive wine. That's where we take the snobs from trust departments that pretend they know the difference between Château Lafite and horse piss. They're doing

68

us a big favor by going to have us pay a hundred and fifty to two hundred dollars a pop for smoked salmon, soft-shelled crabs, a Grand Marnier soufflé.

"I learned to eat all that stuff myself," Joey said, "and some of it's not half bad. But we get for that lunch maybe four to five times the cost in commissions the bank gives us. It's tough business with the bank trust departments. They pretend more than anybody else that it's research and service they pay off for. Don't let anybody kid you; it's the Grand Marnier soufflé.

"The group lunches involve a bunch of traders going to a downtown bar where they have specials like mud wrestling or amateur topless contests. We bet on the outcome between us; the winners get so many shares or so much money in commissions from the losers. Now, we don't make the decisions about what is bought and sold; we just execute the orders. But the power is with the traders on the desks, because we're the ones who move the goods."

"Okay," I said. "What about neutral territory?"

"Well," Joey answered, "neutral territory is usually conventions or special assignments, as we call them. It's the heavy artillery for when we really want to impress someone."

"Give me an example."

"Last spring," Joey said, "we had the annual Eastern traders' convention in New York. We really wanted to get some business from the Midwest Teachers' Pension Fund. It's a pool of capital of over a billion dollars, bonds and stocks. Even a small share of the biz gets up into heavy numbers. There were two guys at the pension fund who controlled the buying, both of them straight as sticks, the kind of guys who wear both suspenders and a belt. We called them Mr. Inside and Mr. Outside and we were being funny, because Mr. Inside never saw the sun in his life, and as for Mr. Outside, we didn't call him that because he was a good salesman. We called him that because we figured you couldn't take him anywhere outside Iowa.

"Also, they always sent back Christmas presents — Mark Cross wallets, sports duffels, simple stuff — unopened. What did these guys want? Well, considering this a personal challenge, I went myself to pick them up at LaGuardia. I had a white stretch limo with champagne stuck in an ice bucket in the back. I didn't touch the champagne myself. But I did have six Saint Pauli Girl beers, ya know, on the ride up, which I didn't heave out the window. I tucked in a bag on the front-seat floor out of sight.

"Mr. Inside and Mr. Outside were both carrying suitcases with stickers of Zion National Park on them, and they told me they'd be happy to take the bus into the city because they couldn't be under any obligation. I smiled and told them that they'd do the same for me if I came to Iowa and that it was just simply the good-neighborliness of the industry. They huddled next to the baggage carousel, stuck out their hands, and said, 'A deal, thanks.'

"You could tell," Joey continued, "that they had talked a lot about the corruption of the city versus the purity of the country. But after passing several sets of graffiti written on the concrete bridge supports and the street kids playing handball and basketball next to the fallen-down houses of Queens, they sank deeper into the cushions of the limo and reached for the champagne. I discovered on the ride that Mr. Inside and Mr. Outside really were terrified of New York. They were afraid of being mugged, robbed, being insulted and abused. I told them that I completely shared their fears and that I hated the city, the Yankees, the Jets, the Giants, and the Knicks. We became brothers outside of the bubbly after that and I promised that we would not travel anywhere out of easy whistle of the limo.

We finished two and a half bottles of Mumm's on the way to the hotel and I had real-life visions of every farmer's daughter and traveling salesman joke I had ever heard. The brotherhood of the grape tends to unite these differences of geography and politics. Mr. Outside and Mr. Inside stuck to me the rest of the evening like shit to the tractor wheel."

Joey told me that they went to the traders' banquet at the Waldorf that night and ate every single bite of every course, including refills on the roll basket and the butterscotch sundaes left untouched by their tablemates, two nervous and dieting traders from the Cleveland Trust.

"After dinner," Joey went on, "we listened to one of America's biggest economists and a former Treasury secretary in a rented tux tell us a lot of statistics we didn't understand and could care less about, for which he was paid five thousand bills. I was hoping no one would ask him any questions, because I was losing the edge, when they stopped serving drinks at the table. The economist was hoping no one would ask him questions either, like 'What the fuck are you talking about,' when Mr. Inside stood up and said, 'Mr. Economist. This was all very interesting but we have specific questions. We trade the stock market all day long. It would be really helpful if you would tell us this: Would you be a buyer of stocks today, and, if you would, what kinds of American stocks would you own?'

"Well, the economist hemmed and hawed and went on for ten minutes and never answered the question. Mr. Outside jumped up as the speaker was gulping some water and Mr. Outside said, 'I'm from Iowa, Mr. Economist, and we don't have the New York advantage of a bar and grill on every corner. But I did some homework before we came east.' You coulda heard a pin drop, but instead all you did hear," Joey said, "was cellophane being torn off the cigars.

"Mr. Inside continued, 'I can understand that you're not going to give us tips on the market about what you are buying, even though that's the one speech we'd really like to hear. I know you believe in the power of the individual and that you follow the philosophy of Ayn Rand. Indeed, Mr. Economist, I read *The Fountainhead* in college and it charged me right up. Trouble is that life tends to beat out of you the glories of the individual. Did you ever get to go to bed with Ayn Rand?'

"The economist covered the microphone with his hands,

spoke briefly to the chairman of the traders' convention at the head table, and left the room to polite applause. When he was gone, Mr. Inside and Mr. Outside got a standing ovation and a tray full of stingers.

" 'Actually,' Mr. Inside said, 'if the speaker were a true follower of *The Fountainhead,* he would have approved of what I did.'

"The stingers were the finishing touch," Joey said. "Stingers usually are. Anyway, the Midwest Teachers' Pension has got roughly three million in commissions to pass out every six months, and money draws a crowd. Morgan Stanley, Salomon Brothers, and First Boston came by after dinner to whisk Mr. Inside and Mr. Outside to private clubs where backgammon was the sport and little sandwiches without crusts were served after midnight. The Iowans declined. 'If Joey from Boston wants to drink beer,' Mr. Outside told them, 'we're obliged to Joey. And we get the feeling that you in New York would not bring us home for dinner. Joey, from Boston, has already asked us to his *house.*'

"Meanwhile," Joey told me gleefully, "I'm jumping up and down in back of the Iowans, throwing the bone to the boys from Yale at Morgan Stanley." Joey got Mr. Inside and Mr. Outside into his limo after two rounds of stingers. He took them to a key club, where there were cheeseburgers and their choice of two dozen ladies who paraded through the cheeseburger room for their viewing pleasure.

"I'm a happily married man," Mr. Inside told Joey, as Mr. Outside walked off into the pool area with a black woman from Montserrat and a graduate student from Sarah Lawrence. They each cleared $175 on a good Wednesday night.

"We have two sayings in South Boston," Joey told Mr. Inside. "One saying is 'Eatin' ain't cheatin'.' The other is 'It ain't a mortal sin to watch.' "

"But what are we talking about in actual dollars?" I asked.

Joey sighed. He hates to get to the point during cocktail hour, and I was buying. "You know," he said, "I was in Texas in the Army. Nuevo Laredo, in Mexico, was only an hour away from our base. I said to myself then, 'Where has this been all my life?' And I realized that in my mind a border town should always be no more than an hour away. Now, New York is an hour away by shuttle and, as a border town, it's more expensive but almost as good. If you think of New York as a border town, it makes it bearable."

The wise slave or servant or jester is as old as Plautus and is documented in drama from Shakespeare and Ben Jonson up to Jack Benny's Rochester and television's Ann B. Davis in "The Brady Bunch." The jester who outsmarts the establishment, who has the last laugh, exists in real life beyond the stage. Joey the Trader, in one twenty-four-hour period in New York, consumed five meals, more than the equivalent of three bottles of whiskey, four bottles of wine, one bottle of cognac, and seventeen cans of beer. I should also mention two boxes of Antonio y Cleopatra cigars. He also charged one Fleetwood stretch limousine, one airline shuttle, one double hotel room, one prostitute from Mobile, who, in lonely moments, continually hummed the country and western ballad "Alabama Rain." Joey's combined tab came to $727.40, which he submitted entirely to his firm.

In a separate travel and entertainment invoice, Joey included his receipt for "hamburgers and birthday party for Midwest Teachers' Pension Fund: $475." Joey's receipt included mention of hors d'oeuvres, birthday cake, champagne, and candygram. The whorehouse cost Joey $300; he spent the $175 difference on several lottery tickets, a pair of Dingo boots, and a day of beauty for his girlfriend at Diego's Salon, which included a pedicure and an introduction to aerobic dancing.

In the first month after the convention, Joey received orders from Mr. Inside and Mr. Outside that generated $47,000 in commissions for Joey's institutional department. Joey received an override on the business, a bonus really, of $1100 before taxes.

I ran into his boss shortly after Joey told me about his coup.

"It's no big secret," I said to him, "how a lot of business is done on the institutional level in America. I think it's interesting that you have a no-questions-asked policy."

Joey's boss went to Brooks School and Williams College. He and his second wife go to Watch Hill, Rhode Island, in the summer. She watches him the way a basketball statistician used to watch Bill Sharman hit free throws. "You know," he said, "Joey always thinks he's putting one over on us. The truth in Wall Street is that if you produce, you can get away with anything. Most of the time I'm pissed that I went to Williams and that I can't get away with going to the whorehouses with Joey. You pay a certain penalty in our business for lining up with management."

I told Joey what his boss had said, and he laughed. "He's a horny bastard, but he's got to be careful, or he thinks he does. Rockefeller can die in the saddle, but he better not croak on a night out with Joey the Trader."

Joey instinctively knows that other people's money will pay off for him. "I got a card from Mr. Outside," he told me. "It was the classic old line, a picture of the Iowa State Fair, and it said, 'You can't beat our pigs.' You know why they give me the business? I'll tell you. They loved getting laid in New York. But New York is evil and Joey the Trader is good. I can sugarcoat the experience because I'm not a hustler the way they think of New York hustlers. I'm in their pocket for the duration. Guilt is a big deal in this business," Joey said. "Today I'm planning on taking two insurance companies and a bank to Nantucket for lunch by helicopter. For that they'll pay off twenty to one the cost of the chopper." He grinned at me. "And the nuns told me I'd always be a bum."

On the ride downtown, I reminded Joey of the story. "Ah, Christ," he said, "it's always a struggle against New York. You know why I'm down here today? I'm down to defend the expense account. Can you believe it? Every time we get a new boss, he starts off being an asshole." Joey let me off at the corner of Wall and Broad Streets. Before he left, I needed to know.

"Are all your charges for real?" I asked.

"What, are you serious?" Joey said. "I do the business, right. Of course the charges aren't real, but people have to be used to how things are. No sense being an asshole when business is *good.*"

No other city in the world reminds you of your own mortality more than New York. The next morning it was one of those freak sunny days in March when you think New York is an Easter Parade and all deals are possible. Feeling on top of things, I was staring down on the Park from my eighth-floor window. Joggers ran the pathways; the horse carriages clomped the streets; people were taking early lunches on benches in the sun.

Suddenly there were yells on the sidewalk below my gaze. As if in a movie, I saw a taxi driver jump from his vehicle and begin to haul two passengers from his back seat. A well-dressed man and woman tumbled out. The man and the driver set about each other, flailing their arms, kicking shins. The woman, in a long fur, jumped on the cabbie's back, grabbing his face, pulling his ear. I could hear the screams but no words. The cabbie threw the couple off, and they circled each other, occasionally lunging out with feet and pocketbook. A crowd gathered in the sunshine. I could see people clapping their hands. The woman dragged her companion away toward Fifth Avenue. The cabbie followed, gesticulating. I had read that morning that a record 9268 handgun licenses were applied for in 1982. That was a thousand more than the previous year. A bellman came into my room to collect my bags. I was catching an afternoon plane. Going home. "There was a fight down there," I told the bellman, explaining the scene. He shrugged. "This is war here, sir. Anyone who doesn't understand that doesn't understand New York."

A few minutes later, on the street with my bags, I believed the bellman. Waiting for a cab, I was lifted off my feet in a bear hug. A voice whispered in my ear, "We eat wimps like you for breakfast in this city." It was Tommy the Boomer Hancock. I hadn't seen him in years, but I knew he had been wiped out with his concept theory in the early 1970s, when Wall Street and the market collapsed. Concepts went the way of Cameo Parkway Records, Equity Funding, and King Resources as the investment business ran with red ink and blood.

Not only had the stock markets declined; the Boomer's source of ideas, the Monk, had died. "When your genius dies," the Boomer said, "it isn't long before it catches up with you. You depend on one person in your life, you're bound to be unhappy. Sooner or later the one person disappears. The Monk got hit by a Brown student driving a Pinto. You always got to plan for that event, and I didn't. Neither did the poor Monk, and he died before he could give me that year's concept."

The Boomer looked terrific. "I look like money, don't I?" he said.

I asked him what he was doing.

"I'm doing what I should have done years ago," he said. "It's a no-brainer that's making me a fortune. I give lunches for heavy hitters. I send out ten thousand letters a month to public corporations. 'Are you happy with the price of your stock?' I ask them. Well, who's happy with the price of their stock? Nobody. The chief executive officer comes in for lunch. I invite key institutions: the big banks, mutual funds, insurance companies, the largest buyers of stock in America. I give them lobster salad, white wine, Poland Spring water, and the best beer in America, Rolling Rock, in long-necked bottles. There is no presentation. The CEO shoots the breeze with the institutions. They ask questions, he answers.

"I don't set fees for this," Boomer said. "Never set a fee, and they'll always pay you more. What do you think is fair? I ask the mutual fund. They always give me hundreds of thousands of shares *more* than I would have figured. You see, most people you meet feel guilty most of the time. Guilty about their elderly mothers, their kids living with the ex-wife, their depraved thoughts, or where they cheated the IRS. If I give them no set fees, they pay me much more than they ordinarily would. Because they're feeling guilty that I may think they're cheap, not big-time enough."

"Why should they come to your lunches? Why can't anyone do it?"

"Hey," said the Boomer, stepping back so that I could admire his double-breasted cashmere topcoat with matching cashmere Borsolino hat. "This is the *Boomer*. These people have no adventure in their lives. Have you ever met anyone who invests money for an insurance company? Be serious. They come for the adventure. You never know when there's a chance to fly with the Boomer down to Palm Beach for a little fishing expedition. A little jaunt to the Flame or the Petite Marmite with two-hundred-dollar hookers who join us for dinner. Huh? In Florida the hookers work part time at the health clubs. Then you take them to the Colony or off to Exuma. That's the big place to take hookers today, Exuma.

"Adventure and lobster salad and Rolling Rock: this is the game of the Boomer. See, if I went bust in Philadelphia or Baltimore or Boston, I might as well leave town for good. No one forgets in those cities; you'll always be the Boomer, who crapped out. But in New York they love resurrection. New York always gives you another chance to walk away winners. You know why? Because she laughs at you. Charlie Bluhdorn died a few weeks ago. [Charles Bluhdorn, who died on February 18, 1983, was chairman of Gulf & Western Industries. He built the company from a small auto-parts concern into a multibillion-dollar conglomerate that ranked fifty-first among the Fortune 500 corporations.] He died on his own plane coming back to New York. His favorite expression was 'What is the bottom line?'

"The bottom line, Charlie, is death," the Boomer added. "New York sweeps them aside and goes on, trying to croak another genius, before his time. And you know the final irony? The stock jumped almost ten points within days of his death.

He could buy companies, but he couldn't move the stock. He dies, Wall Street figures they sell off the pieces of Gulf and Western, it's worth more than the whole. The final joke is the stock jumps when the chairman dies. The bottom line."

I didn't have time to get depressed over Boomer's philosophy. I was late for my plane and jumped into the first cab in line at the Park Lane's front door. "LaGuardia," I ordered and, *whack*, back I went against the seat as the cabbie got us to fifty-five miles per hour before we hit the light at Fifth and Fifty-ninth. I peered at the driver's ID. His name was wonderful: Fux Tilsit. He had a shaved head and a mustache like a Turk-ish lancer's. Away he went as the light turned green, zeroing in on pedestrians, slower cars, civilian vehicles, like a mad Russian guest-star driver on "The Dukes of Hazzard."

"Fux, old boy," I yelled at him, "I'm not in that much of a hurry! I want to get there alive." He answered by pushing a button that locked all the doors and increasing his speed. We were at the Eastern shuttle in twenty-one minutes, and I have never been so terrified in my life. Fux drove as if pursued by every gang in the South Bronx on Harley-Davidsons. I jumped out of the cab with my bags and came to his window. "What the hell is the matter with you, Fux? How long have you been driving in New York?"

"I been driving thirty year," he said, holding out his hand. "What's the matter for you, don't you know this is war?"

Not being from New York, I naturally tipped him. Being from New York, he naturally did not thank me. But Fux did miss my feet as he burned rubber back to the battles, back to the war.

I called the office from my gate to check the price of South-west Forest. "It's off a quarter," Sardonic Sandra told me, and added, "I hope the Texan pays for the ten thousand shares." I said a silent prayer that the Texan would pay for the stock and rushed to join the growing line of people hurrying to escape New York.

4

Such
a Deal

April 4. There is a rhythm to every business, the same way there is a rhythm to a poem or a golf swing. Coming back to the market after a three-day weekend makes me feel a little rusty. April Fool's Day was also Good Friday this year. On Good Friday the stock market is traditionally closed. We close because back in the late nineteenth century the New York Stock Exchange adopted the same holidays as the London exchange. So a three-day weekend is fine, but it interrupts the concentration on the trend of your business.

Crossing the street to my office building I met one of our brokers, Peter the Bargain King. He was carrying an armful of boxes. Peter felt the three-day weekend an intrusion and echoed what many men felt about their office and their homes. "Thursday afternoon at four, *bang*. It stops," he said. "What am I going to do at home for three days? No prices. I read *Barron's* on Saturday in an hour, then I got nothing to do. I hate to say it, but I could live in the office, you know what I mean? In the office I got conversation, I got action, I got the chance to make

79

some bucks, and I can see my prices going by. At home you see no prices going by, know what I mean?"

I asked Peter where he was going.

"You know where I'm going," he said. "I'm going to the Bargain Basement to return all this crap. The best time to go is first thing in the morning, when everyone else is still in shock. I buy bargains for everyone in the family — the three boys, the wife, my mother, my Aunt Betsy. I got all the sizes on a card. Then I bring everything home, we try them on, I bring back most of the stuff the next day."

"Why doesn't your wife or Aunt Betsy return what you don't want?"

"What the hell do they know about bargains?" asked Peter the Bargain King. "My wife wanted to sell my Clorox at nine and a half. Today it's twenty-five. Hey, this stuff is heavy. Need anything? They got Ralph Lauren ties at three bucks. Can you believe there are fools who pay retail for merchandise?"

Peter hurried away. I watched him pick a tabloid newspaper out of a trash barrel and add it to the pile he was carrying. Peter could spot bargains even if they were the wrong size, wrong color, and yesterday's style. Dealing was Peter's vice and his narcotic. He pursued his passion in numerous ways, all small scale. Conversely, of course, he hated anyone who asked him for a discount when buying stocks. "Chiseling bastards," Peter would call them.

We all love bargains where we can find them and we all pursue our deals, some of us secretly hoping to screw the other guy, all of us hoping the right deal at the right time will set us free. In the world of business, polite and fancy names are given to the enterprises that attract the biggest sharks. On Wall Street, these names are investment banking, corporate finance, and venture capital.

Deals in the corporate world are made by people who sit in meetings for hours at a stretch, who love to go hammer and tongs at negotiation without respite. I have a lone-wolf mentality and hate meetings and negotiations and arguments over the last $5000 or the last perk for the outgoing chairman. But in greedy times, you tend to look around. Invariably you see people who are raking it in faster than you. In greedy times, people who make ordinary income taxed at the highest rate get itchy to make deals. I'll tell you the story of Spooner the Lone Wolf setting out to make himself rich on the toil of others. Essentially, this story illustrates the stuff of capitalism: why companies go public and how money is raised for new ideas, for entrepreneurs.

In the late 1960s, a wild stock market ran parallel to civil disorder and the hippie revolution. A I have mentioned, it was possible for companies to form in several months with no assets other than a "concept" that would appeal to frenzied investors. These companies would be incorporated, promoted, and sold to the public at inflated prices plucked from the air. These issues would be often oversubscribed, popping up on the first day of trading to premiums and creating instant wealth for the owners and promoters, most of whom had bought their stock for pennies per share.

I watched this flowing around me as I collected commissions. But I either spent the commissions or had them taxed away from me. I suffered from the disease common to Americans: no savings. At this time, while flying to the Bahamas for a company convention, I met a man who had bought twenty companies public in a four-month period. He had rings on his fingers and bells on his toes. He had a new young wife and a Monte Cristo cigar always lighted.

"What are you, a stockbroker?" he said. "But what good is that? Look at these . . ." He pulled from a briefcase seven or eight prospectuses for new stock offerings. All over the front page of each was stamped the legend *Highly speculative* or *Involves a high degree of risk*. Two of the companies were in the nursing-home business; one claimed to manufacture and sell natural pet food; and one was a proposal for a theme park of American heroes with one exhibit actually showing a wax model of Nathan Hale being hanged.

The man tapped this last prospectus with a forefinger that showed a half-inch of flesh and two inches of diamond ring. "See the offering? One million shares at two dollars and fifty cents a share. It's now three and a half. Theme parks are the hot idea of the future. Learn about American history painlessly. Go down the Thomas Jefferson waterslide. I own fifty thousand shares at a penny. One cent, right? It cost me five hundred dollars four months ago when we put this thing together. Now it's worth *one hundred and seventy-five thousand.* Is this capitalism? Is this free enterprise?"

"But you can't sell this stock," I pointed out. "It's restricted."

Restricted or lettered stock represents securities that must be held at least two years from date of issue. This ruling prevents the owner of inside or founders' *stock sold at a cheap price, in this case a penny, from capitalizing on new-issue frenzy. The two-year waiting period presumably proves whether or not the company in question can survive. For this man with founders' stock, this was an* illiquid *investment, at least for the two-year holding period. He could not buy and sell the security the way you can buy and sell Exxon or General Motors.*

My fellow flier looked at me as if I were a fool. "You don't wait two years to cash in," he said. "Don't you think the banks are greedier than anyone else? I bring the lettered [restricted] stock to a bank. It's considered good collateral. I take a haircut on what they'll lend me to maybe sixty percent of the current value. On this little baby, they give me over a hundred thousand dollars. I pay prime, or seven percent, on the dough. The interest charge is deductible, and I've got the use of all this money while I wait the two years for the big bonanza."

"The only catch," I said, "is if these companies fold or the market goes bad."

"That's the kind of sour grapes you get from someone without a piece of the action. Don't you know concepts are always

82

in fashion? Where you been, son? We're in the middle of a twenty-five-year boom market."

"What's the matter, darling?" my wife said as I slumped back in my seat.

"That turkey," I said, "is making a fortune by throwing beanbags through holes in Benedict Arnold's chest. He's cashing in on recreation rooms in nursing homes. I'm worried about IBM going up or down a few points, and he's selling iceboxes to the Eskimos."

She smiled. "Don't covet thy neighbor's capital gains."

"That's thy neighbor's *wife*."

She took a sip of her complimentary Bloody Mary. "That, too."

I was missing something easy, and it rankled. Why couldn't I add deal-making to my repertoire?

The next week an old friend from college called. He was going to be visiting from out of town and wanted my advice. "Sure," I said, "come on up whenever you arrive." My friend had been a wrestler in school, a wrestler at a hundred and thirty pounds. I remembered that he ordinarily weighed considerably more than that out of season and that he was always throwing up and taking enemas to make the weight for meets. Chas Hooper was serious and dedicated. "Did you just throw up?" I greeted him. "You look trim and marvelous."

"To succeed," he said, "you have to make the weight in life." Then he proceeded to tell me that he and his sister dedicated their lives to helping the high school youth of America learn about their country and build their bodies at the same time. Chas Hooper never smiled as he told me of summer camps in the Rockies and in the desert of Arizona that he and his sister had started. "We've grown in the last two years from fifty kids to five hundred, in four-week sessions. We teach them survival, nutrition, body-building, classical music. And we bring in biggies from government, the law; you know, a Supreme Court justice here and there. They lecture in a low-key way, in jeans, about our heritage. I'd like to talk to you about expanding this dramatically all over the country. To do this we're going to need some big bread."

"You're talking about a concept, right?"

"The biggest concept of all," Chas Hooper said. "The explosion of the buying power of youth."

This was in 1968, and a company named National Student Marketing was one of the hottest stocks in America, having gone from 6 to 69 in a matter of ten months. *Never trust anyone over thirty* was the motto of the generation, and their elders were doing everything possible to try to exploit this nonsense.

I thought to myself, "This is an honest, hard-working man, probably with a good idea. I am not going to advise him to seek counsel elsewhere. I'm going to keep this one for myself."

"Chas," I told him, trying to sound confident, "I think you've come to the right place." I arranged a meeting for that night with Chas at his hotel. I brought with me my accountant and a friend of his, a friend my accountant had talked about for years. The friend's name was Bruce and he was a consultant. "Bruce can turn companies around," my accountant told me. "Bruce can see through the crap in a company better than anyone I've ever met," he added. "Bruce can spin flax into gold."

"I've never found," I told my accountant, "that Bruce is a name I can particularly trust."

My accountant was great with numbers and always spoke in clichés. "Don't judge a book by his cover," he responded. "You got a problem with a company, Bruce can straighten it out."

Bruce looked a lot like Zero Mostel. He was on his way to obese, but not quite there. Long black strands of thinning hair were plastered across his skull. The three of us, Bruce, my accountant, and I, met for a drink in the hotel bar before going up to join Chas Hooper. "I am violating my number one principle in being here tonight," said Bruce first off.

"And what is that?" I asked.

"Never show up anywhere without an understanding of your

84

fee. I never go anywhere for nothing. If you do, your advice is worth just that."

"But you don't even know if you people will get along; if it's a good idea; if it's do-able."

Bruce smiled the smile of experience. "Everything is do-able. Just make sure you don't walk in a room for free."

"Don't keep beating around a dead bush," said my accountant, and we left to go make a deal.

In his hotel room, Chas Hooper mesmerized us with his visions of an inspired younger American generation, strong in body, stimulated by the knowledge of our heritage taught in painless and interesting ways. "I believe I'll need half a million dollars to do this right," said Chas.

Bruce was sitting in a corner, reading Chas's projections of sales and profits for a five-year period. Chas predicted that he could grow from a thousand kids in his programs to twenty thousand in five years, with sales growing from $500,000 to $5 million. Profits would grow from $25,000 to over $2 million.

Bruce jumped from his chair. "You don't need half a mil. We'll raise two hundred and fifty thousand for you, which will buy twenty-five percent of the company. Our little group will take thirty percent of the company for our efforts in your behalf, plus expenses, plus fees for continuing advice. You keep forty-five percent, which is probably more than you should have if we were hard-nosed negotiators."

Chas was furious. "You came in here for only one reason," he said. "You're a friend of my friend John. And you proceed to tell me what I need like you're the sheriff who's going to throw me into foreclosure. You treat me like an idiot and you're going to walk away with thirty percent of my idea? I ought to throw you out of the room."

"Good business sense has nothing to do with emotion, Mr. Hooper," said Bruce.

"Let's not be running to conclusions, Chas," said my accountant.

I got up and went to the bathroom. This was not going the way I had figured, gentlemen of good will moving logically toward agreements that would satisfy everyone. Being a stockbroker was easy. You called clients and recommended a company to buy. In two minutes or less customers made up their minds. They bought or they didn't buy it.

So far, I had made five phone calls to all of the people in the room to make arrangements for the meeting. They all had to give their speeches and rebuttals. I didn't understand the numbers, hated meetings in general, and already knew I probably wouldn't get home until after midnight. I used the facilities and then leaned down to flush the toilet. An enormous *whoosh* came forth, one of the most powerful flushes I had ever witnessed. At the same time, as I was bending over, my glasses, which I had stuck in my vest pocket, plunged into the bowl and disappeared in the middle of the giant flush. I jammed my arm after them and felt a tug that threatened to pull me with them. I began to laugh. The big negotiator with his arm wet up to the elbow. I had a vision of myself in the pipe system of the hotel, searching for my lost spectacles, on my way out to sea. It put the entire meeting into perspective.

The principals were still yelling at each other when I emerged. None of them noticed my arm. I spent the rest of the evening looking at blurs and listening to recriminations. It took three more meetings and at least twenty-eight phone calls to hammer out the terms. Bruce and my accountant would prepare a private offering, a limited partnership, to raise $250,000 for a 25 percent stake in Chas Hooper's company. Each unit to which prospective investors could subscribe was $12,500, which bought 1 ¼ percent of the deal. The company was called Unlimited Youth Horizons. Bruce, my accountant, and I would own a total of 30 percent of the company. My 10 percent interest cost me $10,000, or a penny per share. This was the so-called founders' stock, "penny stock," which was really my fee for putting the people together and, I figured, for making all those phone calls.

86

Bruce would bill the company for any travel, meals, and incidental expenses incurred in preparing, advising, and moving along the deal. Chas Hooper's lawyer would draw up the offering and register it with the appropriate state regulatory authorities. Chas and his sister would retain 45 percent of the company. If the deal was shown to a maximum of twenty-five potential *sophisticated* investors, there would need be no filings with the Securities and Exchange Commission.

This was a private offering, a limited partnership. This meant that the limited partners' loss potential was limited to the amount of their investment. The hope, naturally, was that the company would prosper enough to "go public" — to be traded over the counter or, potentially, on a national exchange. If this happened, stock for which the limited partners paid a dollar could return four, five, ten times the money. The offering also meant that the minute the $250,000 was raised, the stock that cost me one cent was presumably instantly worth $1.00 per share, or a total of $100,000. Who could not like that kind of arithmetic? Here is a chart that details the simple numbers of the Unlimited Youth Horizons' deal.

UNLIMITED YOUTH HORIZONS OFFERING
250,000 shares at $1.00 per share.

Minimum unit is 12,500 shares at $1.00 per share.

The company is to be capitalized at a total of
one million shares, par value $1.00.

After the successful offering, the breakdown of
ownership will be as follows:

TOTAL SHARES	OWNER	COST TOTAL
100,000	Bruce	$10,000
100,000	Me	$10,000
100,000	My accountant	$10,000
450,000	Chas Hooper	Zero
250,000	Limited partners — the investors	$250,000

Ordinarily, if the money is successfully raised, the deal-makers take a commission of from 1 to 2 percent of the proceeds. At my insistence, no commission was charged. This set me up immediately against Bruce, who told me that I was both naïve and a fool. None of the proceeds would go into anyone's pocket. The funds were for expanding the youth camps and for working capital.

"Now the next step," Bruce told us, "is to assemble potential investors into one room, where they'll be captives. Then we get Hooper, the spellbinder, to tell his story. Successful deals eventually depend on mass hysteria. Why should you spend hours calling customers about this opportunity when we can raise all the dough in one place at one time."

"Smooth as gold," said my accountant.

In selling anything, the simpler you make the presentation, the easier the results. Bruce had said, "Fill up the hall with people." What we said to fill the room was this: "Would you like to make an investment in a private company that services the youth market? Did you ever hear of National Student Marketing?" Naturally, everyone contacted had followed the stock market progress of the hot company. And we were in an incredibly greedy climate, where doubling money seemed easy and a tenfold return was theoretically not beyond reach. All you needed was the right concept.

We had an investors' meeting in a private dining room in Chas Hooper's hotel. There were twenty-four people in the room. "Don't worry about that twenty-five sophisticated investors' rule," Bruce had said. "In the first place, there's no such thing as a sophisticated investor, only smartasses who always say no and greedy ones who always say yes. If the deal is intriguing at all, there's usually one guy in the room who'll demand the whole thing. He stampedes the rest of the group, and you wind up oversold."

Each person in the room received a manila envelope with the terms of the offering, the financial projections for the company, statements of intent for the business, comparisons of

Unlimited Youth with different companies in the field, and four-color brochures on the existing youth camps. The twenty-four potential investors were either clients of mine or of my accountant.

"I don't bring money to a deal," Bruce had told us. "I bring expertise. Other people's money is the only way to operate in life: the bank's money, the insurance company's money, OPM — Other People's Money."

I was liking Bruce less and less. My accountant was constantly trying to calm me down. "You don't have to win popularity contests to cut a fat hog in the ass," he said. "That's a Southern expression." I told my accountant that I believed him.

Sure enough, at the meeting, Chas Hooper gave his revivalist speech about kids' energies being channeled into constructive and profitable activities. When he finished his presentation, which was earnest, convincing, and utterly honest, a fat man who spoke with spittle forming at the corners of his mouth got up, flicked his cigar ash onto the floor, and said, "All right. With all the bullshit aside, what do you think you can get for the company in two, three years?"

Bruce jumped to his feet. "I think I can answer that," he said. "National Student Marketing sells at forty-five times earnings. If we can meet projections and earn a dollar a share in three years, then twenty-five times earnings is twenty-five dollars a share. Okay. Cut that down by a lot. Make us, say, fifteen times earnings, which is *nothing* for a growth stock. Figure it out. If we were public, fifteen dollars a share would be reasonable."

"It might even be cheap," said another potential investor, a client of mine who raced sailboats.

"Would there be a lot of objection," the fat man said, "to my taking the whole kit and caboodle?" That started the clamor. We could have raised a million dollars before the fight was settled between the fat man and everyone else in the room.

Bruce rapped on a water glass with a spoon. "Naturally," he

said, "we are pleased with your response. We want you to read over the material and think about what you have heard. You can call Mr. Spooner at his office with your decision, and we'd appreciate your doing that within the next forty-eight hours. Sober reflection is what we want you to remember; sober reflection."

The meeting was over, and the fat man came directly to me. "Look, kid," he said, "I've never done business with you before, but you look like a bright guy. You want to do some swinging with me, I buy stocks in chunks: five thousand, ten thousand, fifteen thousand shares. You set aside the *man's* share of this deal for me, and my commissions will make it worth your while. You know what I mean, kid? These other guys are pishers. You're going to step up to the majors with me. As for you," he said to my accountant, who was also his accountant, "you I can fire if you don't take care of me."

"I did you a favor," my accountant pleaded. "I had to drag you to this meeting. I told you it was a great story."

"The only great part of a story is the punch line," said the fat man, "and the punch line is *Get me the stock*." We gave the fat man four units, $50,000 worth of stock. He bitched and moaned and threatened his accountant. Because of the fat man's antics, raising $250,000 was a breeze.

We all celebrated at an Italian restaurant where they serve the house wine in Coke bottles. "Now you go out and sell the shit out of these programs," said Bruce to Chas Hooper. "You got responsibility now to all kinds of strangers who love you today but can be out for your scalp tomorrow. I gave them forty-eight hours to make a decision. You don't want people thinking too long about spending money. When the glow fades, the tendency is to zip up the pockets. Give a definite time period in a deal and stay with it."

"John will tell you," said Chas, "that I go after life like a bulldog. Your people's money is in the hands of an honorable man."

90

For six months after the offering I spoke to Chas Hooper on a weekly basis, long distance to Colorado. For six months, every investor called *me* on a weekly basis. "How's our company doing?" they would all ask. "How are the numbers on the youth ranch?" People always called to ask about the investment when I was concentrating on some more immediate problem. There is a rhythm to life, as I have said, and a rhythm to every business. But the stock market has an immediacy like few other businesses. Often, buy-and-sell decisions have to be instantaneous, and concentration is essential. Every call about Unlimited Youth was insidiously timed to destroy my concentration. The calls also came at home. They came during dinner, during climaxes in sporting events or mysteries on television. "How we doing out in Colorado?" they would say.

"If I hear another word about Unlimited Youth," my wife said, "I'm going to lock myself in the bathroom until Christmas."

"It'll be worth it, sweetheart. A penny in will be four or five dollars out," I said to her. But I was no longer quite so sure, especially when my accountant called and told me, "The fat man is leaving me to go with Price Waterhouse. He said you insulted him."

"Look," I said, "the fat man must think everyone is an idiot. Before we gave him his allocation in Unlimited Youth, he called me to do business. But his idea of business was to ask for shares in every hot new issue that was coming out. When I told him that I reserve new issues for my established clients, he ranted and raved and swore he'd call you."

"He called me. Did you tell him to go and fuck himself?"

"Absolutely not," I said. "What I told him was to go take a flying fuck over the moon."

My accountant sounded baleful. "That's why he went to Price Waterhouse."

I decided that 10 percent of the deal was nowhere near enough.

91

Nine months after the money had been spent, National Student Marketing collapsed. Massive fraud was charged, and the stock dropped from 50 to practically nothing. The stockholders in Unlimited Youth called to ask "How is *your* company doing?" It was no longer *our* company. If any problems arose, if anything went wrong, it was my fault.

There is a truth about private investments. If you can't see the price of it daily, as you can with a listed stock, after a while you forget you own it. Smaller private investments, in restaurants, in Broadway plays, in boutiques, public oil and gas programs, engender tremendous interest when the money is first in. But as time goes by and there is no special news, no momentous developments, and certainly no price in the papers, the small private investment fades from one's consciousness. The longer the time goes on in a small deal, the less the investor remembers it. The process is like buying a new car. You itch for the car, you can't wait to buy it, finally drive it with pride, polish, it, baby it. With time, you take it for granted. The car after a while becomes dull, routine, a means of transportation. It is often unreliable and sometimes a downright pain in the ass.

I spoke to Chas Hooper on the phone. "National Student Marketing collapsed," I told him.

"That's too bad," he said. "But I don't read the financial pages. I'm too busy running my business. Besides, what's that got to do with Unlimited Youth?"

"Nothing, I suppose," I said.

"Well, I'm glad you called anyway," Chas said. "We've had a couple of problems."

He told me that one of his congressional speakers at camp, there to talk about separation of powers, had seduced a fourteen-year-old camper. Her parents had sued Unlimited Youth. Heavy rains in Colorado had also washed out a complete obstacle course that could not be rebuilt for six months. "It was an integral part of building the whole adolescent," Chas complained. "I think I can use about another hundred thousand to keep things on an even keel."

"Where do you think you're going to get it?" I asked.

Silence. "Where do *you* think?" Chas said. "You're my man. I gave you the deal; you and your fancy advisers who have lost me thousands of dollars in fees."

"You forgot something, Chas," I said. "We raised a quarter of a million dollars for you."

"Yes," he said. "But now I *really* need it."

Chas Hooper came to town and met with Bruce, my accountant, and me. "The facts of life are," said Bruce, "that youth as a concept may be dead. Since we raised your money, kids are taking over the universities, rebelling against all authority. They're not going to summer camps, coming-out parties, or to Europe on tours. They may be buying records and drugs, but they're not buying flag-waving sessions where they get to do a hundred pushups after the lecture and sing 'God Bless America.' "

"Are you being sarcastic about my country?" said Chas, standing up.

"Your first loss is your best loss," said Bruce.

The meeting dissolved and Chas stayed in town several days, calling on stockholders. In trying to raise more money for Unlimited Youth, he struck out completely. We had lunch before he was to take a plane back to Colorado. "Bruce already sent me a consulting bill for our meeting the other day," he said. "It was a dark moment when I first came to this town. Most of the investors were sympathetic. But no one offered anything except to say they were tapped out. I didn't believe them for a minute. The fat man told me he was going to sue for misrepresentation. All I wanted to do in this deal was make money by servicing the public and carry my stockholders along with me. Now I've got to go to the banks to bail me out, fight off the courts, and on top of it I get a consulting bill for advice that put me in the shithouse."

93

Chas Hooper left town. Six months later Unlimited Youth folded. Chas, only because of his good character and hard work, managed to find a buyer for his campsites, a cult leader from Abilene, Texas, who promised refuge to Christians who believed in making heaven on earth through exposing their bodies to the elements. Chas could have washed out the investors entirely. But he paid them all back approximately fifty cents on their investment dollar, a wash, or break-even, for people in the 50 percent tax bracket.

I saw the fat man in a restaurant not long after that. He was eating two fifteen-pound lobsters. As I walked by, he looked up, butter running down his chin and onto a large bib tied around his neck. "What are you selling this year, cancer?" he said. I ignored the fat man but later told a friend of mine about the incident, a friend who had also invested in Unlimited Youth.

"When you count your money before a deal even starts," he said, "it's going to be a disaster. Or, if not a disaster, at least unbelievably difficult. Before you ever do something outside your normal area of expertise, always ask yourself one question: 'What do I need it for?' "

I didn't lose any clients as a result of Unlimited Youth. But for a while I lost some credibility, some of my edge. Because clients and customers and patients expect us to be perfect. And, of course, we are not.

I tell you the story of my attempt at deal-making because we are back in the climate of the 1960s. It is, as I write this, springtime in a Republican administration, and every engineer with a degree and an idea wants seed money to start his own software company, his own hardware company, his own used-computer store with video games in the restrooms. Throughout America there is the smell of easy money.

Sardonic Sandra, my assistant, greeted me after the long weekend with distasteful news. "There's someone waiting in your office," she said. "I checked your calendar. No one is scheduled. It's someone looking for money or advice. No one who knows you comes in early to give you business."

Sardonic Sandra is the best in the city at what she does. But, like all long-term people who fall under the heading "executive secretary" or "sales assistant," she owns me. Sardonic Sandra has worked with me for six years, and she treats me alternately as her lover, friend, child, or enemy, depending more on her mood than mine. She is married to a salesman and they have no children. I am always trying to get her approval, especially since the time I nominated her for Secretary of the Month at a local radio station. She was to receive a month of flowers, a trip to Atlantic City, free movie passes, and a case of champagne. The radio station called her at her desk to tell Sandra that she had won the contest. She was furious. "What's wrong?" I asked. "I thought you'd treat it as a lark."

"All contests are demeaning," she said. "Do you think of me as Secretary of the Month? It's funny when it happens to other people." She saw my surprise and softened. "I won't leave you; I'll drink your champagne. You can consider this a warning, and you and your *wife* of the month can take the trip to Atlantic City." It's typical in life that we apologize for absurdities. I apologized, and the flowers kept arriving for Sandra every day.

"Watch me get rid of this guy in record time," I told her about the visitor, and marched into my office. There on my couch was Fast Jerry Goldstein, my high school buddy who used to give boy-girl cellar parties and who had become quite wealthy by saving troubled companies, turning them around, and bailing out at favorable prices. "It's time I opened an account with you," he said. "High school blood is thicker than water. This means you'll think twice before fucking me over. That's what friends are for."

Fast Jerry had gone bald in college, as if he wanted everything in life accelerated, catching up with the speed of his mind and his mouth. "I want to buy good-sized positions in several small insurance companies and in a few savings and

loans I know about. I want to buy these companies on margin."
(He wanted to put up 50 percent of the cost, borrowing 50
percent from the investment firm at a rate approximately 1 percent over the prime.)

"My whole life and career is based on leverage, Johnny. You
buy these stocks for me and I'll explain the second reason for
my being here."

While I placed the orders, he told me that he had borrowed
heavily from the insurance companies whose shares he was
purchasing. "While I'm in their pockets," he said, "they see no
conflict in hinting to me that they're on the verge of being
acquired by some sharks at a higher price. They feel that drop-
ping hints to me is good business. It assures them that in the
future I'll stay on board to borrow from the sharks. The savings
and loan companies are friends of the insurance people and
they tell me their prices are cheap. If you want to make money
in a deal or in a stock, never buy on a whim."

"Who's the stockbroker, Jerry, you or me?"

"In this case, you're merely the middleman. Notice I didn't
ask for your advice. No risk. Execute the order and take your
outrageous commission. Notice I didn't even ask for a discount."

"I gave you ten percent without your asking," I said.

"You always were a cheap bastard," Jerry said. "I remember
in high school how you'd always collect gas money."

"Okay, Fast Jerry. Now give me the hook."

"The hook," he said to me, "is that our twenty-fifth high
school reunion is in June. I want to make sure that I'm named
the most successful graduate of the class."

I went to a large suburban high school. My graduating class
numbered over six hundred students. My wife claimed that
every time an item in the newspaper read, MAN FOUND DEAD
IN TRUNK OF LINCOLN AT LAGUARDIA AIRPORT, THREE
BULLETS IN HEAD, I swore the dead man had been a high
school classmate. We did have our share of characters: several
bookies, a mob hit man who killed people with Louisville

96

Sluggers, a television comedian, a governor of a Midwest state who would leave the room if he heard an off-color joke, a call girl who had been the mistress of an oil sheik.

Our twenty-fifth reunion was to be at the end of June and I was in charge of "Who's Who." This was a list of personalities: who had been the most beautiful, who was the most beautiful now; who had been most athletic then, who now; who had been most likely to succeed, who was now the most successful. The current choices were to be subjective, my choices. I kept track of the past: where people had gone, what they did. It was my curse.

"This is the last thing I would have believed of you," I said to Fast Jerry. "You don't care about stuff like this. Remember you started that club in high school, the Antibullshit League?"

"Yeah," said Fast Jerry Goldstein. "But there's a big reason why I want to be named most successful, other than the fact that there's good excuses for it."

"What's the big reason?"

"That it shouldn't go to that prick Harold Newman."

Prejudices of the schoolyard die hard. Harold Newman wore ties to high school, which was unforgivable. He was a stuffed shirt. He didn't play sports. He was the confidant of the girls and giggled with them in the cafeteria. His mother made him weird lunches, like peanut butter and banana sandwiches, like mayonnaise, sardines, and matzoh — in January.

"I've been head to head with the little bastard lately," Fast Jerry told me. "And I want to do to him what you should never do in a deal. I want to fuck his ears to the ground. He's still got that tight curly hair, you know what I mean?"

"Harold has done amazingly well," I said. "In the last few months I've read about him in *Barron's* and *Business Week*. I haven't read a word about you in the national magazines."

"Are you pulling my chain, or what?" Jerry said. "The heavyweights stay *out* of magazines. I've got six major banks that have a hotline to Fast Jerry. Any troubled company and

97

big bad loans that aren't in African rain forest countries, they call me first. Save our bacon, they tell me. And I do. I'm like the old WASPS. I don't talk about it. You got a good deal here, but I could buy and sell you twenty times."

"Maybe Harold Newman could buy and sell me fifty times."

"Are you negotiating?"

"Are you trying to bribe me?"

"You took the order, didn't you?"

Sardonic Sandra came into my office. She was under standing instructions never to give anyone meeting with me more than twenty minutes. "Excuse me," she said, which was part of our rehearsed routine, "you have those people from Houston in the conference room." We didn't even have a conference room. Up-Your-Gross Smith took every available inch of space and gave it to producing brokers. We were doing $2.5 million in commissions a month with fifty-five salespeople, and conference room space was dead space. You wanted to meet privately with a client, you took him to a restaurant.

You want to sell something? Let people know you have limited time, limited product that is on allocation, and people from out of town who have come all the way to see only you. Always make the million-dollar buyer think there is someone twice as big waiting in the next room.

Fast Jerry got to his feet. "You sit here," he said, "basically being a whore. I'm going to earn my award. I'm going to give you an education in how to make yourself a fortune at the same time you pull people's bacon out of the fire. You want to take the day off?"

"I'll take a raincheck."

"I mean it. I want to show you why I'm the most successful in the class."

"I promise I'll come out with you some night."

Fast Jerry gave Sandra a dirty look and left. I started ripping open the morning mail and figuring what orders I wanted to place. The phone rang. "It's that Jerry Goldstein on line three,"

Sandra called out. I picked it up. "I'm in the lobby," Fast Jerry said. "Just want to let *you* know that *I* know you don't have a conference room. Also, why would anyone from Houston ever come here? Unless it was to go to a hospital."

Later that morning I received a call from New York, from Harold Newman, or rather, "Harold Newman calling," the voice said. "Will you hold for a call from Mr. Newman's secretary?"

No longer do we deal directly. A little power produces layer upon layer of interference and protection. This was the ultimate, an assistant calling for a secretary. The secretary finally came on. "Mr. Newman wants to know if you'll be available for a call at three P.M."

"Only if it's for ten thousand shares," I answered. People didn't ordinarily answer Mr. Newman's calls this way. Silence was followed by "I'm not sure of the nature of Mr. Newman's call."

"I'll be here at three," I promised.

"What are you screwing around with my secretary for?" Harold Newman said promptly at three o'clock. "I'm running an operation here, not screwing around." He was talking on a speaker phone, a device guaranteed to annoy anyone who has ever been called on one. Voices bounce at you as if the caller is in the middle of a tight aluminum box.

"Harold," I said, "is that any way to greet an old friend?"

"I greet old friends after business hours," he said. "This is business. Do you want to do a trade for me? Twenty percent [discount] will be fine." He ordered twenty-five thousand shares of a robotics company, Rapid Robot, selling at 19½.

"This is very nice of you, Harold," I said.

"It'll be nicer when you name me most successful in our high school class. Which, by the way, I deserve. But I believe in crossing all the *t*'s."

"Do you really think I'd respond to a bribe?" I asked him.

"You're a stockbroker, aren't you?" he answered.

99

"Do you really think that twenty-five thousand shares is going to buy you a title like most successful?"

"Hey, there's more to it," he said. "I don't mind if you *tell* people that I'm a client of yours. You remember the man who approached the Count de Rothschild to borrow money? The count said, 'Come, I'll walk with you through the Bourse. Take my arm. Once they see you walking with me, you will get all the credit you can stand.' You mention my name, John, and it should be good for a hundred grand a year, easy."

"I'm not sure everyone knows your name in this town, Harold."

"Are you kidding me? Did I tell you that *Forbes* magazine has me listed in the next issue among the five hundred wealthiest Americans? This is not the five hundred wealthiest in our home town. This is in *America*!"

I spoke very quietly into the receiver. "Jerry Goldstein gave me *forty* thousand shares."

The truly aggressive person never skips a beat when challenged. Harold picked his voice up an octave and went on the attack. "Forty thousand shares of *what*, a fifty-cent stock? Where could he borrow the money to buy stock? I figured he'd be slipping his oar in, pretending to be a big man behind the scenes. Don't tell me he's even in the same league as I am. He's not even in New York, for Christ's sake."

"He's done very well, Harold."

"Who else is in the running now? Come clean. Any surprises in the class, or have we got what I always thought we'd have: cops, teachers, and people who've inherited family discount furniture stores. Hey, buy another twenty thousand Rapid Robot. I see it on my machine, offered at nineteen and three quarters. *Carefully*, now."

After I finished talking to Harold Newman, I went to blow Jimmy Minot's police whistle. I also gave a shake to Mad Mark's cowbell. This had been a spectacular beginning to April, and I could only wish for a twenty-fifth high school reunion every year.

Even the most cynical of us respond to childhood, to tales of our past. Our children love to hear even stories of their own childhood and can listen endlessly to repetitions of their adventures and misadventures as babies. When I called my old classmates back to give them the reports of their stock purchases, I told them that I would arrange to spend some time with each of them to judge their success.

"This is terrific," Fast Jerry said. "I worked for all these years and I'm haunted by a guy who came to my cellar parties. Just remember, I live in your town; I can get back at you."

Harold Newman said, "Have your assistant call my assistant. We'll fit it in."

Not only was I getting new business; I was about to receive seminars in how deals are made in America.

A week later, Fast Jerry Goldstein picked me up outside my office at 7:00 P.M. He drove the largest Lincoln available, a white Continental. "Don't tell me it's big and loud," he said. "That's my nature. You can't get away from that. But you see also I'm wearing old khaki pants, an open-neck shirt, and a ratty sports jacket. When you do a deal, you always have to be a surprise, keep everybody off balance. So no one really knows what to expect." Jerry was taking me to visit the owner-developer of an adult sports world complex that included a golf course, tennis courts, condominiums, and gymnasiums. The complex needed a big infusion of cash, and Jerry had been approached to see whether he could help. "The guy had a great idea," Jerry told me. "Everybody in America today thinks they can have great bodies, live forever, and they'll pay a fortune to string themselves along believing it. Remember the cellar parties in high school? Guys are getting twenty years in the slammer for stuff we did on Saturday nights in those days."

"Times change, Jerry."

"It's all bullshit; people never change," he said. "And most people you meet, thank the Lord, are dumb. This guy with the country club, he's got two hundred acres, half-built apartments, fancy locker rooms rusting out, because he started to build with money at eighteen percent. You die fast with money at eighteen percent.

"But he's got great land, possibilities to really turn the complex into something. He paid eight million and he's choking on his own blood. He's being squeezed; the vultures are circling. If I come in as his partner, I can solve all his problems, promote the right way, get the banks off his back. I also got a buyer down south if I get my hooks on the place, a buyer for ten mil who wants to turn the place into rental units. Of course, no one knows about the buyer, but he's in my pocket."

"How did you get the project, with all the vultures circling?"

"What I'm going to tell you is the secret to effective deal-making and why I'm the best at what I do and also why you're picking *me* as most successful." Jerry was driving in the middle of the road at about seventy miles per hour, as if he were cruising through the Nevada desert with nothing in sight. Cars honked their horns; people spun out of the way, cursing. "I had that Chevy convertible in high school, remember?" he said. "And that hair my mother would die for."

"At least you drove the same way then," I said. "But you always had five other people in the car to help you out of scrapes. What do you do now?" I asked, buckling my seat belt, "when people pile out of cars looking to punish you for reckless driving?"

"Reach under the seat," he said. I reached underneath my seat and slid out an ax handle.

"Fits under there better than a baseball bat. You'd be amazed how discouraged people get when they see a big bald-headed bastard come out of a Lincoln with an ax handle."

When we got to the country club, a short fat man in a black suit that fitted him like a sausage casing grabbed Jerry as he emerged from the car, hugging him and kissing him on the cheek. "Jerry," he gushed, "how much alike the Jews and the Italians are."

102

"If you mean that the men like to kiss each other, I suppose you're right."

The fat man laughed and hugged Jerry again. I was introduced to Sal Bartolo, the developer of the complex. "I'm not a very good ad for my health community of the future," he apologized.

"Hey, Sal," Jerry said, unbuttoning his shirt to the waist, "you got the vision. Don't worry about how you look. You got *me* for the cover of the brochures."

Over wine and cheese and crackers, Fast Jerry Goldstein got 40 percent of the entire property, plus all the concessions, for an infusion of two hundred thousand, cash. "You know what sold me on Jerry," Sal asked, "when everyone and his mother was knocking on my door? When Jerry first came to see me, we sat on the rocking chairs that I had on the clubhouse porch. Jerry didn't say anything for a while. We rocked and looked out, up the eighteenth fairway. Then he said, 'Am I seeing what you see, Sal? I'm seeing Bartolo's dream, aren't I?' Jerry was right. Anyone who could see that this was Bartolo's dream was going to be my partner."

We drove away after the handshake. It had taken three hours of conversation about almost everything but the deal. "This looks like chicken shit to you because you got on suspenders and a white shirt," Jerry said. "But you add it up and it's chicken salad. I'm only telling you this," he went on, "but my net worth is approaching nine million dollars, all of it made the hard way." He drove another forty-five minutes to an old factory town with a river running through it that bubbled from pollutants like Wisk in a washing machine. Fast Jerry parked opposite an old mill outlined against the spring sky like a book jacket for *Das Kapital*.

"They used to spin yarn in that factory," Jerry said. "Yarn for most of the sweaters in America. Now I'm going to put forty apartments in it. Yarn Spinning Green, I'm going to call it. All rental units. That's what America needs today, apartments for rent, not more condominiums. No one can afford to *buy* housing. We've been working on the city's zoning laws for a year. Got one more stubborn son-of-a-bitch on the city council to push over the edge before it's mine. Never buy a building with a dream in mind until you make sure the local power wants to allow that dream to come true. But I like to come out and watch and poke around. I like to touch the brick."

Jerry got out of the car, went around the back, and opened the trunk. He came back with a small cooler, from which he handed me a cold Budweiser. Disdaining the pull tab, he opened his beer with an old church key, then took a long drink, chugalugging. "See," he said, "contrast is everything. I got a net worth of nine million but I always keep a six-pack of Bud and a blanket in my trunk. High school taught me that you can never tell when you might get lucky."

Sitting and finishing the six-pack, I listened to Fast Jerry's rules for dealing:

"Number one, first a rule of life. You want to kiss off a pain in the ass, lend him money. This is the cheapest way to get rid of someone. Lend money to someone you dislike; he'll never come back.

"Number two. Never deal with people who do things like pay twenty-five hundred dollars for a week at adult baseball camp to play ball with ex-major leaguers. These are the types who can never make a decision, who masturbate a deal to death.

"Number three. Poke childhood and get common with people. The tough part in a deal is establishing a relationship. 'Who started in right field for the fifty-seven Dodgers?' Whatever it takes to find mutual territory, hammer away at that. A good deal should be a fair trade for a fair trade. Some guys are whores; some aren't. But you have to find that common ground immediately. I always ask myself, 'Do I dance with his daughter?' If I answer yes, I'm going to succeed.

"Number four. When I buy a business, all I need to know is the gross of the business, that is, what are the sales? I don't care what he nets or what his overhead is, because I know I can control that better than he can. I know I can make more profit per dollar of sales. The key is not what you pay for earnings but what you can do with those earnings.

"Number five. Always make a deal that makes sense with the long term in mind. It's amazing how many guys go for the whole leg. In business you're either a healer or a destroyer. There's no sense in cleaning a guy in three years, because then you deal with the devil himself. The person on the other side should always be able to say 'You know, he took three of my toes but I'm still walking.'

"Number six. I've accumulated a lot of money by being second. I don't want to innovate; I'm happy with a medium reward that I get for bailing others out of their mistakes. How do you get more with less is my motto. Let me tell you, I see companies where they've hired guys for a hundred grand a year just to turn out the lights.

"Number seven. You have to go through the rituals. I know two partners who can only negotiate while screaming and yelling at each other. They scream everywhere — in restaurants, on tennis courts. It's their ritual. Another chief executive officer I know only speaks in whispers; everyone has to come real close to him. This guy's breath stinks, and what's more, he knows it. But the deal and the meetings go superfast, because no one can stand him. If you don't go along with their rituals and understand that each character needs to strut his own peculiar style, then you won't end up shaking hands.

"Number eight. Misdirect the people on the other side, and above all, never let them know that you care. Your heart is thumping out of your chest, but you have to act as if the whole business is ho-hum and bacon for breakfast. This is like saying to a woman in a store, 'Are the shoes too small?' She'll fight like hell to buy those shoes no matter how much they pinch.

"Number nine. Get the opposite side to spend a night at your house. No one can resist common ground; you have to establish that personal relationship early. Because very few people in business *ever* have that.

"Number ten. Don't fuck 'em completely, because people never forget."

This last bit of wisdom Fast Jerry told me as he finished off the final Budweiser. He pulled the Continental back onto the highway and again moved into the middle of the road and kicked the speed up to seventy.

"If you don't mind my saying so," I said to him, "everything you've told me seems suited only to mom and pop operations, to people like Sal Bartolo."

"That's the point, you schmuck!" Jerry yelled at me while frightened drivers scattered around us to the right and left. "Don't you know that dealing with Ford or IBM is exactly the same as dealing with Sal Bartolo? The rituals are different and the size is different. But the rules are exactly the same. Common sense is the key to business dealing. Remember, as Kipling said, 'The colonel's lady and Judy O'Grady are sisters under their skins.'"

"You know," I said, "this exercise is supposed to be a contest. Harold Newman has completely changed since high school. He talks differently; he's all smoothed over. You wear high school and the past like a letter sweater."

"I'll tell you a little story," Fast Jerry said. "There was a gigantic fire in the forest. Everything was burning up and all the animals were at the banks of the river. A beaver was swimming in the river, safe from the fire. Mr. Scorpion was on the bank, about to be burned, and he called out to the beaver, 'Beaver, you've got to rescue me! Give me a ride to the other side.'

" 'Forget it, Scorpion,' said the beaver. 'You'll get on my back and sting me to death.'

" 'Why should I sting you?' said the scorpion. 'If I sting you, we'll both die, because I'll drown. And besides, if you give me a ride, you'll be doing a good deed for your fellow creature.'

106

" 'Hop on,' said the beaver, thinking that this made sense. They got to the middle of the river and the scorpion stung the beaver. As he was dying, the beaver looked up and said, 'How could you do that? It's all over for both of us.'

" 'I'm sorry,' said the scorpion. 'I couldn't help it. To sting is my nature.' "

The Continental hummed on as Fast Jerry made his move to pass every car on the road.

If that was deal-making, I knew I'd stick to buying and selling Southwest Forest at 11½. It was faster, easier, and I was liquid. And I didn't have to go to meetings.

Still April, with markets still greedy, and I had completed the sessions with Jerry the Deal-maker. Now it was time to hear the pitch for venture capital, raising funds for new enterprise.

Harold Newman met me at LaGuardia with a limousine. Or rather, the limo met me. Harold was too busy to come to the airport. The driver put my bags in the trunk and apologized, "Mr. Newman had an emergency meeting. But he requested that I play a cassette he recorded especially for you."

I expected it to begin "Good morning, Mr. Phelps," the way "Mission Impossible" always kicked off. Actually, this tape began, "Good morning, John. I realize that Jerry Goldstein still takes public transportation. But I couldn't resist giving you a taste of the good life. Do you know that forty billion dollars in corporate securities offerings came to market in the first quarter of nineteen eighty-three? This compares with seventeen and a half billion a year ago, and it's obviously an all-time record.

"This has been a great new-issues market, with companies raising money for such varied operations as rare coins, gambling advisers, horse breeders, and shrimp-farm developers. There even is an offering by an ex-convict who wants to run bingo games on Indian reservations. Venture capitalism is the hottest financial business in America today. And I am the best in that business. On paper right this instant I am worth almost one hundred and sixteen million dollars. When I see you, I'll tell you how I got to this point.

"Until then, you may mix yourself a Bloody Mary from the bar located in the compartment to your left. I thought a little Mozart also might help you to concentrate on what you could do with one hundred and sixteen million. You didn't know what a cultured son-of-a-bitch I've become, did you?"

There is never an accurate predicting of success in life. Harold Newman was always a prig in high school. There was something studied about him. Nothing he ever said or did seemed spontaneous. Blue jeans seemed as uncomfortable on him as business suits, as if he were perpetually being caught between costume changes. Feeling uncomfortable as an adolescent, he would leave himself open to ridicule by inventing lives for himself beyond our teen-age drag racing and going for egg rolls after the movies on Saturday night. "I'm going for polo lessons," he would say, or "I'm going to look at prize cattle, in case we move to a ranch." Or "I have to have instruction in Spanish dancing; we're going abroad for spring vacation." The girls loved to listen to him. The boys called him "Never-Never" Newman.

I had read about him in business journals. I heard the cassette in the limousine. But I wasn't prepared for our reunion in his office at Rockefeller Center on Fifth Avenue. It was like the inside of a planetarium, dark, dark, with pinpricks of light from baby spots throwing beams onto small sculptured objects. A larger beam illuminated Harold Newman sitting behind a mammoth desk of black lacquered teak.

"I call my office the black box, get it?" he said. "People bring new inventions, black boxes, to me. I find the money to make their dreams come true and, in the process, it makes *my* dreams come true. The venture capitalist is the wizard of the eighties. Every one of these spotlights falls on products I have funded that have prospered and grown and returned megabucks to the owners."

For several hours after I watched Never-Never Newman operate. His essential business as a venture capitalist was simple. Someone was referred to Newman, someone with an idea or product that needed money for developing or expanding. Newman raised the money for the idea or for the product in exchange for fees and a percentage of the company he was helping. Then he provided continuing advice and support, nurturing the company through its expansion. If and when the company went public or sold out to another company, and Newman owned 50 percent, he could create instant wealth for the venture capitalist and his partners. Percentage ownership multiplied by dozens of companies that succeed gives you wealth expanded proportionately.

Newman was a small man whose tight dark curly hair was cut close to his head. Watching him operate was like watching the caricature of a dictator. He had decided somewhere after his first success that God was a bully. "You know what you get with this five hundred thousand?" he was telling a potential client as I watched. "You get me riding your ass. And if you screw up, it's *my* company, and you're back in the oil patch begging someone to take you on at three hundred a week."

"I still think I need a million," the man said in a west Texas drawl. "I can get a million in Boston and give up only forty percent. You're going to give me half a million and take sixty percent of the business? That's a pretty fancy spread for towns two hundred miles apart."

"Fine, go to Boston and take the million," said Harold. "But with the half million you get me on the board, me in your pocket. This is not an adversary relationship; this is going to be love. You've just got to understand who the man is going to be in the marriage. You are the beautiful girl, but I'm the fucking breadwinner."

The potential client had a black box of his own, a device that could be flown over potential oil or gas fields and register like sonar when black gold was to be found underneath.

"I do believe I'm going to take this little fellow to Boston," said the man.

"I've played poker in Amarillo, you lying son-of-a-bitch," said Harold, who in high school had never dared to say "damn" to anyone. "Boston never offered you a million. I happen to know that you've been bounced out of half the venture offices in the country. They tell me you're a nut. But I've got faith in the right kind of nut. That's why I'm giving you money. Free money; you don't owe it back. I should take *eighty* percent of the company and get the title 'President for life.' But I'm doing you a favor. Take it or leave it."

The Texan looked Harold in the eye and said, "Fifty percent."

Harold looked over at me. "I'm worth *nine* figures, and he's chiseling me for ten percent." To the cowboy: "Go to the Texas banks. Tell them you want to borrow a million to fly over the Rockies to look for oil when there's a glut on and half the loans to energy companies are looking like greenbacks with pictures of Jefferson Davis."

I watched the Texan sign the deal. Then we had a drink in Harold's office: single-malt Scotch without ice.

"I swear to God he's got something that works," Harold told me. "I've had my people test it independently and it works. I can take a chance on a nut, because we've got so much money in the pot. When you've never had a loser, they're hanging from the chandeliers, fighting to give you everything in their piggy."

A buzzer rang. "That man is camped in the lobby, Mr. Newman," a secretary's voice said. "He refuses to leave till he's seen you."

"This guy," Newman said, "had twenty-five thousand in a fund of mine three years ago. It's worth a hundred thousand today and he's pushing every week to give me more. Every

110

time he comes to New York he camps at my office. You and I are going to walk to '21.' I'll show you this guy, American capitalism at its best."

Waiting in the reception area, which had copies only of the Paris *Vogue* and the English *Country Life* on the tables, was the fat man, my investor in Unlimited Youth Horizons. He didn't recognize me. He had eyes only for Never-Never Newman. The fat man jumped up. "What kind of shit is this? You remember the people who bankrolled you when you were knocking on every door? You're going to return five times everyone's money in the next few years. I read the *New York Times*. I brought cashier's checks with me. I want *in*."

"I can't talk money when I have lunch on my mind," said Harold. "You have to call; make an appointment."

"What is this, a fucking bakery? I have to take a number?"

"I have four hundred thousand left open in the newest venture fund of twenty million," said Newman. "I have promises to all kinds of people."

"Never mind your promises," said the fat man. "I'll take it all."

"See my assistant," said Newman, very cool, and we walked out to lunch.

Along Fifth Avenue, Never-Never Newman lectured me. "If anyone ever talks to you about the quality of money that he wants in a deal, remember this: it's all bullshit. It's the *quantity* that counts. The fat man walks in, greed up to the eyeballs. I've got four hundred grand open. Why should I worry about getting in my uncle or some friendly lawyers I owe a favor to for fifty thousand when I can clean up what's left in one chunk? Get the money; never worry about whose it is unless it's delivered in a violin case by a guy with stickers on his bags from Palermo."

Never-Never Newman's Fifth Avenue rules for venture capitalists:

"Number one. What I take is always in relationship to the

uniqueness of the idea and the quality of management. For instance, if a guy comes in who can change wood to gold, the guy would probably retain eighty percent of the business. An ordinary company, the owners keep twenty percent to forty percent. Who decides how much? Me. I've got the money, and you always have to pare the supplicants back to a realistic amount.

"Number two. In figuring a deal, you have to start with a goal: what you want to make. I won't go in unless I think I can see four or five times my money in three to four years. Of course, this can vary. A real risky company, I'll want ten times my money. An ordinary operation, three times is the target I'll expect. One fund of ours five years ago started with ten million. There are thirty companies in the fund and seven are now public. One company making large computers is already equal to our entire investment. Two others are real winners and ten others fairly good. If I could liquidate the fund today, it would be worth forty-one million. *Now* is the time I begin attacking the problem companies. If you're in this racket, ego is everything. I don't want to be wrong."

Venture capital is a greedy business. Industry average looks for a five-times money reward within four to five years. This is over 60 percent compounded annually. In other words, $1 million should translate to $5 million within three years.

"Number three. It's not throwing darts that determines what we take for our efforts. Here's a general formula: a client owns discount dress stores. We take a survey of public dress store companies to determine how many times earnings they sell for in the marketplace [the price-to-earnings ratio].

"Say the industry sells for ten times earnings, and say we project third-year earnings for our company at one dollar per share. Multiply the earnings of one dollar by ten, and we value the company *three years out* at ten million. Since that's when we're looking for our payoff, and we put in one million originally, we want our million to be worth five million. So we negotiate for half the stock or what we think will be five million dollars' worth. The number of shares of stock is irrelevant; it's nothing more than a breakdown of the economic value. What's your *percentage* is what counts. When we take it public, we decide how much we want to value the company. If we want to value it at ten million, then the underwriter would bring it public at ten dollars per share, for one million shares. This makes it simple."

I interrupted him. "Except nothing is really simple. Nothing happens the way you plan it."

"Hey, look," Harold said. "I work my tail off on my companies. I work eighteen hours a day and I dream in Technicolor about the problems I've got. Everybody who works in America each week comes home exhausted. But most of them come home exhausted with two hundred and eleven dollars and forty-nine cents. I put in the same hours and can have a five-million-dollar payday. One success, and everyone wants you. These days anyone who was a banker and can do a spread sheet thinks he's a venture capitalist. Know one thing: the more sophisticated the investor, the faster he goes for the deals."

Newman watched several businessmen walk by, nattily dressed and engrossed in conversation. "Do they have half as much as I do? I doubt it. I love to watch people go by in the street and know I can buy and sell the shitheels in this town up, down, and sideways."

* * *

The Myth: There are sophisticated investors of great wealth who move money into real estate, oil and gas, and venture-capital deals with great expertise.

The Truth: There are no sophisticated investors, only greedy ones, who, outside their own businesses, are easier marks than daddies at their daughters' lemonade stands.

* * *

Men still drink cocktails at lunch in the "21" Club. Harold Newman had two Gibsons and ordered wine by the glass with his turkey hash. There are times when you can feel drunk on one glass of sherry; other times when eleven Scotches and stingers until two in the morning give you nothing but bar chits. Never-Never Newman was drunk on his first Gibson, snapping his fingers for service, demanding a better table, and working up to something he desperately resisted: nostalgia.

"I hated everyone in high school," he said. "I was the ugly duckling, never realizing I was a fucking swan. All those girls with whom I was best friends, you know, all I wanted to do was touch them, screw them, anything. Even the ugly ones. I would have paid every dime my parents put out in riding lessons, dancing lessons, just to look at a tit. Not even touch one. You know, just look.

"Confidentially," he told me, "I always knew women would love me. For instance, do you believe that I came eleven times last night? I was with an actress in the soaps, just turned twenty-two. I came *half her age* in times last night. Don't ever believe that they all don't want to fuck someone with a hundred million, even if he comes only once."

During his second glass of wine, he said, "I'll admit something, since we'll probably never see each other again after I pick up my award at the reunion. What happens to you in life is an accident. I started out as an engineer. But I also had an M.B.A. What I knew about life was that you buttered the bagels before you put on the cream cheese.

"A lawyer I knew came to see me with some guys who had a system for competing with A T and T on long distance. These guys had a great idea and they knew less about life than I did. Three guys, all inventors. One never said a word, the second wore one blue sock, one brown one. The third talked nonstop, but you couldn't understand him. I personally put in fifteen thousand dollars and raised three hundred thousand for the company, little by little — ten thousand here, fifteen thousand there. You know what happened. My fifteen grand became a million and a half, the company went up a thousandfold, and

114

I'm an expert. If I knew then what I know now, I'd have never put in a penny. And I'd never be in '21,' pushing people around and screwing actresses. By the way, I'm not paying for that privilege either. All they want to do is sniff the power."

Waiting for us on the street after lunch was the fat man, who jumped in front of Never-Never Newman. "What's *he* doing with you?" he yelled pointing at me. "I *thought* I recognized him, and it's bothered me for the last two hours. Spooner stiffed me years ago, and if he's feeding you companies that you're putting in the fund, I'm going to have to rethink . . ."

Newman said, "John Spooner was my best high school friend. I never confuse business with friendship. Furthermore, I'm going back to the office to rip up your checks." Newman motioned me toward a waiting limousine. He patted me on the bottom and gave me a wink. Then he walked toward Fifth Avenue, with the fat man running after him.

"I'm sorry, Harold," the fat man was calling. "I'll pay a penalty. Anything. But don't shut me out."

The limo driver said, "Mr. Newman mentioned that you might want to stop at a place he knows, on the way to the airport. He says the place is special."

"Can I come there eleven times?" I asked.

"Excuse me?" the driver questioned.

"Never mind," I said. "The airport will be fine."

* * *

Shortly after I returned home, I wrote to another old high school classmate, Sister Catherine, who lived in Central America, informing her that she had been chosen the most successful graduate of our class. Sister Catherine was the former Elsie Roberts, whose stepfather was a bookie. Elsie had been a cheerleader who had found Christ, gone to convert the Indians of the Amazon, and ended up in a small village in Central America. With the peasants of the area she manufactured, for sale abroad, products for cooking that have become world famous as Sister

Catherine's Heavenly Sauces. She refuses to come back to the States and lives only to improve the souls of her flock and the bite of her sauces. I sent copies of my letter to Fast Jerry and to Never-Never Newman. Newman's assistant phoned Sardonic Sandra to close Newman's account. I received a note from Fast Jerry Goldstein. It said, "You'll never grow up. Still a sucker for a cheerleader."

*   *   *

April 27. The market closed last night up 22 points at an all-time high of 1209 on the Dow Jones average. Volume was almost a hundred million shares. Energy stocks were particularly strong, and I was blessing the Leprechaun for his foresight. This was a time when dreams were coming true. It was also a time, perhaps, to become nervous. You always look for clues to a market top when money becomes easy to make. In my business, clues are always available, if you believe them.

"This looks like a big one," Sardonic Sandra said to me, marching into my office. "There's a man I thoroughly approve of, for once, waiting to see you. You never see anyone wearing a proper hat anymore."

"He must be a mutual fund salesman who played tennis in college," I said to her. She made a face and ushered him in.

"I'm J. Joseph Barron," he said. "But my name doesn't matter. It's my product that counts, the product that's going to make me rich and, I hope, can do the same for you."

"How did you get my name?" I asked.

"Several people in town mentioned that you were someone to see about raising money for special businesses."

"Several people were wrong," I said. "I manage people's money. I don't do deals."

"This isn't a deal," J. Joseph Barron said. "This is the opportunity of a lifetime."

How could I pass up the opportunity of a lifetime? "What have you got?" I asked.

116

"Well," he said, "I need about a quarter of a million to develop my revolutionary product. It's a device that allows women to pee standing up."

"Out!" I yelled at the inventor. "What is this, a joke?"

"Look," he said, "here's the prototype." He handed me a plastic cylinder that looked like a ten-inch piece of rigatoni cut on the bias at each end. "Think of the applications: on camping trips, skiing, on boating expeditions. What's two hundred and fifty thousand dollars to you; we'll make millions."

"Out, Mr. Barron," I repeated. "I am concerned with earth-shattering subjects, like whether or not Phillips Petroleum will be taken over at sixty dollars per share."

"They laughed at Edwin Land of Polaroid," he said.

"Okay," I answered, "when you produce an instant toilet, come back to me."

When the promoter left, Sardonic Sandra got in her last words: "That's why you'll never make a fortune in deal-making. You're a lousy judge of character."

5

California 1: "Birdies Sing and Everything"

It was May, and, with the advent of spring, the American stock market was going crazy on the up side. In our office Sebastian, the messenger, was miserable. The price of gold was falling, inflation was falling, unemployment was down. He had a T-shirt printed for himself that said on the front *Gold is the only thing to Hold.* Paul the Bachelor took a big risk by saying to Sebastian, "The *only* thing? What about that inflatable rubber doll in your apartment?"

Sebastian would surely mangle his mail, lose checks, rip open love letters.

Whenever there was frenzy in the securities market, up *or* down, I felt the need for perspective on what I do. I felt the need to travel and listen to people who make the economy move: business people, mechanics, airline personnel, car salesman. It was a good time to fly to California to see clients and to do some elephant-hunting: the pursuit of big new orders.

The Dow Jones average reached the 1200 mark for the first time in history; it had closed the previous week at 1226.20. Oil and technology stocks were particularly firm. For the first time in many years both stockbrokers and their customers seemed equally happy. Mad Mark the Institutional Salesman had grabbed me in the office Friday afternoon. "How can you go away?" he said. "You don't leave a business when you're raking it in hand over fist. One of my clients is Moon Fund, you know, a specialty mutual fund that puts money only into emerging high-technology stocks. Two years ago it started with five million and a dozen investments. They're suddenly up to a hundred million and two hundred companies that they've put money into."

"What does that tell you?" I asked.

"It tells me that my commissions are bigger than any time in the last dozen years and that sooner or later the blind hog gets the acorn."

"It tells *me*," I said, "that when the public is begging the fund managers to spend their money, it's time for a breather."

"You take a breather," Mark said, "and Jane the Impaler will push you right out of your office."

Of course, he had a point. Up-Your-Gross Smith published the commission figures of his brokers every week on the bulletin board directly over the water fountain. Broker of the Month received a case of steaks from somewhere west of Lincoln, Nebraska. The prize was given each month for the broker with "the best attitude." This usually meant that you stayed late in the office making cold calls or enthusiastically approved of every product the firm was merchandising. Loyalty without question was good for at least several marbled sirloin dinners.

There are few businesses where you lay it on the line on a daily basis, where you can be always both a hero and a bum. Except for weekends and holidays, the ticker tape never stops. Many businesses shut down for several weeks in July or have seasons that are slack. The stock market tickers run all day, five days a week. During lunches. During vacations. During business trips. The person in the investment business has a compulsion to *know*, to know every eighth of a point, every penny of earnings; the compulsion to be a hero every day. When I'm away from the office, I check in on the phone several times daily. Even if I am out of the country, I check in, for problems, for messages. But I am really checking *prices*. Was I right today? Am I a winner? Do my clients love me?

As I got ready to leave for California, I thought of the ego involved in needing to know prices, needing to be right. Earlier this year a West German investment adviser killed his wife and himself after having lost almost $50 million in the stock market. "I announce to you, full of pain and shame, the total loss of security deposits managed by me," his suicide note read. The adviser had miscalculated the bull market, selling short in the expectation that prices would fall. The market rally had wiped him out. A college classmate of mine committed suicide during freshman year, at Christmas vacation. His note said: "The line between life and death is very thin."

But the winners kept thrusting along with the boiling market. Sotheby Parke Bernet in New York just had its all-time record week, with sales of almost $55 million. An Alexander Calder mobile sold for $159,000, twice what it was figured to bring at auction. High-tech stocks were selling at fifty times earnings. I had just noticed an advertisement in the *Wall Street Journal* for an all-wool tropical worsted suit. "Our $1000 Hickey-Freeman speaks for itself," the ad said. A thousand-dollar off-the-rack suit. It was a good time to go elephant-hunting in California.

Why California? If there was a clamor for stocks and bonds in the East and an atmosphere that encouraged speculation, then that frenzy would be much wilder in the west, where freedom is a low-rider on Hollywood Boulevard or a fifty-cent stock that you *know* will go to $10 a share. I had a strong feeling that prices had moved too far, too fast, and if this feeling was reinforced in California, I would come home with new perspective and would sell.

I first visited California in the early 1960s, hitchhiking west from San Antonio after a short stint in the Army medical corps. I was looking for a job in the movies: writing, directing, acting. It didn't matter. Of course, I felt qualified, having played the female lead in drag in several undergraduate musical comedies. The experience featured a road tour during spring vacation with stopovers in the houses of the rich, where food, liquor, and local daughters were free, plentiful, and abundant, in approximately that order. This is what show business was meant to be.

I was further bitten by an evening spent with Richard Burton after his first American theater appearance in a Jean Anouilh play, *Time Remembered*, with Helen Hayes and Susan Strasberg. I was rooming at the time with James MacArthur, Helen Hayes's son, who later starred in "Hawaii Five-O" on television. We were invited to the opening of the play, then back to the Ritz in Boston for the cast party. Susan Strasberg spent most of the party getting drinks for Richard Burton and sitting in his lap. My roommate and I were annoyed that he was giving us no chance at all for the attentions of Miss Strasberg, and we retaliated by punishing the liquor supply. I remember getting into an argument with Burton about Dylan Thomas and telling him about my own acting aspirations, which he laughed off. "There's more to acting than freeloading off your friends," Burton said. "You don't want to go through *half* of what is necessary to be an actor. My advice to you is to go into the family business. Leave the acting to the British and continue to freeload as much as you can." Susan Strasberg began to kiss him then and effectively shut off any rebuttal from me.

At the studios in Los Angeles I received almost the same story. Through friends' influence I had interviews at Paramount, Columbia, Twentieth Century–Fox, with heads of production, presidents, and directors. In the office of one producer, who was clad in a giant yellow terry-cloth bathrobe at his desk, having just come out of his private shower, I was allowed to sit in on a story conference. Several writers were pitching a television series idea about two brothers in the American Civil War. The producer was leaning way back in his La-Z-Boy chair. His eyes were shut, hands folded over the tummy of his terry-cloth robe. In the middle of the writers' presentation the producer jumped forward. "I see two helicopters," he said.

"You what?" one of the writers exclaimed. "This is the Civil War. Eighteen sixty-four."

"Look," said the producer, "I know what I see, and I see two helicopters. What can you do with it?"

When the writers left, the man said to me, "You don't want to go through what it takes to make it in this town, kid. They're all liars and thieves and assholes. Do yourself a favor. You've got a good education. Go into the family business. What do you need the aggravation for? You don't want to have to take showers in the middle of the day because everyone around you smells of fear. You can't wash off fear." He kept knotting and unknotting the belt of his robe. Not able to come up with a creative solution to two helicopters in the Civil War, I left his office.

No one in power wants to give you credit for being able to persevere. "You won't have the guts to do what I've done," they are saying. But they are also saying: "I don't want to be supplanted by the next generation. No one's going to push me out of the corner office or the chairmanship or my perks." So when, as a recent graduate, you interview for jobs, look around at the trappings of power: the private showers, the yellow terry-cloth robes, the Orientals on the floor. Look at what you can have if you're willing to bust your tail. Don't listen to discouraging words. They come from people who don't want competition or reminders that power changes hands.

I didn't return to California until ten years later, promoting on radio and television a book I had written, *Confessions of a Stockbroker*. In Los Angeles I stayed at a marvelous place on Wilshire Boulevard in Westwood, the Cavalier Hotel. It no longer exists, having been supplanted by condominium towers that replace with cynicism and ugliness that which was special. The bad drives out the good. The Cavalier was really a motel with two levels, arranged like a horseshoe around a swimming pool. Each unit was a small suite, with living room, bedroom, and efficiency kitchen. Writers, actors, visiting celebrities who would be in town for more than a week, were the majority of its residents. Theater touring companies would stay for months, as would film editors from New York or directors who came to town to save a project.

Los Angeles was the first city I had encountered that had the Stock Exchange ticker tapes on television. I would wake up at the Cavalier, flick on the TV, and watch prices roll by. Above the tapes, various commentators would hype the stocks or commodities or services they offered. I particularly liked the moments that prices sped by while music played. My first morning watching those tapes, I remember monitoring the market while listening to "Dancing in the Dark" in the background. Life follows art.

A black dance company was in residence at the Cavalier that week. At breakfast, around the pool, they did their warmups — stretching, jumping in the water — playful in the sun before serious rehearsals. I went down to watch them, the only person among the many in beach chairs carrying a *Wall Street Journal*. While the troupe did athletic routines, a man, obviously not of the company, was doing fancy dives off the pool's board. He had long black hair, which he shook off his forehead after every dive, side to side the way a puppy shakes himself after a bath. He practiced only two dives, a swan and a front roll. But he did them gracefully.

One of the dancers called to him, "Hey, man, that's all you do?"

"That's all I need to do," the diver said. "I'm the master of the short-term relationship." When he finished practicing he walked by me and stopped. He flicked a few drops of water on my *Journal* and said, "Don't tell me an actor with money? You must have inherited it or you're sitting here waiting for an agent and the newspaper is a cover."

"I'm a stockbroker," I said to him.

"Obviously unemployed," he countered. "Sitting in the sun at eight-thirty when the market in New York has been open for an hour and a half." That was my introduction to Eric the Actor. He has been a client since that day at the pool. He taught me how to appreciate Los Angeles. "To understand the Hollywood community," he told me, "is to understand that your value is strictly what other people think you're worth."

He gave me a tour of the city that night and eventually drove us up to the top of Mulholland Drive, parking in a vacant lot between two half-million-dollar houses. We got out and looked at the stretch of lights way below us that made the valley look like a giant video game. "Where else," he said, "does the sentence 'He lives in a sub-three-million-dollar house' make the person who *does* feel like a shitheel?"

Eric the Actor is, as he said, the master of the short-term relationship, which he claims is the only way to survive in California. "Whenever you meet anyone in Los Angeles, for instance," Eric says, "don't use normal conversation; use a story. Here's an example to set anyone up for what you want from him."

Eric's story: "You know about values in Los Angeles and about real estate? This actor I knew struggled for years, small parts, walk-ons, and ads. Finally he makes it big, a series of his own. He's earning twenty-five thousand a week. He's got the Rolls-Royce; he gets his teeth capped. Now he needs a house commensurate with his star status. His agent, Irving, drives him through Beverly Hills. They see English Tudor mansions, sprawling stucco ranches, glass and steel creations.

"In Holmby Hills, the actor sees a castle, complete with drawbridge and moat. It's got a FOR SALE sign done in Old English stuck onto a tree in front. 'Stop the car, Irving, this is it!' says the actor. 'Go in and negotiate for me.' " (Once you're a star, explained Eric, you can't do anything for yourself.)

"So Irving, the agent, goes into the castle. A half-hour later he comes out. 'I got good news and bad news for you, kid,' he says.

" 'What's the good news?' asks the actor.

" 'The good news is it's only a million three, with moat and swans and everything.'

" 'That's great!' says the star. 'What's the bad news?'

" 'You've got to put a thousand dollars down.' "

Eric the Actor's philosophy allows him to be a survivor in a business where 99 percent of the people are usually unemployed. Eric went through life doing "routines" that made him memorable, made producers hire him for the colorful way he led his life. He was in the stock market, for instance, to talk about it, not to make money. He was a broker's dream, someone who never stayed in a stock more than a month. He never lost a lot of money that way. But he could never make money, either.

"I'm a soldier in the trenches of Hollywood life," he told me. "I care much more about the skirmishes than the war itself, and I go AWOL every six weeks for three-day drunks with the natives." Concentrating on the minutiae of life, Eric taught me the sidebars of California and of the movie business.

He had been booted out of college for pulling a fire extinguisher off a wall at a mixer and spraying the dancers, the chaperones, and the aged security guard. He never went back to school, outraging his family and, as he said, "what is worse, friends of the family. People escape to California as much to get away from their families as they do to escape failures in business and personal lives. California émigrés are the boat people of this country.

"You know," Eric told me, "if you fail as a child of the middle class, you can trade off your parents' respectability all your life. Their conscience is guilty enough so that they always provide money, introductions, plane tickets. They can't refuse you, because they don't know where *they* went wrong. Better yet, their friends can't refuse you either, because that allows them to report back to your family the favors and kindnesses *they've* shown. This way everyone is happy. The friends of the family can reinforce how wonderful they are compared to you; the family can keep their guilt going. They will also keep kicking in the bread to keep you in California; they prefer you out of sight. Is this being a prick? Sure, but it's being a harmless prick, because it's giving people what they want."

Aside from his diving, Eric can play "A Foggy Day in London Town" on the piano, "House of the Rising Sun" on the guitar, and the first eight bars of "Flight of the Bumble Bee" on the violin. He also carries a pair of castanets in his glove compartment. "I pull them out at parties where I want to make an impact. *Nobody* plays the castanets, so everyone remembers me."

Once I asked Eric the truth about drug use in the entertainment industry. "It's easy to answer why we do it," he said. "Of course, it happens in varying degrees. Do you know why we do coke and grass? The same reason that all the restaurants are pitch black. So that we can't look at each other in the light. You can get laid on a banquette of any great L.A. restaurant, and nobody knows the difference because nobody can see.

"The main reason is that we're all young and we're all skinny. Even if we're old, we're young, you dig? Getting high is essential to coming back day after day in this business and getting your brains beaten in. Drinking puts weight on and adds wrinkles. No one in the business drinks booze except the writers, and they don't matter. We get high to keep up the fight, because as soon as you show any weakness out here, they holler, '*Next!*' "

Eric was obsessed with adding to his routines, as he was obsessed with his health and his youth. He had been a vegetarian for five years. He took Okinawan karate and no alcoholic beverages except for Oriental beers. He went to scalp consultants to make sure he kept his black hair. He owned a BMW, a scruffy Volkswagen convertible, and a Harley 1500 cc bike so that he could adapt his wheels to any social event. He rolled his own cig-

126

arettes, his tobacco a mixture of Virginia blends. He smoked dope because he thought it was therapeutic and helped him to think of new routines. He dated a lot, women for their celebrity value or women who would get him a job.

One night some years ago I had a few vodkas at Eric's house in Topanga Canyon, where, legend has it, remnants of the Manson clan still hide out, waiting for their messiah. His date that night was a young actress with several peculiarities. She would not eat anything that "ran in a zigzag."

"What runs in a zigzag?" I asked her.

"Like chicken, for instance," she said. She went to a favorite drugstore three times a day for cosmetics, shampoo, lipstick, nail polish. She bought three of everything every time she shopped, and she would use only the top third of each product. A psychiatrist who saw her professionally in Cleveland, where she was born, and who also subsequently dated her, told her that all United States–manufactured products in bottles, containers, or cans were spoiled beneath the first third of the packaged product. I smoked with them, weed that Eric grew in the back of his house. The actress would smoke only the first third of each joint.

One great thing about the management of retail money in the stock market is that business meetings can be decidedly unconventional. When we were rolling on the floor, hysterical over our discussions about what top third areas the actress would sample, I realized that I was probably out of control.

"Time to get you some new accounts," Eric announced. "Let's go up to Nicholson's."

Eric had appeared in several of Jack Nicholson's movies and had been given beer privileges in perpetuity because of his good humor on one of the sets. Beer privileges at Jack Nicholson's was one of Eric's best routines. Whenever he revealed it during a reading or an audition, it was always good for at least six weeks' work.

"I've lied to Nicholson for years," Eric said, "about how

much dough you've made me. Be cool, and you'll walk away with some major money. He's only good for four or five mil a year." Nicholson had just received the Academy Award for *Cuckoo's Nest,* and Eric was charged up on top of what he had been smoking. He drove us to Mulholland, gripping and ungripping the wheel nervously as if it were red hot. He was also singing snatches of rock and roll songs from the fifties, a few lines and into the next, a medley of top hits from the past.

Indeed, Eric did have beer privileges, and Jack Nicholson greeted us as if we were expected. He was wearing a white linen suit, open shirt, and white Italian shoes with no socks. He had the killer smile and Moosehead beer in the refrigerator. Several friends sat around with him. One topic only was being discussed, the imminent earthquake that would destroy Los Angeles. One of the guests regularly went to a psychic who predicted that the next Tuesday would bring cataclysm. Everyone there in animated conversation was actually making plans to leave California before Tuesday. Nicholson was the only one who continually chided the others. Everything he said was touched with irony, as if he gazed on each situation as an outsider looking in. I thought everything *I* said was charming, interesting, and tinged with secret wisdom.

After I'd had two beers and the bottom two thirds of Eric's date's brew, we left. Eric's life depended on timing. He always left a party too soon, knowing that effort alone would probably get him invited back. Now *I* was energized, singing rock and roll songs from the fifties. Eric was silent, driving slowly down the canyon as we headed for Beverly Hills and some Chinese food.

"What's wrong?" I asked him.

"You blew it," he said.

"Whatchoo mean, I blew it? I was charming and witty."

"First of all," he said, "I'm the one who does the routines, not you. You know what Jack said?"

"What did Jack say?"

"He said, 'Why the hell should I give *him* any money to manage? He acts just like all the brokers in *California.'* "

You never go blind into a new town unless you're a fool or looking to get married. I always go on the road for specific reasons, to meet with existing clients, to make sure those clients are feeding me new customers through referrals, and, what may be most important, to observe what people in other parts of America are thinking, saying, and doing. Most people on the road in America are out there to sell something. I'm out there to sell but to also get perspective on why the market may move certain ways in the future. If you get your opinions from local newspapers and network television, you have no real idea about what is going on in America. The energies of the people, the willingness to work hard and to strive for accomplishment are apparent only when you can be out listening and observing. If you manage people's money, you should not do it in an atmosphere of printed reports and Wall Street gossip. You must talk, not to brokers and securities analysts, but to people in business and to consumers of the products and services.

If you don't travel much, you'll be surprised to find that a whole segment of the population is on the road from early Monday morning until late Thursday or Friday afternoon. Tens of thousands of drummers are loose in the land, Willy and Wilhelmina Lomans, on airplanes instead of in automobiles. I was flying first class, where I was usually able to create some new business for myself. Does this sound cynical? Number 1: The stock market players fly first class. Number 2: People in first class are much more likely to talk to one another, to be social. If people feel, rightly or wrongly, that they share either privilege or a certain degree of wealth, they are curious about one another. They will mix, feeling comfortably elite, in front of the curtains that separate classes. In tourist there is much more of a tendency to mind your own business. In tourist, the person who *will* chat with you is most likely interested in ten shares of IBM. Is this elitism? I'm not going elephant-hunting for ten shares of IBM.

As the plane flew over Cleveland I got up to use the lavatory. Both of the rest rooms were occupied, and I stood near the doors with a young woman in jeans, running shoes, and an expensive red sweater. She was in her mid-twenties, with long blond hair pulled back into a ponytail and the minimum of make-up save for a zap of blue eye liner. She was eating raisins out of a cardboard box. "If I give you some raisins," she said, "will you go back to your seat? I can't stand anyone outside the john when I go. I don't want anyone listening."

"What if I cross my fingers that I won't listen?"

"I know you boys; you'll cross your toes or something." She threatened, "Okay, no raisins."

"I'll go back to my seat."

Later in the flight she came back to find me. "Did you notice," she said, "that people can make love to each other for years and still lock the bathroom door, pretending that those bodily functions don't exist?"

"I have a friend," I said, "who pees in the sink at parties rather than make the noise of the toilet."

She laughed. "Know why I chose you?" she asked.

"Because you think I'm going to make you rich."

"I don't care about being rich," she said. "I'm twenty-seven years old and I've never missed a meal in my life. I chose you because you're the only person in first class who brought his own food." For years my wife and I have taken food on flights: pâté, cheese, French bread, cold boneless chicken breasts, fresh fruit. It invariably leads to interesting conversations, with passengers and flight crew alike. It certainly improves the ambience of long passages.

* * *

As the plane flew over Detroit, I thought of the syndrome that best characterizes the investment business, the If Only Syndrome. In November of 1979 I was in Detroit, seeing a client who was an automobile designer for Chrysler. Chrysler stock was then selling for 5. The client's wife drove me to visit the factory in Birmingham, Michigan.

"I was with Lee Iacocca's wife at a party last week," she told me. "Iacocca's wife took me by the shoulders, looked me in the eye, and said, almost like a priest, 'We're gonna make it, kid!' I felt like telling her, 'I don't give a damn if Chrysler makes it; I want my husband home more than two nights a month.' But I didn't say anything. Corporate wives don't say anything unless they want to be ex-corporate wives."

I remember being impressed by the spirit in the factory, impressed by the enthusiasm of everyone I met, as if Chrysler were a hot new computer company knowing it was going to knock IBM on its ear.

"Should I buy the stock?" I asked my client.

"Christ, the optimism alone in our crew should be worth six points."

When I got home and told everyone that I was bullish on Chrysler, I was pounded from every quarter with conventional wisdom. "Are you crazy? They have to go bust all the way."

I said, "Lee Iacocca's wife told my friend, 'We're gonna make it, kid.' " My peers looked at me as if I were certifiable. I never bought a share. Chrysler closed Friday at 32. If only . . .

* * *

The blonde with the ponytail introduced herself. Her name was Estella and she was the cohost of a television afternoon magazine show. She was traveling to California to do a segment on commodities companies that called around America trying to whip people into gold and silver futures' contracts.

"I'm named after the heroine of *Great Expectations*," she told me. "My father always told me as I was growing up what Estella was told in Dickens' novel. 'Break their hearts,' she was told. And that's what I was told. My father wanted me to break their hearts."

She reached out and touched my hand and looked straight into my face so intently that it made me uncomfortable. Quietly she said, "So tell me about gold and silver trading."

131

"How do you know I know anything about that?"

She pointed to all of my reading spread out on the neighboring seat: research reports, market surveys, *Barron's* magazine. So I told her about commodity scams, the phone hustlers who promise to double and triple your money in thirty days by investing in options to buy precious metals: gold, silver, platinum. With Estella staring into my eyes I told her about the romance of gold, the mines in South Africa, Sir Harry Oppenheimer, Eastern Europeans hoarding the metal in anticipation of wars and pogroms. I told her about world anxieties and fear of inflation forcing up the price of precious metals. I told her about hedging bets in life and why she should probably own a few Krugerrands or Canadian maple leafs just in case someday she might have to bribe herself across a border.

She interrupted me at one point and said, "Is this the best time you ever had?" That drove me to new heights, explaining what I knew about the gold standard, the price fixed at $35 an ounce for so many years, William Jennings Bryan and his cross of gold speech. As I was spinning tales of the gold rush and the Forty-niners and Sutter's Mill, she excused herself, pointing to the flashing seat belt sign preparing us for landing at Los Angeles Airport.

Estella exited before me, and I pushed around people in the aisle, trying to catch up with her. Somehow I lost her in the crowd. When I saw her again, she was watching for her luggage at the American Airlines carousel. Her bags were picked off the turntable by a tall man wearing a string tie and a ten-gallon hat. He wore these items with an Armani suit. One of the wonderful things about Los Angeles is that no one worries about inconsistencies. I moved behind them to hear the man talking. "John D. Rockefeller was one thing," he drawled. "My granddaddy drilled down in West Texas while Comanches were killing his one mule and my grandma was delivering my daddy with one hand and checking soil samples with the other. But I can tell you about that on the way. The real story is the truth about those rug merchants in Abu Dhabi. Why, one time I was drinking Jack Daniel's out of a water bottle in front of the Great Mosque when . . ."

I saw Estella touch his arm, stopping his monologue. "Is this the best time you ever had?" she said to him. I ducked behind several Shriners in town for a convention and saw them walk, arm in arm, toward a silver limousine the size of one of the Trucial states.

Since Estella had broken my heart, I decided to pamper myself on the trip to my hotel. Limousines are always waiting at Los Angeles Airport for people who will never arrive, who change plans, who are late, or who break appointments. An artist friend of mine who grew up a surfer in Laguna Beach and claims he discovered the original model for the Gidget movies has told me that the only sentence to remember about California is "Something is always about to happen." On the sidewalk at the American terminal a young woman dressed in chauffeur's cap and gray miniskirt approached, carrying a stenciled sign reading *Dr. Foster.*

"Dr. Foster?" she asked.

"Not me," I said.

"If he doesn't show up in ten minutes," she said, "you can be Dr. Foster. Limo to West L.A., glass of wine, twenty bucks." She walked on down the sidewalk, chanting, "Dr. Foster, Dr. Foster . . ."

As I watched her, a voice said at my shoulder, "Hey, gringo, looking for a good time?" I turned and saw a young man smiling at me. He was dressed like a British advertising man: gray pin-stripe double-breasted suit, polished black shoes, a white broadcloth shirt with a gold collar pin, and a particularly handsome red silk foulard tie. He had a fresh red carnation in his lapel. "Paul, of Upper Class Limo at your service," he said. I settled into the rear leather cushions of a 1958 Rolls Silver Cloud. We rolled out of LAX and onto the Santa Monica Freeway. The air conditioning was broken and the atmosphere was as sticky as the

shirt in which you play squash. "I suppose you think I'm an unemployed actor," Paul said as we slowed down in the heavy
Sunday traffic.

"Isn't everybody?" I said.

"They call me Paul the Player," he said. "I've got money
down most of the time on anything that can make me nervous
for an afternoon. You know those things, the endorphins, that
runners release when they go through the wall of pain? The
endorphins give you the highs that make you think you can run
forever. Well, laying risky money down releases my endorphins.
I get high on point spreads, football and basketball and the
Dodgers. But this year I laid money all over the stock market,
small pieces. But enough so I can get a rush at the end of the
day."

We were stopped completely because of an accident somewhere up ahead. Paul turned around and looked at me. "You
know, I used to want to be a millionaire. I was a stockbroker in
Chicago. I lived on the Lake and I drove a Three-twenty SL and
I did some trades for Hugh Hefner. In nineteen seventy-four the
market destroyed everyone. I had sold everything I owned to
buy General Cinema at ten. Then I borrowed unsecured from
clients at some banks to buy more at eight. Then I went to the
sharks to meet my margin calls.

"I had an accountant who was my bookie for football games.
He introduced me to a shark. A nice guy who said he'd give me
some brokerage biz; he'd scratch my back if I scratched his. On
one Monday I lost seventy-five hundred dollars on the Patriots
and I owed the loan shark twenty-seven thousand, five hundred,
and General Cinema was under five bucks a share. My brokerage
firm sold the stock out from under me, and the loan shark, my
buddy, let me have a taste of thirty-eight-caliber revolver, recently oiled, which he told me to eat while I was in the back
room of a bar in Cicero.

"An uncle of mine who I had put into General Cinema paid
off the shark, and I left town after twice trying to put my head

in the oven. Funny thing was that each time I tried to kill myself I thought of all the fabulous food I had made in that oven.
Then I thought of all the fine restaurants I hadn't tried, and I
turned off the gas and went out for pasta. I also knew that
General Cinema would have really come through if I could have
held it. Today, nine years later, it's selling on the basis of a
hundred and fifty dollars a share, if you don't figure splits. This
is from four and a half in 'seventy-four. Name anything else in
America that has returned *that* in ten years."

"If ifs and buts were candy and nuts, we'd all have a hell of a
Christmas," I said.

Paul laughed. "That's the trouble with the stock market. You
can see prices every day. It drives people nuts. No one can wait
it out. Every year I sent my uncle a Christmas card and wrote
the price of General Cinema on my greeting. 'Merry Christmas,'
I'd say, 'fifty-seven after three splits,' or something like that.
Finally I called him after five years. I'd been sending him small
checks to pay him back.

" 'I'll be patient,' he said to me this time. 'I would have made
millions in General Cinema. What do you like now?'

"I told him that I liked the nachos at El Cholo Restaurant
on South Western Avenue and that I wasn't in the business
anymore of giving market tips. Everybody's looking for their
guru," he added, "someone who produces magic for them on
the road."

Traffic opened up and we accelerated onto the freeway. Paul
told me that he'd come to California because it was the most
anonymous place he could find. "People stand in long lines at
Hamburger Hamlet and never talk to one another," he said. "In
my first six months in L.A., I never met anyone who was born
here. Native Californians hide away behind Spanish monastery
walls or something. What do you do when you're busted out
with champagne tastes in a strange town? I was banned from the
investment business and I wouldn't sell real estate. Good money
in real estate, but it takes too long for people to make decisions.

Do you want to buy a stock, *bang*, you make up your mind in thirty seconds. You want to go with the Raiders over Chicago, *bang*, you lay it down.

"So I drive a cab and eat one meal a week at Chasen's or Ma Maison in my Chicago clothes. Once a week I drive up to the top of Benedict Canyon above the Strip and look at the lights. I watch and wonder about the God that squeezed me out of General Cinema before its time."

I registered some surprise that he still drove a cab. "What happened to your dream of making a million dollars? You're still young."

"A Beverly Hills shrink came into the hack one night," Paul said, "and, can you believe, complained about waiting in line at Hamburger Hamlet where no one talked to anyone else. He was from Newton, Massachusetts, and I told him my story. For six months after that I'd take him from his house on North Canon to Jerry's Delicatessen in Hollywood for breakfast, and for free he gave me therapy. He told me I had to be satisfied with little hits, little highs, and that my personality wanted to consume everything at one swallow. This would destroy me forever if I gave in to it. So I eventually bought my cab. I drive it when I want, and I take little hits, little bites of everything. I even eat half a bagel at Jerry's, half a slice of lox."

We hit Wilshire Boulevard and drove past miles of new construction, condominiums that were to be priced at $1 to $3 million apiece when interest rates took off and the economy plunged in the early nineteen eighties. The half-completed construction projects looked like stage sets for a dozen disaster movies. "But you're in the market now," I said to Paul. "How do you pick what you're buying?"

"I pick what my clients tell me. When the air conditioning is working, I get the biggest movers and shakers in Los Angeles. That's how come you're lucky enough to have me today. One of my regulars who owns half the cable in the valley got out when the AC went off."

I tried to be casual. "So what are you buying, Paul?" I saw his eyes flick up at the rearview mirror.

"Every time I take one of you guys," he said, "I get real nervous that I never should have left the business. You'd be a natural customer of mine. Greedy, but pretend not to be. When I drop you off I've got to call my shrink. I'll give you a lay-up, but it's going to cost you a twenty-five percent tip."

"What's a lay-up?"

"A lay-up," he said, "is a sure thing. Something that is a *given*, a have-to-make-money, guaranteed winner."

"You've got your twenty-five percent tip; let's have the lay-up."

"El Paso Natural Gas," Paul said as we turned into Bel Air at the West Sunset Boulevard gate and the smell of humidity was instantly overpowered by the smell of flowers — hibiscus, lilac, new-mown grass — as if discomfort were barred from Bel Air by the owners' security systems.

"The stock," he went on, "is sixteen and seven-eighths, down from twenty-eight at the height of the energy crunch. It's yielding almost nine percent on dividends alone, and a Big Board rail company, Burlington Northern, owns fifty percent of the stock, for which they paid twenty-five not so many months ago. Even if the company goes from seventeen to twenty-three in the next year, that's almost thirty-five percent, *plus* a nine percent dividend. You're talking about over a forty-five percent return with virtually no risk. That's a lay-up."

Paul eased into the Bel Air Hotel's parking lot. Lauren Bacall was just getting into the passenger seat of a Mercedes coupe. "Ho-hum, right?" said Paul of Upper-Class Limo. I gave him his twenty-five percent tip and checked in, wishing it were Monday and the market open so that I could climb all over El Paso Natural Gas.

The Bel Air Hotel reeks of old California to the extent that I almost expect to see Zorro leaping over its roofs. At the very least it is a place of silks and linens and bespoke suits, a place of the 1920s with men in two-tone shoes and beautiful women emerging from yellow motor cars. It is a place of old money and a reverence for the past. The construction is low white stucco topped by red Spanish tile roofs, buildings obscured by the California fig trees, the plantings of hibiscus and azaleas, of impatiens and bougainvillea. A stream travels through the property, and swans (the logo of the hotel) sail the stream and its ponds as if in aristocratic oblivion of their surroundings.

The hotel had recently been sold to the daughter of H. L. Hunt, and the rooms were all being refurbished. My room was on the pool. It was a large single with dressing room, fireplace, and furnishings covered to make you think you were in a garden — greens and yellows and blues.

I did some laps in the sunshine and watched the guests around the pool. California is unlike any other part of America for this reason: it's easy to forget why you are there. A young lady with the longest legs and the shortest shorts I had seen in years wandered by and asked whether I was enjoying my stay, what restaurants I liked, and if I had lately been to the movies. She loved all of my answers, and I felt the sunshine and the flowers and the chlorine had made me both brilliant and funny. I was about to ask her how long she had been a guest when she moved on and asked the couple on the chaise longues the same questions. Then I saw her take a small basket and begin emptying into it the ashtrays around the pool. The man on the next chaise laughed at me. "She works here," he said. "In California they resist uniforms. No helmet law for the motorcyclists. They believe in total freedom. It even creeps into the Bel Air Hotel from time to time."

At the far end of the pool an older man with a dark tan and a tight black pair of trunks poured several splashes of his drink onto the shoulder of a much younger woman lying beside him. She jumped slightly as he leaned over, licking the liquid where it ran down her upper body. If I were home now, I mused, it would be light sweater weather, with people's faces pushed up at a sun barely giving hints of spring. At home it was clean-up weather; each season in the East promises more of work to do than pleasure. None of my friends or clients would be licking drinks from young shoulders in New York or Boston or Washington. My artist friend was right: something was about to happen in California.

At six o'clock I was picked up by my client, David Wisser, in his Cadillac El Dorado with the vanity plate COUCH. David Wisser owned some of the largest furniture showrooms on the West Coast. His business did a volume of over $35 million a year. When business was good and when the stock market was up, David loved you to pieces; everything was the greatest. When business slumped and the market was down, he would turn on himself, cursing his luck and the fates and the Congress. David's account was up over 47 percent in the first four months of the year and he had generated better than $17,000 in commissions. If timing is everything, this was a good time to visit a manic depressive client.

"How are you, John-Boy, you old dog, you," David Wisser roared to me at the entrance to the Bel Air, a canopy at the end of a small bridge over the swans' stream. "I've got Helen in the back seat, so you and I can get real close and talk about money." David Wisser was a big man in his early sixties with close-cropped gray hair and Brooks Brothers clothes. He had come to California in 1955 and bought a house in Brentwood with a swimming pool for $38,000. It was a brick New England Colonial and had a whitewashed split-rail fence circling the property. "I was offered a million three last year by some fag in a TV series. I've got a thing about selling my house to a fairy," he told me.

There was only one trend in America of which David approved. That was the trend to condominium ownership, which brought with it a new market for home furnishings. David had seen me some years ago on "Wall Street Week" and had called to see whether I would handle his account. "I'm in home furnishings," he had said, "and I see you wear blue wool suspenders with a pink knit tie and a Sea Isle cotton blue and white striped shirt. If you're not afraid to be unusual and you're from the East, I like your color combinations enough to want you to take a run at my money. I can't stand the West Coast hustle, and your colors are my colors." Tell me that I'm in a rational business.

On the ride to Brentwood, every time David paused for breath, his wife, Helen, in the back seat would say firmly, "Ask him why he's not up *fifty* percent for the first four months," or "Apple Computer has doubled since January. That's a hundred percent. We don't own Apple." David ignored Helen, but I was getting nervous.

"We'll have a drink at the house, then to one of our favorite restaurants," David said. "I really want you at the house so that I can show you my clothes." David gave me a tour of his house, telling me the decorations changed every three months. "We live in a miniature showroom," he said, "a reflection that the world is really just one enormous showroom. I change the colors and the furniture to brighten up our outlook and to write off the house for tax purposes."

"We also own oil and gas for tax purposes," Helen said. "But they never send the K1's [the reports of income and/or loss for the 1040 tax form] until April fourteenth, and it destroys our lives because we always have to file late." David drank Cutty Sark and soda and showed me his dressing room, throwing open his closet doors as if displaying long-lost cave drawings. Racks of suits hung symmetrically, six inches apart. Polished shoes in shoetrees filled the racks along the closet bottoms. Shirts and sweaters were piled on shelves, row on row, color-coordinated, the folds exactly aligned.

"Americans lead sloppy lives," David said. "We are reaping the harvest of the welfare state that Roosevelt created to turn us into a Russian satellite. I own a hundred acres in the Arizona desert. When the pinko commie fag hordes and the spear-chuckers come over the walls into Brentwood and Bel Air,

Helen and I will be helicoptered to Arizona, where we have a light stucco bunker stocked with the right weapons, canned food, fresh water, and everything we'll need to survive."

"What about your shirts and suits and shoes?"

David was looking at me to see if I was serious just as Helen came into the room. "An Lac went out onto Wilshire today," she said. "She met three cousins and an aunt."

"Well, Jesus H. Christ," David said. "After I told her never to show her face on Wilshire. The police are picking up anybody who looks like they came off a raft." He slammed shut his closet door and ran from the dressing room.

The United States government claims that there are four to five million illegal aliens in this country living fearful lives in destitution. That's three out of every hundred people in the U.S.A. I followed David into the kitchen, which looked as if it were made to serve all of Robin Hood's men in Sherwood Forest. There were industrial stoves, hundreds of copper pans hanging from hooks, a deer's head over a walk-in fireplace, game prints of elk and moose and partridge and duck. A young Oriental girl was sitting on a high stool, sobbing into her hands. David was talking slowly to her. "No go on Wilshire," he said. "Bad mans there; take Annie away to bad place." The girl stopped crying and slowly brightened as David went to one of the refrigerators, which was disguised to look like part of the wall. It was covered in a blue chintz fabric with only the door handle giving a clue as to its real identity. "Heavenly Hash?" David said to her. "You will be a good girl and no go with bad mans?"

"Annie good girl," she said. "Heavenly Hash." As David spooned out her ice cream, Helen Wisser motioned me from the room. "David knows how to handle these situations," she said. "Annie would kill for Heavenly Hash, and David has made her believe only he can provide it." There was no emotion in Helen's voice, only a statement of the facts. "We paid seventeen hundred dollars for her and she does *everything*."

"Doesn't she get time off?"

"Are you kidding? After she cleans and cooks she's got acres of time. She can swim, use the tennis bangboard if she wants. She can be visited by relatives and they can use the exercise equipment. She's freer than she probably ever was in Cambodia."

"But she's a slave," I said.

"Please," said Helen Wisser. "You want to talk slaves, the Mitchells three houses away paid five thousand dollars for a family of three from Vietnam and those people don't get a minute free. Sally Mitchell doesn't even let them use the outdoor Jacuzzi. And she's threatened to trade the daughter for a better laundress."

"These people are here illegally and they're virtually shut up. They're prisoners."

"We take better care of these people than anyone would," she countered. "God, without us they'd die on the streets of East L.A. Believe me, they're a lot better off."

We went out for dinner. As we walked out the front door I saw magazines arranged on a mahogany hall table; *Architectural Digest* lay next to *Soldier of Fortune*.

We ate in Westwood Village, a restaurant that specialized in bratwurst, because David said that he "felt like something Wagnerian." He expounded on captive nations and colonialism and why it was all right to buy a Cambodian alien for $1700 from the agencies that handled these sorry people. "History is waves of influence," he said. "I go up, you go down. In the future, yellow and black waves will engulf us, and when that happens, I hope some Asian master is kind enough to serve *me* Heavenly Hash ice cream." Helen seemed to pay no attention to David's speeches, but she interrupted at random and said things like "We own no high-technology stocks. I still think we should have some Apple."

"I think you should always go with your instincts in the market," I said. "Your opinion is as good as anyone's in America when it comes to what will go up and what will go down."

142

"The Asians will go up," David said. "That's why I feel no guilt in employing them now."

There was a folded card on every table in the restaurant. The card read: "Join us in our expansion. Units available in our limited partnership for more Bratwurst Centers. $10,000 per unit. Inquire of your waitperson." Only in California would limited partnerships be advertised at your table and sold to you by your waitperson.

After dinner, David drove to the Bel Air and got out, walking with me halfway across the stone bridge leading to the hotel's main entrance. It smelled like the islands, lush with the heavy scent of earth, vegetation, and flowers. We leaned over the bridge. "With Hunt's daughter in control," David said, "there'll be no more pinko commie fags at the Bel Air Hotel." I left him musing on the bridge, his order to buy five thousand El Paso Natural Gas in my pocket.

I had left a wake-up call for 6:00 A.M. so that I could ring my home office when it was nine o'clock in the East. I was calling Mad Mark the Institutional Salesman to get his blessing on El Paso. This is a business that is always seeking reassurances. Am I right? Will it go up? Is it a good idea? It is a business of paranoia and self-deception. "It'll come back; we should buy more at lower prices; someone will take it over for its *true* value."

"On the other hand," Mark said, "Burlington Northern does own a chunk of El Paso at twenty-five. And we own a lot of Arkla [Arkansas Louisiana Gas], which sells at twenty-seven. El Paso's price should be closer to Arkla's than it is now. I would say it's okay to buy. On the other hand, natural gas prices are lousy; El Paso has always had its problems, and there's no guarantee that Burlington will ever come in for more."

"What about the dividend? I'm getting nine percent while I wait."

"Dividend will be maintained," Mark said. "Worst case: you get bored waiting. Should I send you a bill? You're the big broker and I'm holding your hand on Monday morning."

"You forget I'm in California. They drink Margueritas on Sunday nights. When I'm away from my machines I'm full of anxieties."

"Plenty of shrinks in Beverly Hills," he said and switched the call to my office.

* * *

A few words about how so-called big producers in the investment business do their numbers, their commissions. Virtually every stockbroker with significant production (I would place this now at over half a million dollars in gross commissions) controls his clientele. This generally means that the brokers buy and sell at their own discretion, without first contacting clients for their permission. It is almost physically impossible to do major commission business with a wide variety of customers if you have to speak to them about every decision. There are documents at each investment firm called discretionary forms that clients can sign. They give the brokers permission to trade "at the broker's discretion."

I was able to buy twenty-five thousand El Paso at the opening price (17 ¼) in one block. Then I could allocate the shares to people who I felt should have the stock in their portfolios. The distribution would be at my discretion, as was the purchase in the first place. If I had to call a dozen people, tell them my reasons for wanting El Paso, then place a dozen or more orders, the process would be inefficient, time-consuming, frustrating (some would buy, others would hesitate), and the price could conceivably run upward, spoiling my plan. When the stock is bought all at one price, at one moment, the process is efficient, nondiscriminatory (small buyers get the same price as the large buyers), and it enables me to handle major numbers of clients as if they were only one large customer.

This describes the optimum way to run a stock brokerage business. Of course, when all is said and done, with discretionary orders you'd better be right. The most important rule of the

144

New York Stock Exchange, the one with the greatest implica-
tions for abuse and misuse of relationships, is New York Stock
Exchange rule number 405: "know your customer." Unless you
have a firm understanding of whom you are dealing with, dis-
cretionary orders can bring big commissions but even bigger
trouble.

*   *   *

I told Sardonic Sandra to buy twenty-five thousand El Paso at
the opening price (the market begins at 10:00 A.M. in the East)
and went back to sleep, feeling very spoiled. I was beginning to
act like a California broker, which should have had me worried.
But California can make you, very easily, forget everything.

6

California 2: "It's Cold and It's Damp..."

With a short week in Los Angeles in which to accomplish a lot, I was determined to make the rounds as much as possible. This meant not only visiting clients, but checking with other people in the investment business as well. I told you that we are always looking for our heroes.

No trip to Los Angeles is ever complete for me unless I drop in on the man who calls himself Sonny the Options Maven. When I think of discretionary accounts, I always think of Sonny. He works for a regional West Coast firm, but he trained with me in New York when we were both youngbloods scrounging for meals and learning that A's in college math had nothing to do with success in the stock market. Sonny left the firm we trained with soon after getting his broker's license and started his own company, based in Beverly Hills. He was not the kind of person who worked well for somebody else.

Sonny had gone to Hollywood High, wore his black hair

slicked back like Valentino's, and grew up going to birthday parties where ponies were given as presents and Hopalong Cassidy would come out of the cake shooting cap pistols. Sonny dropped names the way you and I daily drop brain cells. And Sonny was a gambler. The firm he founded closed down when Wall Street collapsed in 1970. At the end he had used customers' funds without their permission to try to shore up his company's sagging finances. But back-office chaos and falling prices put Sonny on the bricks with no capital, several dozen lawsuits, and an official ban from the securities industry.

If you flunk out of Harvard College, they will let you back at least twice; they don't want to admit they made a mistake about you in the first place. Time also heals most wounds in the securities industry. I have known several sharpsters, churners, check kiters, and outright frauds booted out of investment firms to find homes in other offices, in good grace, with the blessing of their new firms and the regulatory authorities. Wall Street hates to say no to people who produce commissions. Sonny, after five years in the wilderness, trying to start retail men's stores, selling cable TV franchises, and being a partner in a Tarzana Mercedes dealership, was welcomed back to the securities industry, no longer an exile, the past forgiven if not forgotten.

I walked into his office at nine-thirty, the New York Stock Exchange having already been open for two and a half hours. Sonny's firm was on Wilshire Boulevard, a block from the Beverly Wilshire Hotel, near the corner of Rodeo Drive, where, among other shopping delights, you can buy a gold-plated thirty-eight-caliber revolver at Bijan for $10,000, along with silk neckties for over a hundred dollars. White wine, as you select your merchandise, is free. I walked through a large board room to a closed oak door. There was a framed sign on the door, done in calligraphy. It said: *You come to play, or you go away.*

I walked in and was greeted by the sight of Sonny pedaling

around his office in a large toy car, a Bentley, complete with headlights and windshield wipers that worked. A sound system played in the background. It was the Beach Boys singing, "Help Me, Rhonda, Help, Help Me, Rhonda." Sonny had gone completely gray, but his hair was still slicked straight back like Valentino's. His silk shirt was open to the waist, and he wore designer jeans over lizard boots from Tony Lama.

"Johnny," he yelled over the music, "what a nice surprise even though you've come to use my phone and pick my brain! Besides, you're a yellow dog because you've never gone out on your own the way anyone who claims he's an entrepreneur would have done long ago." He got up from his toy and kissed me on both cheeks. "Remember how I used to put underwritings together, do the big deals, take stock down, and wait for my yacht to come in?" Sonny asked. "Well, finally I've gotten smart. I have discovered the formula for getting rich as a stockbroker. I am now Sonny the Options Maven. That's how I advertise myself. My license plate says MAVEN. I can give everyone a shot at glory even for a few thousand bucks. Options are what the American dream is all about."

"I've always found that options are a stockbroker's dream and a customer's nightmare," I said.

"You obviously don't understand America," he said. "And you certainly don't understand California."

* * *

An option contract basically is the right to buy a certain stock at a certain price for a specific period of time. A desire to buy would induce you to be interested in a call option, giving you the right to call a stock to yourself from a seller at a specific price. The desire to sell a stock or to sell it short, hoping to profit from a decline in price, would interest you in a put option, where you could put your stock (or the option) to a buyer at a specific price.

For instance, you might buy a call option to buy a hundred shares of XYZ at 30 for a three-month period. If you bought a hundred shares of XYZ now at 30, it would cost $3000 plus commissions. The option to buy a hundred XYZ at 30 may cost you only $300 plus a commission, the $300 being the premium you pay for the option contract.

The premium you paid ($300) gives you the right, for a ninety-day period, to buy a hundred shares of XYZ at $30 a share. If the stock moves up to 40 in that time, you could exercise your option to buy the shares at 30. Because of the enormously popular listed options exchanges, there is an active market in trading the options themselves. If XYZ stock moved to 40 from 30 (a little over 30 percent), it is conceivable that the option contract would have moved from 3 (the $300 premium) to 6, or 100 percent on your money.

Options are much more volatile than the underlying stock and provide enormous leverage. What is leverage? If a hundred shares of XYZ cost $3000 and the option on a hundred shares costs $300, you could buy options on a thousand shares of XYZ for the same cash you would put up buying only a hundred shares of the common stock. Thus, with a hundred shares moving from 30 to 40, your profit would be $1000. With options on a thousand shares for the same money, the option moving from 3 to 6 would give you a $3000 profit (3 points times a thousand shares), triple what the stock would bring. But if the stock did nothing in three months, at least you had a piece of paper still worth $3000. The option, however, being a wasting asset, would decline little by little as it reached its expiration date. The premium would wither away and eventually the option itself would be worthless. The most you could lose would be the premium you paid for the option, $300.

Ninety-nine percent of all option contracts done this way expire worthless, a broker's dream, because the commissions would be comparable to the stocks selling at the same prices ($3.00 or $6.00), and options contracts tend to be held for very short periods of time, sometimes days, sometimes hours. They are a customer's nightmare because they are volatile and the customer can't put a time limit on a stock and be a consistent winner. *He can be a consistent* loser *only if he trades for the short term. And if, because of the leverage, he makes a big score, no one walks away from the table. He'll come back until he gives it all away.*

This is a basic explanation of how call options work. These listed options are by far the most popular area, with almost four hundred Big Board companies trading active options on the Chicago Board of Options Exchange or the other exchanges offering contracts in Big Board stocks: the American Exchange, Philadelphia, Midwest, and Pacific. Why are options so popular? Why is the lottery popular? What saved Las Vegas from the desert and Atlantic City from the sea? Greed and the lure of action. If everyone loves a $2.00 stock, and everyone does, then options are a wonderful way for the average person with a thousand dollars burning a hole in his pocket to have some fun. *Note the roman. I said "have some fun," not "make money." The money in this instance is reserved for the stockbrokers, the same way the profits in a casino are reserved for the house. Every young stockbroker, investment executive, financial consultant, registered rep, or whatever title they're lurking behind these days, every one of them who sits in a row of desks in a board room, loves the option markets. Rapid turnover of positions, high percentage commission on low dollar volume trades, and great volatility produce strong revenue for the broker and for his firm.*

Up-Your-Gross Smith loves the option-oriented brokers, even though he has to supervise them very carefully to make sure the action is desired by the client. Occasionally he will click on his announcement microphone, which broadcasts to every corner of the office. "A day without options," he will say, "is like a day without sunshine. Today's special is the IBM March one thirties selling at only half a buck." (Translation: You can buy a call option to acquire a hundred shares of IBM at $130, the strike price, until the end of March. Assume the cost is $50 per option on a hundred shares. If IBM moves up, the leverage

150

on the option is terrific. And if everyone loves a $2.00 stock, imagine how he feels about one selling at fifty cents!)

*   *   *

"What do you mean, I don't understand California," I said to Sonny. "It's a place where you get huge olives in your martinis and you go people-watching at supermarkets at one-thirty in the morning." He didn't laugh. California is also a place where they take their views of Utopia seriously.

"Look," he said, "you want to know how to do business in California, you have to understand that most people who have come here in the last twenty years — and there are millions — came here because they were losers somewhere else. I was born here. But even my father was a bust-out cloakie from Paterson, New Jersey. In California he sold women's clothing and eventually started a chain of stores that were bought by Allied for two and a half mil. Dad found much less resistance to sales techniques out here than back East. He would say, 'Madam, this hemline is all the rage in Paris,' and she would say, 'Okay.' '*Okay*,' my dad would say, is the word that describes California best. Why not try *anything*? That's why I'm Sonny the Options Maven; I'm giving everyone something chic to try."

I used one of Sonny's three phones, the only one that looked like a phone, even though it was pink. The two other instruments offered a choice of Walt Disney's Pluto or a plastic oil derrick, left over, I suppose, from the time my host was Sonny the Oil and Gas Maven. Sonny heard me checking on El Paso, and he instantly punched out the option prices on his Quotron machine. "Hey, you like El Paso? That was a dog ten years ago. You still sitting in positions until your customers die or go to E. F. Hutton?"

"I think it's a good idea," I said, "and on top of the twenty-five thousand shares I bought at the opening at seventeen, I ordered another ten thousand at sixteen and seven-eighths if it touched that price."

Sonny asked me why I liked the stock and I told him. He cut me off in midstory. "Okay, okay, I get the gist. All I need to sell is two sentences." He immediately began dialing customers and giving them what he called his forty-second pitch. Here it is.

"Dr. Saul? Sonny the Options Maven. El Paso Natural Gas September twenties at half a buck. The stock is seventeen; Burlington Northern owns a chunk of it and probably will go for the entire company. If they paid twenty-five for the rest, we could quadruple our money, that's four times, Doctor. Four hundred percent. And money market's paying only nine percent.

"How about we buy one hundred calls, that's options on ten thousand shares. You put up five thousand dollars. If the stock even goes to twenty, we probably can double. Let me do it while it's still cheap. Just say do it; I've got to get the order in while we're still on the market."

Leave ten seconds for a response; then, "Thank you, Doctor. I'll keep you informed."

Forty seconds produced a sale, with a gross commission of $395, and the trade was treated as if the client were buying ten thousand shares of stock at fifty cents a share. Sonny proceeded to make the same pitch five times while I watched. He was successful five times. After placing each order, he would give an imaginary teammate a high five, jumping in the air and slapping an unseen hand. Then he would pedal his little car around the room, jump up again, and call another client.

Stockbrokers all have nervous habits. The pressure of continuously selling yourself and doing so in a short span of time, plus the pressure of wanting to be right and so many times being wrong, makes for jumpy personalities. In our office, Jimmy Minot licks his lips constantly, as if trying to lubricate his selling skills. Mad Mark the Institutional Salesman arches his eyebrows after each sentence; Paul the Bachelor winks his right eye like a conspirator; Jane the Impaler clears her throat every fifteen words, as if she were winding herself up. Sonny the Options Maven rode around his office, glowing with adrenaline.

I play squash four times a week to calm myself down from the pace of trading and phone calls and the pressure of being all things financial to all people. It is a business for the half-crazed. "You know I love to see you, John," Sonny said, "but social niceties take time from the trading day. Every forty seconds I chitchat with you probably cost me three hundred and fifty dollars gross. Friends are for after trading hours."

"Except you probably owe me," I said, "for giving you your idea of the day."

"Well, don't think I don't appreciate it. But I'll tell you, when I don't have ideas, I trade market futures, the Standard and Poor's Five Hundred. Why play individual stocks when you can bet which way the market itself is going?

"The Standard and Poor's Five Hundred average trades now the way individual commodities like soybeans or corn or wheat trade. The S and P Five Hundred is on the Chicago Mercantile Exchange. I put up six thousand dollars' margin for each contract. Every point the S and P moves up or down, it's five dollars per point. So if the S and P moves fifty points a day, which can be normal, that's two hundred and fifty a swing. On several contracts the leverage is great, and my clients love the action. Most of my customers, thank God, have no idea about pork bellies or corn or soybean futures. But they love to gamble on which way the stock market may move. Play it long or short, I could care less."

"You're in the right business, Sonny," I said. "I remember when we were training in New York and you'd want to bet how many minutes it would take the next IRT train to come into the station."

"Look," Sonny said, "I earned these gray hairs the hard way, learning about life through my mistakes. Here's the formula I worked out and here's the truth, whether you like it or not. The sexual revolution is largely something someone made up on campuses at Berkeley and Cambridge, Mass. As far as I can tell, the people who always would get it, get it. And the people who never had a prayer are still pulling their puds. Sex is probably no more available to the mass of people than it ever was. So if the average guy and woman don't stand a chance for exciting sex lives, they want a substitute. I'm their substitute for sex: the options market, the futures exchanges, a chance for some excitement.

"You never stay in an option longer than a few days or a week. It's legal and respectable. You don't have to go to a track or casino. You don't have to use a bookie. You can wear a three-piece suit, a designer dress — and a thousand bucks can be five thousand *fast*. I'm selling cheap kicks to people cheated by the sexual revolution."

"This has taken more than forty seconds," I said.

"Are you kidding? That's my speech when I give seminars. The firm rents me a hotel suite and we advertise the seminars as 'Bored by sex? Try options, the ultimate turn-on!' People flock to the podium after I'm done. Believe me, what I've got, Americans want."

Three people walked into Sonny's office, two men and one old woman. She was bent over, using a walker. One of the men looked very nervous. "Sonny," the nervous man said, "can we be alone?" Sonny took one look at the trio and got to his feet. "No," he said, "my friend Mr. Spooner can stay; I want him to stay. Mrs. Wilson," he gushed to the old woman, "here, I'll pull around your favorite chair. Is this your boyfriend?" He indicated the second man.

"No," said the nervous man, "this is Mr. Hegenbart from the SEC."

"My lawyer made me do it, Sonny," the old woman said. The nervous man was a partner in Sonny's firm, a partner in charge of compliance with SEC and Stock Exchange rules. "Mr. Sonny," the SEC man began, "Mrs. Wilson has revealed to us that over the last year and a half, you have taken forty-eight thousand dollars of her money, supposedly for use in her declining years, and turned it, through excessive speculative options trading, into twenty-three hundred and seventy-five dollars. Commissions during this time have totaled almost eighteen thousand dollars, more than a third of her original capital. There is no defense against this. There is no justification. This is criminal."

Sonny didn't miss a beat. He went over to Mrs. Wilson and kissed her on the cheek. "Have we had a grand time, Mrs. Wilson?" he asked.

"They say you've lost all my money, Sonny," she whispered.

"That's absurd, darling," he said. "Look," he snapped at the SEC man. "Number one, you expect me to roll over because you persecute people with your inquisition tactics? Mrs. Wilson has signed a bona fide discretionary form, giving me authority to trade in her account. Second, you are discriminating against elderly people. Mrs. Wilson should sue *you*."

The agent was incredulous. "Me, discriminating?" he said. "You turned this poor widow's life savings into dust. You speculated in high-risk vehicles for someone who should be getting income with safety . . ."

"Stop!" Sonny commanded. "You see? You're telling *her* what's good for her. Just because she's eighty-two years old, isn't she entitled to a little *fun*? A little excitement? Mrs. Wilson" — Sonny was passionate — "I've got a little situation on the Big Board called El Paso. The options are only fifty cents. If we're right, they're cheap enough to recoup everything plus."

"I ought to have you in jail," the SEC man said.

Mrs. Wilson stood up, supported by her walker. "Wait," she said. "If Sonny thinks he's got something that's really good for . . ." Sonny was sweating from the enthusiasm of his pitch. I patted him on the back and headed out of his office. The Beach Boys' tape was still on in the background; they were singing, "And we'll have fun, fun, fun, till your daddy takes the T-bird away."

I took a quick punch of his machine on the way out. The market was getting crunched, down almost twenty-three points near the close of the day (twelve-thirty in Los Angeles). El Paso was down a quarter of a point and I was trying to get myself psyched for lunch at a time when Morgan Stanley had issued a sell signal to their clients. "To hell with it," I said to myself, stepping out into bleary skies that made my eyes water. "What does Morgan Stanley know about California?"

* * *

The Beverly Hills Hotel rises out of Sunset Boulevard like a castle out of Grimm's fairy tales. Except the Brothers Grimm never would have thought of a pink castle, with its knights riding Jaguars and Rolls-Royces and abandoning the fair damsels to the dragons, or at least to the agents. I was going to the Beverly Hills Hotel for lunch with Harry the Producer. Everyone who has ever managed other people's money has several magic clients for whom they can do no wrong: every stock they buy goes up, every market timing move is correct, every interest rate prediction comes true. Usually the magic clients for whom you can do no wrong have a total of $4700 under your control. On the other hand, the key people in your life — your parents, your uncles and aunts, the chairmen of the board who can set you up for years — are put into loser after loser and every one of your predictions fades into old promises. Broken dreams of capital gains lost echo the classic situation: the sure-thing short-term play that turns into a "fine long-term investment."

Of course, these are the people who can do you the most good. They can also do you the most harm, moving big money your way or becoming folks you must avoid forever in clubs and bars and restaurants. Because they will say in loud whispers, "There's the guy who stiffed me in Zymos or in Pizza Time Theaters or in Fortune Systems." For whatever reason, the gods of the stock market smiled on me. For Harry the Producer I could do no wrong. And he was a biggie. Your best clients bird-dog for you; they get you other clients — their friends and relatives. You become their pet; they brag about you. Harry the Producer was going to give a party for me, to show me off to his friends as his house money manager. We were having the ritual lunch at the Beverly Hills Hotel to allow him to demonstrate his power in action.

The true beauty of shades, of sunglasses, is that they allow you to watch other people without being obvious. No one entered or moved in the Polo Lounge of the Beverly Hills Hotel without everyone else noticing. But the women and men who wore shades indoors at lunchtime didn't have to move their heads to check out the new arrivals. "Mr. Harry the Producer," I said to the maître d'.

"You don't hear him?" the maître d' asked, a response you would hear only from maître d's close to the entertainment business. I heard Harry before I saw him. He was swearing into a telephone at his table in a booth against the center wall of the lounge. He saw me and jumped up, the phone falling onto the table. He bounded across the room and called out, as loudly as he could, *Angel!"*

Harry the Producer was a redhead. He had a thick shock of hair that would have done credit to Rusty Jones. He was a former fat man turned skinny from fad diets. But the fat man was always eager to get out, and Harry would go on binges of eating, his weight jumping up and down, up and down, with the fortunes of his latest movie. Harry picked me off the ground in his hug and gave me wet kisses on the cheek. "Angel," he repeated, "you're the only one in this town I can trust. And you're not even *in* this town." Harry had new pet names for people every few months. If he called me Angel, he called everyone Angel. Soon it would be replaced by Darling or Precious or, my favorite, Delight. It is very pleasing to a stockbroker to be called Delight. Although I can live with Angel.

Harry virtually carried me to his booth, hugging me and

pinching my cheeks all the way. "Angel, my genius," he said, pushing me down onto the seat. "I'm going to parade you around like the star you are; you're going to meet everyone: Warren, Jack, Spielberg. But first you meet Mr. Lipsky. Mr. Lipsky, this is John Spooner." Mr. Lipsky was a little old man, very frail, with a carefully groomed gray beard and steel-rimmed glasses toned Brooks Brothers gray to match his beard. He had a dry, firm grasp. "Mr. Lipsky is dining with us because he likes to talk about money," Harry said. "Mr. Lipsky has at least a toe into everything that happens in this town important."

Mr. Lipsky nodded. "I got a theory about the stock market that always works," he said. "I only buy companies where my friends run the company. Over the years I owned lots of stock in Warner Brothers, MGM, Paramount, savings and loans, the West Coast department stores, the Pacific Telephone, the land developers. I know all the owners and they would tell me to buy their stock."

"Those stocks go up and those stocks go down," I said. "Did they tell you when to sell?"

Lipsky nudged Harry. "He has to come from the East to tell me stocks fluctuate. You see, I can use East Coast words. Fluctuate. Junior, if you do business with friends, they stick to your life," he said to me. "If I buy the stocks of their companies because they tell me to and I *lose* money, I know they will find a way to pay me back. They give me pieces of their deals, I own acres in the valley because Louis B. Mayer lost me money on a stock. Friends have to make you whole, because a loss is on their conscience. Friends stick to your life. That's why, one way or another, I always make money in the stock market."

The phone kept ringing for Harry and people kept coming by our table to pay respects, sip from anyone's glass of white wine or Poland Spring mineral water, ask about current projects, or drop off scripts. Harry's films had received four Academy Award nominations the year before, and everyone knew it was all right to be nice to him. Our booth filled up with people. After a while eight bodies were shoved tightly together, trying to nibble various salads without getting pieces of vegetable stuck between their teeth.

The female lead in one of Harry's movies was pressed against my right side. "This is one of the major people out here," she said staring past me at Harry. "He said to be nice to you. What are you, one of the money guys?"

"I manage Harry's money."

"Oh, I've got a business manager too," she said. "We all have business managers out here. Mine has me on an allowance. It's wonderful. The checks I get have pictures of Pilgrims on them. You know, really solid stuff. He buys gold bars for me and stores them in underground vaults somewhere in the Rockies. Really solid stuff."

Harry was screaming into his phone. "You cocksucker, the accounting was right to the penny. With the flight on the Concorde you got more than you're entitled to." His face took on the color of his hair, and his nose was as inflamed as if it had just erupted with adolescent skin problems. He hung up and tapped on his wine glass with a spoon. The table conversation dampened.

"A man is lucky," Harry said, his nose dimming, "to be surrounded at lunch by people he loves. Now I want us all to cross our arms and hold hands with our neighbors. Go ahead." I crossed my arms and held the hands of both the actress and Harry. "Now kiss the cheek of the person on your right and the person on your left." We all kissed. "Now we shut our eyes and all wish for unlimited projects that work, for never giving a percentage of the gross, and for confusion to our enemies." He opened his eyes. "Switch seats to give us all a crack at each other."

There are rituals everywhere. I know a hostess in Boston who keeps a silver bell by her right hand at dinner parties. When she rings the bell, you must turn to the person on your left.

159

She rings again fifteen minutes later and you have to turn and converse with the neighbor on your right. In the new arrangement I found myself sitting next to Mr. Lipsky and a man who was cutting a cucumber slice into four pieces and carefully chewing each tiny piece.

"So, what are you buying?" asked Mr. Lipsky.

"I bought a chunk of El Paso Natural Gas today. About seventeen," I said.

"I can't buy anything from you," Lipsky said. "I've got no stake in you. You've got no reason to make me whole if you give me a bummer."

"I've never given Harry a bummer."

"You're young," Lipsky said. "No one is ever right all the time. And if you make a mistake, I want to look you in the eye when you're a loser. I want to look you in the eye at the Polo Lounge at lunch and see what you're made of. I don't like bad news over the phone from three thousand miles away.

"Harry has made a lot of money and he rides in a limousine and has made some good pictures. But he rides in the *front* of the limousine because he's still unsure of where he belongs. He doesn't know how to impress people the right way. In Harry's office," Mr. Lipsky said, "you go in and he says to his secretary, 'Get my father on the phone. I'll take it on the toilet.' "

"Who's the vegetarian?" I asked Mr. Lipsky about the man on my right who silently chewed his cucumber slice. The man was poised over his plate, looking like a gargoyle. He was in his mid-twenties and everything about him seemed clenched, as if having lunch were an order to do isometric exercises. "That's Chill," said Mr. Lipsky. "He makes sure nothing happens to me."

People kept coming up to the booth. A man approached, wheeling cases of wine. "Put them in my trunk," said Harry. The man bumped into a table and I heard the crunch of glass. Harry reddened and immediately squeezed by everyone on his way to confront the man. Harry ripped open a case and screamed at him, "Do you know what this wine cost? Do you

160

know what overbudget means?" He went on for minutes. I had never heard anyone carry on so violently over something so trivial. He looked at us. "People screw up, you have to let them know." I slid out of the booth myself and grabbed Harry by the hand as he picked through the broken glass. "This wine was a gift," he muttered. "But there are principles to establish."

"Harry," I said, "thanks for lunch, but I have to check in with someone at the hotel. I bought you a lot of stock this morning. Would you treat me this way if I gave you a loser?"

"Hey," he said, kissing me suddenly on the cheek, on the neck. "You're my angel, aren't you? I only treat my angels great. What do you think, I'm a one-way guy? What did you buy me? Here" — he bent down — "take a couple of bottles of wine. It didn't cost me anything."

There's always a fancy automobile with a hired driver outside hotels in the big cities of the world. For cash they will take you where you want to go while their patrons dine or rendezvous in the hotel. I grabbed a black Lincoln stretch limo to take me to the Bel Air. As I was getting comfortable in the rear, I asked the driver, "Who are you waiting for?"

"This is Harry the Producer's car," he said. "Can you believe that wherever we go he sits with me in the front? But I'm a happy cowboy," he added, "because it proves that in California everyone's equal."

I leaned back into the cushions, wishing I were home in the East and that someone would ring a little silver bell. I was beginning to worry about what would happen if I gave Harry a loser.

I had called my old friend Eric the Actor earlier in the week, and sure enough, he was invited to the party Harry the Producer was giving for me on Friday night.

"Harry loves me because he knows he's getting a cheap court jester," Eric said. "He's a great negotiator, you know. I was in several of his films, and once I thought I'd gained a little edge, I asked him for a percentage of the film.

" 'I don't give percentages in my deals,' Harry said. 'Where'd you get those shoes?' That was the end of the conversation."

On Friday, May 6, Sardonic Sandra called me at the Bel Air. "This is what happens when you go away on a pleasure jaunt in a service business," she said.

"What's wrong?" I asked. "Never mind the preamble."

"El Paso just cut the quarterly dividend to seventeen cents from thirty-seven cents, more than fifty percent. The stock stopped trading at sixteen and one-half."

I had been buying the stock over the phone since Monday morning and had accumulated over a hundred thousand shares at prices ranging from 16¾ to 17⅜. One of my main selling points was that El Paso's dividend gave to the buyer almost 9 percent, comparable with money market rates, if not favorable. With the dividend cut in half, the credibility of the entire story became suspect, and me with it.

*　*　*

The Myth: Brokers don't care what happens to stocks. They get their commissions whether you buy or sell.

The Truth: Stockbrokers bleed over their decisions. They spend sleepless nights worrying about your money, about your stocks and bonds and annuities and tax shelters. It's true that commissions are charged whether people buy or sell. But when a stock is purchased for someone at 20 and it goes down to 10 and is sold, the commission at 10 is much less than at 20 per share. And after the loss the customer invariably says, "Sell it at ten and send me a check for the proceeds. There'll be no more business in my account. I'm through with the stock market and definitely through with you." Bernard Baruch could say, "You can't be God for a commission." But the scars of losers and mistakes never quite heal.

*　*　*

The morning haze was burning off the Bel Air pool. The day was turning beautiful and I was going crazy in California with

$1.7 million of client money in a stock that probably would reopen on the New York Stock Exchange 2 points lower than its previous sale price. To complicate the situation, my source for the stock was Paul of Upper Class Limo. Try explaining *that* to your customers.

I frantically dialed Paul's number, got his service, and told them this was an emergency. Sardonic Sandra called again, telling me El Paso had indeed reopened 2 points lower. I didn't want to go to Harry's party. I didn't want to have my avocado salad by the pool, pretending I was a producer waiting to be paged to come to the outside phone. After two hours of waiting, Paul reached me in my room.

"Remember me?" I pleaded, "the guy to whom you gave the lay-up? El Paso Natural Gas at seventeen? They just cut the dividend. It's dropped two points."

"Hey," Paul said, "I wouldn't worry about it. Burlington Northern is still lurking in the wings. You should probably buy on the bad news, not sell it."

"I could be stuck for a hell of a long time," I said. "Who knows when or *if* Burlington Northern will ever pick up the rest of the company?"

"I'm not a stockbroker," Paul said. "You want a tour of the valley or a driver to Universal Studios, I'm your guy. You take the advice of a barber or a bartender or a chauffeur about what stocks to buy, don't expect them to hold your hand if it goes wrong. You want to book the car, or what?"

I hung up the phone and thought of an article about Los Angeles I once read. I looked out my window at the sunshine and the swimming pool and the flowers. Waiters were bringing drinks on silver trays to guests who looked skinny and rich. The line in the article was "Another shitty day in paradise."

Eric the Actor, full of good spirits, picked me up at six-thirty to drive me to Harry's party. "I'm having my midlife crisis," Eric told me. "I've reached an important milestone."

Eric would never understand about El Paso. It was difficult for me to focus on his good mood.

"That's wonderful," I told him. "What's the milestone?"

"I've reached that point in my life and it is now time to develop fuck-you money. To this cause I'm going to devote myself full time."

Maybe he *would* understand about El Paso.

Fuck-you money is a concept often bandied about in the investment business. It is also bandied about in the entertainment business, which will give you some idea of the similarities between these two occupations. The term is self-explanatory; it represents wish fulfillment. It represents the accumulation of enough liquid funds and personal net worth to tell anyone at any time what he can do with himself. Fuck-you money is financial freedom.

"How are you going to accomplish that?" I asked Eric.

"I'm going to be smart, for a change," he said. "I'm going to switch to the producing side. I'm going to suck up to the Harrys of the world to cut me in for a piece of the action. What's the point of being in a film for scale? I work ten weeks, I make a living. I'm getting older. Suddenly I can't get the young parts. Routines don't mean a thing if they've got to shoot you through cheesecloth. When I start choosing the darkest booths in the darkest L.A. restaurants I know, it's time I started moving in back of the cameras, away from in front of them."

Harry the Producer lived in Bel Air, high on the canyon above the hotel. His Mediterranean-style villa was ringed by cedar trees. Attendants from UCLA were taking cars. "Angels," Harry greeted us, with hugs and kisses. He seemed somewhat restrained toward me, but it was probably my imagination. This was supposed to be a cocktail party honoring Harry's East Coast stockbroker, but indeed was an excuse for him to throw a large payback for people in the film industry.

Eric moved to the garden for a drink. Harry pulled me aside to tell me about my role, where I stood with him. "You're my precious," he said, "and I'm not forgetting it. And this party is for you; I'll give you a toast and speech and everything. But the world is cruel. The truth is that if you make a lot of money

164

for me, I don't want you handling any of my friends. The more you pay attention to other people, the less time you have for me."

"Harry," I protested, "service is what I'm selling. I pay attention to all my clients."

"Angel," he said, "save the bullshit for the folks who inherited their dough. This is Harry you're talking to. Go get some smoked salmon, some stuffed mushrooms. You're the guest of honor, but lay off the hustling at the party. You're *mine*."

The house had belonged to a silent film star. Walking through it and around the garden, I had the sense that this was not life but rather a place where the cameras were always rolling and the sets would be struck at midnight, the marble pool and the sculptured lawns, the antiques and the people, carted away. In the morning, it would all be a vacant lot.

Harry wore a velvet smoking jacket and black tie. I was amazed that he carried neither a long cigarette holder nor a megaphone. I wandered around nibbling the hors d'oeuvres and drinking Absolut vodka with Clamato juice. Big Hollywood parties are unique in that no one in attendance, be he a dentist, doctor, banker, or stockbroker, talks about anything other than show business. Even at lawyers' or doctors' conventions you can hear conversations about books or schools or the children or nuclear disarmament. At Hollywood parties, the doctors talk reconstruction of breasts for actresses, dentists talk teeth-bonding for soap stars, bankers talk funding for "the package," and lawyers talk deals of the clients "in turnaround." We are all on the set in Los Angeles.

I talked with a young actress for a while who told me, "Nothing ever stops a party out here, I mean, nothing is too outrageous unless you do something to offend one of the five people who count. There are only five people in this town with any power. Everyone else is always playing catch-up.

"I was at a party once," she went on, "hiding in a bathroom with Olivia Newton-John, because everyone was hitting on us. People are always hitting on you out here. We were looking out a window and George Segal and Robert Wagner were roasting everyone. Ray Stark was there and he's one of the five people in town who count. Before they got to him, he stood up and said, 'That's about enough of that.' That was the end of the roast and really the end of the party. We got hysterical in the bathroom, because this never happens. By the way, you're not hitting on me, are you?"

I listened to Eric the Actor explaining to a small group of people about sex in Los Angeles. "These days," he said, "I call it 'doing baloney pony.' There are so many names for cock in this town because it means so many different things to people."

A competitor of Harry's, another producer, Brooklyn-smart and sleek as an otter, leaned against a statue of Pan by the pool and talked to an audience. "Don't kid yourself, we're out here for the uncertainty. Once I tried to buy one of the big Vegas hotels for twenty-three million. I got the Teamsters to put up eighteen million for the first mortgage and I could write a check myself for the rest. Everybody loved me. This was in nineteen seventy-four. I produce a couple of turkeys, the stock market plunges, and I go from aces to C.O.D. overnight. C.O.D. is when nobody wants to know your name. Hey, son" — he noticed me — "you taking notes or you want to eat part of our deal?" There is no relaxing in Los Angeles. Everyone works a party.

A lighting designer in the living room lounged full length on a couch done in soft brown corduroy. "Brown is the color this year," he said. "I, for instance, have seventy-six shades of brown in my apartment. Brown is safe."

A consultant to Twentieth Century–Fox emerged from an upstairs bathroom and offered me a snort from a traveling inhaler he carried in a side pocket of his safari jacket. I showed him my glass of Absolut. "This is all I need," I said.

"Just a onesky with this puts the icing on the cake," he said. "A onesky never hurt anyone. Just a little afterdinner mint, some nose candy."

"What do you consult?" I asked him.

166

"I consult life styles." He winked at me. "I consult as long as I provide. You dig? I grew up out here," he told me. "I was visiting my grandma once in Westwood. Next door lived Fred Astaire's mother in an upstairs apartment. Stairs outside the apartment led up to her door. One day I'm visiting my grandma and the upstairs door opens. Fred Astaire walks out, says good-bye to his mother, and tap-dances down the stairs. That's my vision, and it's a vision I try to bring to the business when I consult."

"Do you think cocaine enhances or distorts that image?" I asked him.

"Could you say that again?" he said.

After several hours I cornered Harry the Producer.

"This is a great party, Harry," I told him. "But I'm not sure that if I shook everyone here upside down I'd find more than a dollar seventy-five."

Harry was uncharacteristically silent. He sipped champagne from a tulip glass. "Come on," he said, "I want to show you something." He took me into his screening room, a recondi-tioned area in his basement, with twenty reclining theater seats and a white front wall. He shut the lights and clicked on a slide projector. *Harry's Latest Score* flashed in big letters across the screen. For the next five minutes, shots of pipelines and refineries and homes comfortably heated with natural gas snapped by in a logical procession. The final slide showed Harry tossing wads of money at the camera and his mouth forming the words "Thank you, El Paso Natural Gas."

Harry put the lights back on. "How the fuck can I show this?" he said. "How the fuck can I parade my angel when El Paso cuts the dividend and the stock goes in the shithouse?"

"Harry," I said, "don't you think this is a little dramatic? It's where we *sell* a stock that counts, not what happens while we own it. We've bought plenty of companies that went down for a while, and we always ended up winners."

"I never made a film about *them*," he said. "It's like finding out my wife wasn't a virgin when I married her."

I went to find Eric the Actor. He had just taken out his castanets and was clicking away for the daughter of a major movie lawyer. Between beats he told me, "I can't leave yet. Acquiring fuck-you money requires serious attention."

I walked down the canyon, away from Harry the Producer's house. No one walks the streets of Bel Air at night. Like Los Angeles itself, the suburbs of the West are driving territory. I thought I heard coyotes up in the canyon, and I remembered news stories from several years past about the animals coming down from the hills and attacking people. I could see the head-lines: STOCKBROKER CARRIED OFF BY COYOTES. JUSTICE SERVED.

I quickstepped down Stone Canyon Road, passing by the burned-out shell of Kareem Abdul-Jabar's house. A fire had re-cently gutted the dwelling, surrounded by a wall with wrought-iron Art Deco basketballs topping the pylons. How quickly the possessions, the physical proof of a man's life, can be destroyed! Vodka was making me maudlin, but I was looking forward to a nightcap in the safety of the hotel. Crossing the bridge to the lobby, I saw a man leaning over the rail, being sick. As he straightened up, I saw that it was Sonny the Options Maven. "I was prepared to wait for you all night," he said, slurring his words. "The hotel kept claiming you were out. I thought you were ducking me."

"You've got to get control of yourself, Sonny," I said. "You're a *pro*. You've been through the ups and downs hundreds of times."

"Yeah," he said. "But the downs hurt more and more each time, and you never get used to them. Besides, I took my last stand on El Paso options with Mrs. Wilson. We pushed it all on red. I'll be banned from the business for good." He went over the rail one more time. I hoped the swans were not swim-ming under the bridge. Sonny wiped his mouth and stared at me.

"I don't want any excuses or explanations. That's all we get in our business. I just wanted to look you in the face so you'll remember the night Sonny the Options Maven went in the tank for the last time." He lurched away toward the parking lot and I went into the bar for a Scotch, something strong that didn't taste healthful like California. I nursed my drink. A man on the next barstool leaned over and said, "I'll be honest. I'm a promoter. But wouldn't you pay forty-five dollars for a device that screws into your phone and can tell you if anyone is listening?" I signaled for the check. The bartender rang it up, pointed to my drink, and said, "Take it with you." It was the nicest thing anyone had said to me all day.

I flew home the next morning but had to return to California right before Memorial Day. I was at Pebble Beach, in Monterey, delivering a speech to a group of corrugated-box manufacturers. A client of mine, the kind of man who lists his occupation as "private investor," had a house along the eighteenth fairway, one of the most famous holes in golf. Mortimer was his name. He was a man of strong opinions, and no one called him Mort.

We played golf together and he insisted that we tee off early, just before seven in the morning. On the first tee the fog off the ocean was so thick, I couldn't see the ball washer. "This game is easy," I said, "as long as you hit it straight." Mortimer didn't laugh. He was as serious about his golf as he was about his money. "I tee off early," he explained, "so I can beat the goddamned Japanese." He ranted on about the Japanese for three misty holes. "Oh," he said, "this nation is slipping into the toilet and there's no doubt about it. Just in California I can see the signs; I don't even have to go east. In Detroit, General Motors pays its workers seventeen dollars an hour. The Japanese get fanatically loyal people devoted to screwing on a windshield wiper for twenty-five years at nine dollars an hour. I tee off at seven because by ten A.M. a thousand Nipponese are banging balls in every direction. They drive me crazy, and they're taking over the West."

"How about Silicon Valley?" I asked Mortimer, trying to take his mind off the Oriental challenge.

He snorted. "Silicon Valley is symptomatic of what's wrong in America. First of all, Santa Clara Valley pumps one thousand ninety tons of noxious fumes into the air every day. Second, those kids running these so-called hot companies think it's all fun and games.

"I went to a fancy dinner party recently in San Jose, given by a man who has loaned millions to the high-tech geniuses. It was the most amazing party I've ever been to. Everyone there arrived in his or her Bentley, Rolls, Jaguar, Excalibur. They were each worth anywhere from five to seventy-five million on paper, and they couldn't spend it fast enough or in more conspicuous ways. At cocktails the men were bouncing off the walls, men so excited that they were talking in tenor voices, squeaking. What are they talking about? Bytes and logic and mega and user and shelter and compound and everything except *anything* human. At dinner there were twelve tables set up. I swear to God all the men moved en masse to the tables, no place cards, and sat down en masse with each other. The babble kept up in high tenor with all of them taking notes: what accountants, what venture capitalists, what money managers, what automobiles, what interest rates. The wives *sat by themselves.* They had been paid off; all of them given stock and each was worth a million plus in her own right. I heard one of the women say, 'I wouldn't look at a dress selling for under six hundred dollars.'

"This is Silicon Valley. And you talk about your cosmopolitan San Francisco. This is a town so nervous about what the East is doing, they can never enjoy themselves. San Francisco is a town where if an Italian moves in and puts 'Count' in front of his name, they'll give him a party once a week for a year and push their daughters at him to catch one of his diseases. They think driving around in Lamborghini at three in the morning with the top down is tantamount to *dolce vita.* I'm worried about our republic."

Mortimer had lost eleven golf balls by the time we reached the eighth green. The fog had burned off; there was no wind, and the greens grabbed the iron shots as if catching them in a glove. It mattered not to Mortimer; he was into decline and fall. "Holy shit," he said on the thirteenth as a ball whistled over our heads. We looked back and saw two foursomes, eight Japanese whipping golf balls in enough directions to guarantee Bing Crosby a good spin in his grave. Mortimer swore and screamed at them.

We played on, and it began to rain at the fourteenth. "You can't escape," Mortimer muttered. "It's destiny. And is it revenge to sell my house to them for a million six? It's revenge on their neighbors. They can babble to themselves 'Arigato' and get millions of yellow patriots to work for nine bucks an hour."

On the eighteenth the Japanese hit into us again and Mortimer snapped. "Get out," he said.

"We're not up to my drive yet," I said, having hit my biggest tee shot of the day, avoiding the ocean that dogged us on the left.

"Last night," he said, "I was in a bar in Carmel. The place was loaded with Japanese. The piano player asked for requests, and one of them asked for 'This Land Is Your Land, This Land Is My Land.' They all *stood* and sang it. Get out."

I got out of the golf cart. Mortimer roared in the other direction and I saw him stop in front of the eighteenth tee. He began to grab golf bags from the Japanese players' carts, run with them to the cliff edge, and throw the clubs into the sea. The two foursomes descended on Mortimer; I could barely see him in the distance through the mist and the rain. He had taken a club out of his bag and was flailing about, against great odds, probably against history.

My month of California research had convinced me that I should scurry home and probably start to raise cash in some of my portfolios. Sebastian would be thrilled to learn of my anxiety. He would buy more gold and check on the price of silver coins, which, I was sure, he hoarded underneath a pile of black ankle socks and old photos of Rudolph Hess.

7

How to
Make Love to
a Stockbroker

June 1983. Back in my office, with California comfortably be-hind me. Too much accumulates in a very personal business when you are away: too many calls to return, too much cor-respondence to answer. In all my years managing peoples' money I have never been away for more than seven business days in a row. Is this obsession? People want the doctor; they don't trust a strange voice. When you are selling service more than anything else, you'd better be available. Besides this, when you are not in your office, you are not making money.

And it was getting too easy to make money. The stock market was approaching an all-time high. One of the youngbloods in the board room caught me at the water fountain. "I see where Crossin is making you look like a rookie." Crossin was a broker, in the business for three years, who recently joined us from another firm. He had been putting big numbers on the board, creating commissions that so far this month had been exceeding mine. The troops in the board room loved to lean on the occupants of private offices. The shootout mentality bristles in the investment business, and it is easy to keep score. It's not how the clients profit; it's what the brokers produce. Up-Your-Gross Smith published our figures daily, and at any signs of faltering, the youngbloods would buzz around, digging, pushing in, waiting for the kill. "I know," I said. "Crossin's been doing great. I've channeled some business to him because I closed my books for the year on June first." When you push for sales in a business like this, it is a mistake. And when *everyone* is making money, something is wrong.

Crossin was a cutie. He was in it for the money. You might say everyone's in it for the money, but you'd be mistaken. Most of the people in the securities business are in it for the anxiety, the uncertainty, the action, the flow of people in and out of their lives. As Adam Smith put it, "They are in it for the game." Crossin was in it to turn a buck in whatever aggressive manner he could. I knew him well, because he had been a client of mine. Crossin never figured up his profits and losses; he kept track of his commissions. "Where has this been all my life?" he said several years ago. "I gave you seventy-five hundred dollars in fees in the last twelve months."

"You were up thirty-nine percent on your portfolio," I answered. He ignored me. "If *you* can make it in this racket," he said, "I'm coming in. My father said that a stockbroker's first rule should be 'Never let the profit exceed the commission.' "

Crossin was an intimidator, the kind of person who would point out your weaknesses to you. "I see you're combing your hair forward to hide your bald spot," he would say to someone he had just met. Or "Your breath could be improved a lot." To women, he was likely to say "You ever thought of breast implants?" Or "Why don't you try getting out in the sun a little more, do some exercises, firm up that chin?" Most of us are cowards; we resist confrontation. People were always very eager to say yes to Crossin, figuring it was the easiest way to get rid of him. He was a great salesman because he exploited weakness. People wanted Crossin out of the room quickly, fearing he would turn on them.

We all have known someone like Crossin. If he were bumped in a car lightly from behind at a traffic light, he would jump out of his vehicle, swearing and threatening murder. Most of us would wave on the offending vehicle, smile, and call, "No damage, no problem." Not Crossin. The first month he was registered as a stockbroker, he called me. With him you had to attack first. "I don't have time to give you my ideas of what to buy, Crossin. Call your own research department." He laughed. "I'm just calling," he said, "to tell you a story about why I'm going to be producing more than you in a year." I figured I'd listen or he'd come over and tell me in person.

"I'm driving home alone after dinner in town," he told me. "Up Route Eight ninety-six [a major commuting road] when some bastard in a BMW cuts me off and really nicks my driver's door. I mean big nicks. Naturally I blow my horn and he digs out. I lean on it and chase the son-of-a-bitch. He goes up to ninety and I'm right on his tail in my Firebird. He exits and I'm still on his bumper and he panics and spins into a fence at a dead end. I jump out of the Firebird with a three-foot rubber flashlight in my fist; I'm going to kill him.

"I get over to the BMW, and the driver is looking wild at me, panic in his face. I peer into his car and he's wearing no pants. He's naked from the waist down. But not only is he naked, his pecker is hooked to an attachment plugged into the cigarette lighter. No wonder the bastard ran me off the road. He starts crying and saying he'll pay for any damage or inconvenience. I tell him, 'Let's have your license and registration,' which is difficult for him to produce, hooked up to the cigarette lighter. I take his info, and by God he's the executive vice president of a microchip manufacturer, a hot company.

" 'I'm married with kids,' the guy says, sobbing. 'Just give me a break. I'll pay you. No one has to know about Auto Suck.'

"I gave him my card," Crossin said, "told him to call me in

a few days. By then I'd have an estimate on the scrapes to the Firebird. A married high-tech wizard hooked up to Auto Suck, do you believe it? This is what is meant by a service economy. Machines can take care of everything, even a blow job."

"Two weeks in the investment business, Crossin," I told him, "and you're a philosopher."

He went on, "Three days go by and I get no phone call. I take his card and open a new account for him with my firm. I had his Social Security number from his license. I mail him the new account forms and wait another three days. He is dealing with the wrong fucker if he thinks Crossin is not on his case.

"The beginning of the next week, I get him on the phone and tell him, 'Congratulations; you have a securities account with Crossin. I want feedback on the high-tech companies: who's hot, who's cold. I also want clients from your company. You scratch my back, I scratch yours. No one will know about your experiments into space-age sexuality. And my auto repairs will coat a hundred and seventy-five dollars. This is not inflated. I'll send you an itemized list from the body shop. I want our relationship to be based on honesty and mutual trust." He's given me six new accounts so far and some great information."

"It's blackmail," I said.

"Come *on*," he said. "I'd never rat on the guy. We're getting to be friends. I even told him I might try Auto Suck myself."

"What goes around comes around, Crossin."

"You believe that," he said, "you believe in Santa's elves. It's the numbers you put on the board that count. I'm just calling to tell you that I know how to do business and I'm coming after you."

Now Crossin was working in my office, out on the selling room floor, with his desk nearest the main door so that he could comment on anyone passing by or grab the walk-in accounts before anyone else. I was against hiring Crossin after I learned of his coming to us for an interview.

"You don't want him, we don't hire him," promised Up-

Your-Gross Smith. But the chain of command means a lot on Wall Street, and they try to run their shops as major corporations, not as the merchandise marts of yesteryear. Crossin had evidently intimidated someone way up the ladder in New York, and the next thing I knew I came in one Monday morning, wearing a pink bow tie and gray suit, and was greeted by Crossin, who said, "Anyone ever tell you that pink is not your color?"

"I'm sorry," Smith, the manager, told me. "He was shoved down my throat."

"Forget it," I said. "In seven months he won't be here." But as Crossin's production increased, so did his credibility in the board room. The bigger your figures, the more likely people are to say "Maybe he really knows something." Crossin was a great salesman. He understood the one area that was every investor's, indeed every stockbroker's hot button: inside information.

"Crossin is buying Steady Chemical," one of the young brokers told me. "It's selling for eight and a half and Du Pont is going to make an offer at seventeen next Wednesday. We're all buying it. You better take a look."

"How the hell does Crossin know it's being taken over?" I said.

He looked at me, admiration for Crossin shining out of his greedy little eyes. "The best contact of all," he said. "He's screwing the daughter of the chairman of the board."

George Orwell said, "All pigs are equal, but some pigs are more equal than others." What is the easiest way to make a sale in the stock market? Promise inside information, the privileged knowledge that none but a few favored people possess. If you say the magic words to a customer — "Buy Steady Chemical at eight and a half; there's going to be a deal next week at seventeen" — he can't resist. The entire board room began buying Steady Chemical. It rose on fairly large volume to 9⅝, at which point Teddy Loveman, the tape-watcher, stormed into my office. "So," he said, "is it only *your* customers who are the last to know?" I instantly knew what he was complaining about. Rumors travel in a board room faster than they do in the White House.

"Do you want to make money, Teddy," I said to him, "or do you want to fuck around?"

The old shoe dog looked at me. "To tell you the truth," he said, "I already made my money. I want to fuck around."

Everyone loves inside information except the Securities and Exchange Commission. The regulatory bodies exist presumably to protect the public from abuse. What is more abusive in a democracy than someone profiting from special knowledge that you and I don't have? Naturally we should make him give back the profits, pay a penalty, and promise never to do it again. But of course you cannot legislate human nature, and everyone's struggle in life is to somehow get on the inside. Even in the Politburo.

Crossin's efforts at productive pillow talk typify the lengths to which some people will go to make dreams of the sure thing come true. Three recent cases show the temptation to profit in this area. In one situation, recorded on tape by a discount brokerage firm, an employee of a printing company bought shares in corporate takeover victims before the takeovers were publicly announced. He would read the offers as they were being printed, then buy the target stocks. In another situation a typist at a New York law firm specializing in takeovers used his inside knowledge to buy stocks before deals were proclaimed. This scheme worked for five years and took in more than $2.5 million. A Morgan Stanley vice president fled the country for two and a half years after being indicted for profiting on trades in companies where mergers and acquisitions were pending. Another man in the same case pleaded guilty and cooperated with federal investigators. The two had been classmates at Harvard Business School.

I bought five thousand Steady Chemical for Teddy Loveman

at prices ranging between 9⅝ and 9¾. I had been bidding 9⅝ for all of his stock when a five-thousand-share block crossed the tape at 9½. At the time, Teddy was sitting in his usual seat at the front of the board room. One of the youngbloods jumped to his feet and yelled, "It's taking off." That was enough for Teddy, who was now whipped into a frenzy and had to have the stock at *any* price. It closed at 9⅛ and I buttonholed Crossin as he was leaving the office. "You want to get yourself booted out of the business?" I asked him.

"You giving me some friendly advice because I'm outproducing your ass?" he said. A real sweetheart.

"Look," I told him, "you go around telling everyone what a hero you are in bed and what you've supposedly learned, and every stock jockey jumps on the thing; the whole office buys the story. If it comes true, which I doubt, you'll have compliance [the department in New York that supervises potential problem areas] all over us, but especially all over *you*."

"Hey," he said, "I deny any of that stuff. I'm buying the stock on fundamentals. It looks cheap." Then he bragged to me about his new method of picking stocks. He told me that he compiled a list of all the publicly traded companies in our metropolitan area. Then he researched at a business library all the founding families of these public companies. He called all the companies individually, asked for the official in charge of corporate information, for liaison with the financial press, and inquired directly about daughters of the chief executive officer or president, specifically about divorced daughters.

"Divorced daughters," Crossin explained, "are much more likely to spill the beans about mergers or takeovers. They're vulnerable; they've been bruised. It's easy to get them on subjects other than themselves, because they've spent so much recent history on that very subject. It's a relief for them to talk the business, to get outside of personalities. And, after a roll in the hay . . . well, I've had two deals before this one, at my other firm. Now I trust this method a hell of a lot better than a research report from some joker on Wall Street who can't find his ass with both hands."

By the following Wednesday, the day of the supposed Du Pont takeover of Steady Chemical at 17, the stock was selling at 8. No merger was announced that day. In my experience of almost twenty-five years in the investment business, ninety-nine out of a hundred stories offering so-called inside information are false.

*   *   *

Merger and acquisition fever really began in the modern era after 1970, when Wall Street collapsed. At that time hundreds of investment firms folded or were incorporated into surviving huge corporations offering womb-to-tomb financial services. Share prices across the list collapsed also, to the point where, with ever-rising inflation, it was much cheaper for a corporation to buy out another company than to build one from scratch. The takeover game became bigger; large premiums were paid for the assets of the targeted victims. Rumors of takeover interest caused investors and speculators to rush into the stocks of potential merger candidates. If you are tempted (and aren't we all) to buy a story about a deal stock, a takeover, here are some practical guidelines to remember.

If you are told a definite time that a deal will take place, for example, next Wednesday, and nothing happens, sell the stock.

If you start hearing the same story in a variety of places, from more than one person, sell the stock. A well-shopped rumor almost never comes true.

There seems always to be some truth to a merger or takeover story. Perhaps there were discussions among several companies or among takeover specialists involved in the rumored stock. But discussions, even negotiations, are not a final deal. Most discussions or fishing expeditions lead to no deal at all. Above all, when you buy a stock on a supposed inside story, the story of price may be correct, but I have learned that no one ever

179

seems to get the timing right. Howard Johnson's, the ice cream–restaurant–hotel chain, was rumored to be a takeover candidate for years. Every three months for a long period of time I would get calls to buy Howard Johnson's at 12 or 13 or 14 for a takeover "in two weeks at twenty-two." In every case, months went by, the clients bailed out with losses, and no deal came about. One day out of the blue, with the stock selling at 12 and a fraction, a British company announced a tender offer for Howard Johnson's in cash in the mid-twenties. Patience pays off in the merger game, but not one client in a thousand ever stays around for the payoff.

If you must buy a takeover story, buy only those which seem to make economic sense, which are selling nearer to historic low prices rather than at inflated, fancy price earnings multiples. If you buy a tip on this basis, with the target stock selling near its lows, and if no takeover takes place, the disappointed speculators dumping the stock will probably keep your risk to a minimum. The worst mistake you can make is to buy a rumored takeover stock on heavy volume on a run-up in price. Then, when you get caught in a no-deal situation, your loss can be serious.

Remember above all else when buying so-called inside information: buying anything is easy; it is the selling of the stock that is the most important transaction of all. If you buy a takeover story at 10 for a $20 deal, say to yourself, "If I can make twenty-five percent or better quickly, on rumors, I'll grab it." In almost all cases there is a speculative run-up on the same rumors you have heard. The suckers bid the price up to 12 or 13, then it collapses back to 10 when no deal develops. I'm thrilled to put my order to sell in at 12½. If I get it, terrific. I'll take 25 percent on a trade any day.

I must say that stockbrokers are supposed to report all mention of inside information to their firm and/or the authorities. However, this book deals with reality, and we all struggle from our first breath to be as unequal as we possibly can. I have never heard of anyone reporting inside-information leaks to the au-

*thorities unless he had a personal ax to grind. The best advice
I can give you in regard to takeover plays is to keep your losses
short and small. The person who gives you the inside word
never wants to admit a mistake; you have to be disciplined and
on your own, as in dieting.*

* * *

On the day the Du Pont offer to Steady Chemical failed to
take place, Steady Chemical drifted to 6⅞ on a low volume of
2700 shares. Crossin had accumulated over 150,000 shares,
ranging in price from 8¼ to 9½. A lot of that stock had been
bought for people Crossin cold-called, from mailing lists of professionals and street records from wealthy suburban towns. "I
specialize in companies that could be candidates for merger
and acquisition." This was Crossin's pitch. Most people in the
money business give life to stocks they buy. They think of them
as friends if they go up, enemies if they go down. But they
always take them personally. Your stocks become members of
your family, good children and bad children: "That fabulous
IBM; that goddamned Baldwin-United."

"The deal has been put off another week," Crossin promised.
"Keep buying."

At the front of our board room, Harry the Cloud was ecstatic. Harry was the pessimist, forever beset by personal mysterious ailments, predicting the collapse of Western civilization
with every headline, with every twinge of neuralgia. Harry had
sold short Steady Chemical at 9 and covered his short at 7⅛,
almost a 35 percent profit. He competed with Teddy Loveman
on every trade. "It's not just Teddy who's a schmuck," he said,
chortling. "All you guys who chase stories are schmucks. Every
time I get a board room rumor of a deal, I immediately sell it
short. If I use strict limits for covering the short, like twenty
percent down I cover it, I'm a winner every time. Of course,
what good does it do me when it takes me an hour every morning to get my heart started?"

The happiest people in life are those with a plan. Even

Harry the Cloud's hypochondria was part of his plan; it kept him going. So was shorting on rumors part of his plan; it was his system, something he could rationalize and justify.

The next week it was discovered that Crossin was selling Steady Chemical. When you buy a stock, you want plenty of company; you want the world to know, you want to feel the warmth of everyone's support and approval. When you are dumping, you travel in a chilly world of isolation. One of our teletype operators told one of the brokers about Crossin. The broker told his buddies, and five of them marched to Crossin's desk. He quickly opened one of his desk drawers, threw a bunch of executed order tickets into it, and slammed the drawer shut.

"You sucked us into Steady Chemical," one of the brokers said. "Now you're bailing out without telling us."

"Look," he said, "I don't have time to play wet nurse when I've got a business to run. I get an order from someone, there's no time for chitchat."

"Plenty of time to chat when you're buying, though."

Crossin gave the defense of the schoolyard. "It's a free country," he said.

A board room is a small society, as is any business — a community of people working together, a tiny village. When there is disharmony, the community begins to rot. The bitterness began to swell up around Crossin. Teddy Loveman dumped his five thousand Steady Chemical "at the market," the prevailing best price at the time. He got 5⅞, the low of the day. "This is what you do to me," he said. "I buy at the high; I sell at the low. If you'd been my partner at the shoe factories, I'd be picking the lint out of my belly button on welfare."

"Teddy," I said. "You're the one who told me yourself you wanted to fuck around."

"Yeah," he grumbled. "But not at the lows of the day."

I stayed in the office late that night. So did Crossin, and we rode down in the elevator together. "So I tossed and lost," he said. "You know what the bitch told me when the stock started to break down?"

"No," I said.

"She told me that she'd made up the story to keep me dating her. She told me that every guy she's been out with since her divorce she tells that her father's company is being taken over by Du Pont."

"It's a sad story all around."

"Yeah," he said. "The office is pissed. I even bought the stock myself. It'll come back someday, so I'm going to hold. I guess I'd better just keep going down the list of corporate chicks with wealthy daddies."

* * *

Thursday, June 15. The Dow Jones Industrial Average closed at its highest, 1237.27, and greed was seeping out of all the cracks like leaking plaster. Silicon Valley in California and Boston's technology highway, Route 128, were pumping new companies public as fast as politician's promises. The appetite for these shares seemed endless.

A week ago, a California small-computer manufacturer, Eagle, was all set to market shares to the greedy public at 13. The night before the deal, the president of Eagle, coming home from a party celebrating his soon-to-be millionaire status, drove off the road in his new Maserati and was killed. A passenger in the car was killed, too. He was a yacht salesman. The stock offering was postponed, but it came a week later at a lower price, 12. Instantly the stock jumped to 17, investors shrugging off any implications of the president's death in the rush to make some fast money. A year later, Eagle sold at 1⅞.

Nothing is sacred in the world of investments. Indeed, almost everything is profane. No significant news event takes place without jokes about it instantly racing over the phone systems of the nation's brokerage firms. Sacrilege, racism, sex, and what's "sick" are the themes of these jokes. They materialize

183

within minutes of an event or a rumor. The attempted assassination of the pope, the deaths of Princess Grace and Natalie Wood, the candidacy of Jesse Jackson, the epidemics of herpes and AIDS, the scandal of Representative Gerry Studds, all gave rise to jokes. There is only *one* thing to take seriously. How are your stocks doing? What are the prices? Black humor proliferates because everyone in the business always operates on the thin edge of disaster. News means nothing to the history of the world; it has relevance only to the value of portfolios, the movement of bonds and commodities.

During the next several days in the office, Crossin was closeted for hours with Up-Your-Gross Smith and several men in dark three-piece suits, carrying briefcases. Since there are no secrets in a board room, everyone knew that some client had felt cheated in Steady Chemical and wanted his money back.

A week later, Crossin was gone. A plastic surgeon he had cold-called and promised a fast takeover blew the whistle to the SEC and our firm, telling the story of Crossin's use of supposed inside information. When the client appeared with counsel, Crossin did his cause no good by threatening the doctor with physical abuse. The whole office could hear him say, "You rearrange faces? I'll rearrange your face so you'll need two jowl tucks, an eye bag special, and a nose job." Crossin got it off his chest, but he was dismissed from the securities industry. His last paycheck included the deductions for the doctor's stock losses. Rule 405: Know your customer.

Less than 2 percent of the thousands of people I have dealt with over the years ever used the one tool of analysis that is more effective than any other: common sense. Clients use emotion, fear, greed, tips from barbers, stories in locker rooms. Virtually no one thinks about where he is investing money.

Here is an example of common-sense investing based on a prediction of mine, buying shares of companies that have a lot of cash. A simple aid that I use, and to which you can have access by calling any investment firm and requesting one, is the

184

monthly stock guide issued by Standard and Poor. This small booklet contains thumbnail sketches of nearly every public company, its price and earnings history, along with rudimentary financial information. Once a year I scan the booklets for companies that have cash, little or no long-term debt, and current assets over current liabilities of better than 2½ to 1. Ask your broker once to show you how to read this information. After that you'll never forget it, and it will provide you with a simple formula for determining strengths of a company. Naturally this can be simplistic. But I have never lost money in a company with heavy cash, low debt, and a strong balance sheet, and whose stock was selling near a low point in its historic trading range.

In 1977 I bought for my clients shares in Commerce Clearing House at between $11 and $13. Commerce Clearing House issues business and tax reports and updates the law changes, which are filed in looseleaf notebooks. The service is sold on a subscription basis, and I have never been in a law firm or accountant's office that did not have a library of Commerce Clearing's materials. In 1983, it had a cash position in excess of $65 million. Current assets totaled around $177 million; liabilities were under $60 million. Long-term debts totaled slightly over $2.5 million.

That was nothing compared with its cash. First the numbers jumped out at me. *Then* the common sense. The stock was near the bottom of its historic price range. I called a dozen lawyers and asked them whether they still used Commerce Clearing's products. A dozen said they couldn't operate without them. I asked myself one question: Would the tax code and tax legislation get *simpler* as the years went by? I answered what I thought was obvious. Our government and its tax code would get ever more complex, ever more bureaucratic.

I jumped all over Commerce Clearing House between 11 and 13 in 1977. When I buy a stock I immediately set a target for it that seems reasonable, that seems to conform to common sense. Remember, buying is easy in the stock market. When to sell is the difficult part, the side of the equation that gives the most problems. When I buy a stock at 10, I say, after assessing the company and its prospects, "I think I can make forty percent on this stock over the next year." If the stock moves to 14 within that time, I'm out; I sell it. We never run out of inventory. There's always something else to buy. I believed I could more than double my money in Commerce Clearing within two years. By 1979 the stock sold in the high 20s. Four years later it was much higher than that, but I stayed with my discipline.

Seldom do I buy a stock and say, "This is not for sale until someone takes it away from me." Such a stock I own today that I first recommended in December 1979 in *New York* magazine. That stock is Affiliated Publications, the parent company controlling the Boston *Globe*. There is always a danger going public with stock recommendations. As I keep telling you, it is easy to keep score in the market. I quote from the *New York* article to give you an idea of what I emphasize for investors pursuing profits: value.

> Spooner, who under the pseudonym of Brutus wrote *Confessions of a Stockbroker* and is an executive of Shearson Loeb Rhoades, also has a great reputation as a stock picker. So I asked him for his current favorites.
>
> Spooner emphasized that he likes to go for what he considers unusual undervalued situations, and he came up with the following four picks:
>
> Affiliated Publications (recent price, $26 [since tripled]), which owns the Boston *Globe* and some other communications properties. Spooner thinks the *Globe* enjoys "virtually a monopoly" in Boston, and feels that the family which controls the company eventually "will not be able to resist lots of dollars if they are thrown at them for a takeover." But he cautions that this stock is a hold over a period of time. 'It's not going to be a quick play.'
>
> Gillette ($26 [sold at 47]) is beginning to look sharp again, in Spooner's view. In the early 1970s, the old-name

razor company was selling in the sixties. Now Gillette, after some competitive battling, has regained market share, but its stock price has not responded. Spooner sees very little downside risk and the potential for a large reward.

International Banknote ($2.50 [sold at 6½–7]), a low-priced stock that he thinks will benefit from the worldwide outbreak of inflation because its business is printing currency, stamps, and traveler's checks for a number of foreign governments. "They print money," says Spooner, and predicts that someday the stock will go over $6 "and the institutions will take a fresh look and wonder where this stock has been all this time."

Tampax ($28 [sold at 55–60]) is another familiar and financially solid company that has fallen from loftier price levels. It sold for $136 a share in 1972, but was battered when Procter & Gamble and others entered the tampon market. At current prices it is yielding 9 percent, and its earnings this year will be higher than when it was selling for $136. Meanwhile, it has $60 million in cash, no debt, and women are switching back to Tampax products. How does Spooner know? "I have over 2000 clients, and everyone who is a woman and still has a menstrual cycle I ask," he says. "They're not offended by it as long as they can make money." So Spooner thinks that at current prices Tampax is "cheap as hell."

What pervades our lives more than anything else in America? Communications of all kinds. Is this going to diminish in the next decades? A snowstorm predicted in the East is trumpeted at least forty-eight hours in advance over television and in the newspapers. We are whipped into an emotional frenzy before the eventual inch and a half falls. But if you watch, listen, and read the media, you would think we were preparing for atomic devastation. Again, common sense tells me to own a large metropolitan newspaper, particularly one that really serves a much greater area, all of New England, and has a virtual monopoly on ad linage in the city. I still own Affiliated Publications, which has split twice since my recommendation. I believe someone with a lot of money will buy Affiliated at a fancy price, well in excess of where it sells now. In this case my target *is* takeover. So use the common-sense method yourself when considering an investment. Does it make sense? And does it represent true value, not just an overpriced whim?

*   *   *

June 14. We had more to be concerned with than Crossin's departure. Texas Instruments' earnings were a disappointment to the brilliant institutional investors who followed the stock and saw the blue-chip high-tech favorite plummet. In one day it was off as much as 43 points. (Most retail stockbrokers do not deal in Texas Instruments, IBM, or Digital Equipment, because most customers want the names no one has heard. They all want "the next IBM; the next Xerox." But an institutional favorite with bad earnings suddenly makes everyone nervous about the secondary high-technology companies.) Small computer manufacturers were instantly seen as vulnerable, and the selling became rampant. Commodore was down 6¼, Apple 4¼, Tandy 6, and Coleco over 5 points.

When institutions — the pension funds, mutual funds, trust departments, and insurance companies that dominate trading in the stock market — shake their tails, they force violent swings in both directions in the popular companies. You don't want to be in the way when they decide to sell a stock.

An example of institutional thinking is the practice of "window dressing." Basically, window dressing is getting a portfolio in shape before the end of each quarter when the mutual funds have to report their holdings to the stockholders. God forbid it should be seen that an institution owns Texas Instruments after the public saw the headlines about Texas Instruments' disastrous plunge. It doesn't matter whether the fund took a huge bath in Texas Instruments or sold it on the bottom of that 40-point slide. All that matters is that it not show in the portfolio as one of the stocks owned at the end of the quarter. It's very easy to play with other people's money and to be as emotional with billions as the man in the street is with a thousand dollars in his jeans.

* * *

As you've seen, there are many approaches to stock market analysis, many ways of picking winners. Some of them are unusual. But from what I've seen, whatever works for you in life, embrace it.

I hate meetings. This is a symptom of the silent generation, the people who grew up to be too young for World War II and Korea but just too old for Vietnam. The silent generation understands that a meeting is a forum at which everyone present feels he has to contribute. Therefore, all meetings are too long, universally boring, uninformative, and take away the participant's time for being selfish elsewhere. Several times a year senior management calls me and says, "We know how much you want to sneak off and be selfish. But So-and-So is one of the outstanding securities analysts we have and he's speaking to your office next Wednesday. In pursuit of high office morale, we want you to attend." When they put it that way, I go to meetings.

M. J. Vining, who analyzed consumer trends, spoke at one such meeting several years ago. I had read her reports, or, rather, I had scanned them. What does she like? And what does it sell for? These are the points which interest me. All the rest is verbiage. An executive vice president introduced M. J. Vining. She stood up and never smiled. She acknowledged our presence with a nod and went right to work. "Ladies and gentlemen," she said, "it's time to buy Sears Roebuck. I am not tucked away in a cubicle with my charts; I am out in the streets and in the shopping malls, talking to the people. Sears has its act together for the first time in years and I am preparing a major institutional report recommending purchase. I feel that at seventeen and a half there can be a fifty percent or better total return within the next fiscal year."

M. J. Vining wore a navy Oscar de la Renta suit, cut severely. A thin gold chain with a charm attached hung around her neck. Her hair was auburn and cut short.

"That's a real ball-buster," a broker sitting next to me said. "I try to get my clients to buy Sears, which has been a dog since 'seventy-one, and they'll bust their necks transferring their accounts to Merrill Lynch."

M. J. Vining went on with her consumer specialties and mentioned one that made a lot of sense to me.

"I would be a buyer of Tampax," she said. "Under twenty-nine, as a particularly undervalued specialty."

"It can only go one way," leered the broker next to me. M. J. Vining never betrayed emotion. Her voice was flat as she continued.

"What do you think of women analysts?" I asked the broker.

"Look, Spooner," he said, "you've been around the business long enough to know that if you had to kiss a frog who could give you winners, you'd kiss a frog all day."

He was right. M. J. Vining moved on from favorite to favorite, telling us about current earnings, new products, and future projections, adding several specialty companies she liked. Jhirmack Products, makers of natural cosmetics, and Universal Health, a hospital management company recently gone public. Everyone diligently took notes until it was time to break for cocktails.

The broker next to me excused himself quickly to be the first at the bar. "Don't give me speeches," he said. "Just give me the names of the stocks they like and buy me a drink. That's all any broker really wants."

The hors d'oeuvres served at investment products' meetings are always the same: shrimp, which disappear immediately, and chicken livers wrapped in bacon, which last a little longer. People in the investment business devour freebies. Because I don't like to buck the trend, one Scotch tended to lead to another. I found myself standing in a group next to M. J. Vining, who was holding forth on the value of on-the-job training. "Some analysts," she said, "pore over the annual reports, pore over the charts. I'm a brick-and-mortar person. I need to poke around a company, meet the people, lay on the hands. Numbers come after the awareness of the personnel. Are they happy? Do they care?"

"Aside from the psychology," I said, "how's your track record?"

She looked at me curiously. "No one ever asks analysts that," she said. "They just write down what we're recommending."

"As a friend said to me, too many securities analysts came to Wall Street because they failed in the professions they analyze."

"Well, my batting average is a thousand, buster," she said. "You'll never know if I'm telling you the truth until you give me your money. There is no past in this business, only the future."

I nodded, loving that she said that, and turned away for another Scotch.

I left the reception while the brokers were complaining to each other about what a heartbreaking business it was. The hors d'oeuvres were long gone. I was in the elevator alone. While the doors were closing, a briefcase appeared suddenly between the rubber safety strips, popping the doors open. M. J. Vining slid aboard and punched the lobby button.

Without skipping a beat, she said, "I figured that we've got fifty-eight seconds to make love before we get to the first floor. Think we could do it?"

I'm fond of saying that since I was twenty-one nothing has surprised me. But what she said surprised me very much. It took me fifteen of the fifty-eight seconds before I blurted, "Yes, and maybe one and half times more if we rode it back up. We'd have the hang of it by then, right?"

Anyone who says that to you on the elevator deserves to have you buy her a drink. Before she caught a cab to the airport to fly home, I bought her two whiskey and sodas and learned M. J. Vining's secret of securities analysis.

"I ask the unusual question," she said, "for several reasons.

One, to get my foot in the door of corporations that try to avoid women and, two, to get the kind of response that always leads me to an inside story, to special knowledge."

"I buy that," I said. "But you could have said a lot of things that would make me pay attention. Why go to an extreme, I mean, fifty-eight seconds to make love? That's ridiculous."

"I don't know," she said. "I've done it."

That's when she told me that in her private life she participated in orgies, in the swinging life that met for organized group sex several times a month.

"I'm divorced," M. J. Vining said. "The women who swing tell me that this is the usual pattern. A husband, a boyfriend, urges them to swap partners, to include another woman or another man for *his* benefit. My husband," she went on, "kept pushing me to make love to his best friend, because supposedly the best friend had a lot of problems. Makes me sound stupid, doesn't it? But there are stupider things in marriage and more absurd reasons for doing those things.

"It turned out," she said, "that my husband liked to watch, liked to participate in threesomes, and, as it further turned out, was more in love with his best friend than with me. If you're living with one person, your sexual patterns continually repeat themselves. He likes to get on top, she comes if you touch her rear end, blah, blah, blah. You get in a groove and stay there in most long-term relationships. But when introduced to variety, you discover all kinds of positions and new zones of pleasure you never knew existed. What started out as a favor to my husband turned into something that hooked me."

"And you got divorced?"

"Sure we got divorced. A relationship cannot survive swinging. Anyone is naïve who thinks it can, because you're always going to find a short-term pleasure that obsesses you. And obsessions are what blow marriages out of the water. So we split. But I kept doing the group routine; you meet people, you get interested. I began going with a television producer, a bachelor who took literally the male motto of people who run orgies: 'Come not.' " That's the motto obviously because once the man comes at an orgy, you may as well watch cartoons until he feels restored.

"For lots of the men," M.J. said, "that one shot is all he's going to get. But I discovered an amazing thing. I got terrific ideas for investments from swinging."

We were at the point in our drinking where we were taking each other seriously. "Give me a few ideas you've gotten from orgies."

"One of the finest house parties I went to," she said, "was run by a chemist for one of the big drug companies. He had a body shaped like a test tube, almost straight up and down and hairless. It was like he had found the right profession to match his looks. Now, there's nothing written down that you have to bed with everyone at one of these things. But people get uptight if you don't, and they say you won't be asked back. But basically, you screw if you're in the mood. If you don't, you stand around and talk or watch or tell people you're just not in the mood."

M. J. Vining took a long drink of whiskey, a two-fisted swallow. "This chemist is all over me like a tent," she said. "He wants me; I'm the best thing that's ever arrived at his parties; he'll put Bach on the stereo because he knows I understand. This is an orgy, for Christ's sake, not a date. But because he can't have it, obviously he wants it. Anyway, he comes back to me all evening. I'm kind of wandering from room to room, watching the action, and he follows me wherever I go. Finally he says, 'If I tell you how to double your money in the next year, can we make it?' Jesus, American men are getting so pathetic. I'm a good negotiator and I say, 'Maybe. Let's hear your information.' The chemist tells me that the government, the FDA, is going to ban saccharin because it causes cancer in rats.

" '*That's* what you're going to trade for screwing me?' I ask him.

" 'No,' the chemist says. 'You buy shares in G. D. Searle. Searle is going to get FDA approval on aspertame, a product of theirs that's a sugar substitute. When the saccharin flap hits the fan, anything new that's a sugar substitute will go through the roof.'

" 'Every drug analyst on Wall Street,' I say to him, 'thinks G. D. Searle is going broke.'

" 'Every drug analyst on Wall Street,' says the chemist, 'is an asshole.'

" 'That's not good enough to get you into my pants,' I say. 'If I *were* wearing pants.' "

Virtually every drug analyst on Wall Street did dump on G. D. Searle when it was selling at 11½ to 12. M. J. Vining bought the stock at 11⅞ and sold it, she told me, a year and a half later at 28. She still hated the chemist, but the night she met him, when he offered her the tip, she ended up taking him into her mouth at approximately 12:47 in the morning. At the same time she was mounted from behind by a computer salesman from Burlington, Massachusetts. They were her seventh and eighth encounters of the night and she accepted the chemist only because, in the glow of the red bulb that illuminated the room, she could not honestly tell who he was.

"When I come to New York," I told M.J., "I'd like to hear more about this."

"Call me," she said. "I'll bring my boyfriend."

Anyone who doubles her money in a year and a half I will pursue. I called M. J. Vining before a business trip to New York and suggested that she, her friend, and I have dinner. "By the way," she said, "last winter I bought Garfinckel, Brooks Brothers, Miller and Rhoades on the Big Board at twenty-two. There was just an offer by Allied Stores at forty-eight." (It was acquired subsequently at 53.)

"Don't tell me," I said, "you got the idea at an orgy."

"Really," she said. "Half the men were wearing Brooks Brothers clothes. I mean plumbers, computer technicians, lawyers, construction workers, unexpected people. There are always piles of clothing on different beds, and I check the labels. Week after week Brooks Brothers shows up. On impulse," M.J. said, "I buy the stock. Nine months later, *bang*, up fourteen points in a day. And you know the kicker? Garfinckel, Brooks Brothers says '$48 is an insult, it grossly undervalues our assets.' Hey, you could buy it for *months* in the low twenties. How many times can you get laid and get rich at the same time?"

"Not many," I admitted. "By the way," I added, "aren't you ever afraid that this phone might be tapped?"

"Are you kidding?" She laughed. "Who'd tap the phone of a stockbroker?"

On a subsequent business trip to New York City, I made arrangements to meet M. J. Vining and her television-producer friend. I was staying again at the Park Lane Hotel on Central Park South. The hotel makes you nervous if you're not rich: plastic cards open the doors to the rooms; the service and appointments are impeccable; the clientele all look as if they had glided through life on the backs of the peasants. Sometimes it seems, at the Park Lane Hotel, that each of the guests speaks Spanish, French, or Japanese as his first language. The women are all freshly coiffed and always just going to or coming from Bergdorf Goodman. I was in the elevator on the way to meet M. J. Vining and her friend at the bar. A woman riding with me noticed the enamel heart pin I wear in my lapel.

"I'll buy that from you," she said with a Spanish accent. "How much will you take?"

"Sorry, it's not for sale," I told her. "It's one of a kind."

"There is no such thing as one of a kind," she said.

"Where are you from?"

"We are from Colombia," she answered. "But, with troubles everywhere, there is only one place in the world to be. That one place to be is the United States." The door opened at the second floor, where the bar was located.

"Where are you going now?" I asked.

"To Fifth Avenue," she said. "Of course, *there* I can find a pin like yours. One can find everything there."

The United States is now the refuge for all important money in the world seeking stability. This will spill violently into the United States stock market in the 1980s, and if you are aboard, there will be a long ride and major profits. It is always better to be early than late.

M. J. Vining and her friend were drinking Poland Spring water when I arrived. He was Solly Spiegel, producer of a mid-day talk show, twice divorced, and the possessor of a shock of tight blond curls usually described as a Jewish Afro.

"Do you believe we found each other? There's no accounting for taste," M.J. said.

"M.J. is a voyeur," Spiegel said. "Or whatever a female voyeur is called. She'd rather watch than do it."

"It's because of who you have to do it *with*," she explained. "Men in the nineteen eighties don't know whether they're fish or fowl. Mostly foul, I might add."

"It's refreshing not to talk about politics or religion," I said, trying to steer them away from the bickering M.J. claimed characterizes the advanced relationship.

Spiegel said, "I can agree about one thing. American men are fucked up and American women are miserably unhappy. The problem is that we don't seem to be able to do anything about it."

"Sure you do," I said. "You go to orgies. You couldn't do that twenty years ago unless you were in Rome with Anita Ekberg and Dolce Vita."

"We do it," Spiegel said, "but I'm always secretly worried that it's the beginning of the end of the Western world and I'm going to be punished for it."

"Guilt." I nodded.

"Guilt," he agreed. "But it's like masturbation when you're young. You can't tear yourself away."

"Well, you're dressed for an orgy tonight. What happens?" I asked.

M. J. Vining had switched to Cutty Sark and a splash of water. She drank one after another. "The party tonight," she said, "is at a Holiday Inn in Rye. There'll be something like thirty couples. Fifteen to twenty dollars a person pays for drinks, music, cold cuts, and your share of the rooms, which are reserved in advance. It's like any other social group — the Kiwanis, the Rotary, a booster club. We pay at the door and go into the large function room, where there is a bar and a three-piece combo. We have name tags and we mingle."

"There are usually one or two key couples at these things, the organizers," said Spiegel. "Now, I have to tell you that this is super tack and I'd never go for it in a million years if it was for business. But what you get at these things for fifteen or twenty bucks, you tell me where a bigger bargain exists in the world. Sometimes there's a little too much fat on the cold cuts, but what the hell."

"You're not the typical male," I said, "involved in this situation."

"Most of the men are married. The organizers are *always* married, and they're always called Bob and Carol, Ted and Alice, for nicknames. It's the swingers' inside joke."

"So I'm at the bar with my name tag," I said. "Who makes the first move?"

"Usually," M.J. said, "it's one of the organizers. They cut other couples out of the herd and invite them to the private sessions later. One of the Bobs or Teds at my first gathering came up to me, clinked glasses, and said, 'I'd like to taste you later.' That was it; no beating around the bush, as it were. I'll tell you, that may not work on everybody, but it got me all hot to go to the rooms."

"After about an hour and a half or so," Spiegel added, "after the drinking and dancing and lining up of compatible couples, the big function winds down. Between five and six couples move to suites rented for the night. We change light bulbs in the rooms, all red to make things dim but not completely dark."

"The point is to see and be aware," said M. J. Vining. "I've never been left out of the final group . . ."

She was proud of that and she insisted that she never went to an orgy where she didn't get a great investment idea. They told me that no one at these sessions had ever worried about disease, because, as M.J. said, "They're virtually all married couples sleeping around. It's single people who spread disease, not married couples. I never think about problems like that."

They told me that homosexual activities at orgies happen only on the West Coast, not the East Coast. But lesbian relationships are encouraged throughout America on the swinging circuit.

"Traditional macho values from Boston to Atlanta," explained Spiegel.

After we drank for almost two hours, it was time for the couple to drive to Rye. "Before you go," I said, "I want M.J. to tell me, if you had to describe in one word how you feel about your participation in these events, what would that word be?"

M. J. Vining rolled her tongue around the rim of her glass, coaxing out the last drops of Cutty Sark. "Sad," she said; "it makes me sad."

"If it makes you sad," I answered, "why keep doing it?"

"Because" — she smiled — "it is impossible for a successful businesswoman to find a good man or good men who don't feel threatened. Orgies are as impersonal as coffee in an all-night cafeteria. And I have my research."

"She has her research," Spiegel said, getting up and leaving me to sign the tab. "Any chance you'd like to come along?"

"We'd be a woman short," M.J. said. "How about if I go with Spooner?"

Spiegel shrugged. "Hey, we're all big people," he said. "There's always another orgy."

198

I thanked them but stayed at the Park Lane. I was asleep when the phone rang. Out of the black hole of my dreams I checked my watch: 3:30 A.M. It was Solly Spiegel.

"Look, I'm sorry," he said, sounding all excited. "But M.J. got a tip tonight. One of the biggest cable TV companies in America just went public for the first time. She thinks they're going through the roof, and I want you to buy some for me first thing in the morning."

"Who gave it to her?" I asked.

"One of the politicians from upstate New York passing out the cable franchises. I want to buy a thousand shares; what information do you need?"

"Name, address, and Social Security number," I mumbled, reaching for a hotel pencil. M.J. came on briefly.

"It's going to be real good," she said. "Somewhere down the road it's going to be a winner."

* * *

Monday, June 26. I had lunch with one of the smartest portfolio managers I know. He was responsible for running a private pool of capital, currently over half a billion dollars. I told him that I couldn't find any bargains in the market and that it worried me. "When all my brothers and sisters who manage institutional money see their June figures," he said, "they can go to cash and still have an outstanding year. Why shouldn't they do that?" I returned to my office that afternoon and started to sell every stock in my portfolios that sold for more than ten times earnings. If I couldn't find any bargains to *buy*, then weren't conditions overheated? Too greedy?

That night we had an office party at Raffles, a Cantonese restaurant. It was a hangout for the players of the Street. The party was for a record first half-year of business. Since the previous August, corporations had raised a total of $27.4 billion in the equity markets, including a record of nearly $6 billion in March alone. Almost $5 billion was raised in initial public offerings, new issues, since the beginning of 1982, another record. The stock market had been given a $775 billion boost since the bullish rumbles began a year ago.

"We can eat shrimp until the bars close," exulted Paul the Bachelor, who equated endless free shrimp with the bull market mentality. Raffles was a dump that served four-ounce drinks and gave the brokerage business what it loved: happy hours, dim lights, waitresses with black stockings and low-cut tops, video games, lots of pay phones, and Poo Poo Platters. We had its one private area, the Garden of Delights Room, red and black from the lanterns on the ceiling to the lacquered chairs and tables to the outdoor-indoor carpeting on the floor. The gin and tonics were moving like a hot issue. The waitresses were hustling in and out with hors d'oeuvres as if it were everyone's last meal. Sardonic Sandra sipped a Campari and soda, above it all. "I really hate it when you're holier than thou," I told my assistant.

"At least I'm honest," she said. "You pretend you're *not* holier than thou. That's your secret."

Brokers and traders and money managers congregated at Raffles for lunch, drinks, dinners, and late-night rendezvous. Investment people love Chinese food because it soaks up the booze and you can shovel it in in great quantities. It's fine food for blowing off nervous energy; lots of small pieces and something to do with your hands.

Up-Your-Gross Smith was in his element. His share of office profitability for the first half would probably bring him in excess of $150,000, not bad for pushing the troops on to greater sales' triumphs. He was working the room, shaking hands and slapping backs. "A nice job, have a spring roll," he would say. "A fine effort, troops, another round of pork strips." Behind his back the troops were bitching that the party should have been held at a major hotel or a private club on the forty-second floor looking over the city. Peter the Bargain King said to me, "He'll charge the party off on the office profit and loss statement, save at least twenty-five hundred bucks by having it here, get a kickback from the owner for the booze, and probably take spareribs home in a doggy bag. We take the heat and he's too cheap to go to a first-class place. Hey, I eat here every day; this is no big deal."

But everyone was feeling loose. The average stockbroker in the room could annualize his income at better than $75,000, more than the typical president of many a midsized company. A trio came in to play, tenor sax, drums, and trumpet. The floaters, Lisa and Jill, danced with everyone. Mad Mark the Institutional Salesman drank bourbon and kept cutting in on them. Big Jimmy Minot, the trustee, kept badgering the band to play a waltz while he practiced leading them, using a fried shrimp as a baton, the shrimp dripping with duck sauce.

One of our salesmen, whom everyone called Ichabod Crane, was holding forth about the market going to 2000 in the next year. Ichabod was the house expert on everything from arms control to political thought in Rome under Justinian. He also used to be the office censor, running to Up-Your-Gross Smith to report liaisons between brokers and secretaries. "You make vows," he said, "at communion, at confirmation, at bar mitzvahs, and at weddings. We must live our lives as pure as we can. Not as pure as Galahad, but we must try. I cannot work in an atmosphere where there is fornication and impure thought. Speak to the offenders," he would say. "By the way, the Fed will tighten the spigot on the money supply in the next ten days, and there will be extraordinary cold in the Sun Belt next winter. Time to buy orange juice and heating oil futures. Don't say I didn't tell you." Ichabod Crane was six feet four and as skinny as an accusing finger. He ate cucumber sandwiches with the crusts cut off and drank orange pekoe tea at his desk every day, because he wanted to make sure nothing escaped his critical eye. He watched and he censored. Every transgression was reported to the manager.

One day not so long ago, Tony Arena, our margin clerk, was driving home from work on a detour through the red-light district of town. He spotted Ichabod sneaking into a peep-show arcade, the kind with twenty-five-cent porno loops. When confronted with this fact the next day, Ichabod rose up and said, "You have to understand the devil in order to combat him." But he never again blew the whistle on fellow workers. And occasionally he would even go out to lunch and, in the summers, order a salad and a Pimm's Cup Number Two.

At the party, returning from a trip to the men's room, I saw one of our older brokers at a wall pay phone. He was famous in the office for having a few drinks in the evening and calling various secretaries and female bond traders at their homes. He was married. "Come on, Wendy," he pleaded. "A filet and some red wine. Sauce Béarnaise. Asparagus and hollandaise. Just a little conversation. A ride in the BMW, a couple of vodka stingers." He hung up. He put another dime in the slot. "Diane," he started, "how about a late dinner, a little veal Marsala, some champagne? I really need to talk to you about some bond problems . . ."

The party was getting hard core: the serious drinkers, the pairing-off, the time of promises. Smith, the manager, was dancing on a table with one of the new secretaries. The drummer got up and began to put the cover over his drum. Up-Your-Gross had rolled up his sleeves, revealing a *Semper Fi* tattoo on his right forearm. He pulled his wallet from his rear pocket, still dancing, and yelled over the trumpet and saxophone, "Play on, blast it, until I tell you to stop. My wallet tells you to play on. This is a goddamned bull market." The drummer whipped off the cover and settled back into the beat.

Everyone was dancing now, and new arrivals crashed the party from the bar. They were all welcome; they were in the fraternity, and the money was coming at all of us from everywhere. Paul the Bachelor sidled up to me. He had splotches of hot mustard on his tie. "This is from Dunhill's in New York," he said. "Cost me sixty-five dollars. It isn't easy." When I left the party, the older broker was still on the pay phone. It was the time of night when he would promise anything.

The next day, June 27, there was renewed fear in all the

202

press about the return to inflation and the growth of interest rates. The market was off 20 points, the biggest drop in over two months. There was also a bottle of Courvoisier in a gift box on my desk with a note: "Baby, your couch was great. Enjoy." The note was not signed. I thought how money and sex always draw a crowd and how seldom the reaction to either is one of pure joy.

8

Freud Said, "What Do Women Want??"

"I'll tell you what women want," said Seymour the Shrink. It was July, and we were seated outdoors at an Italian restaurant, eating pasta and drinking wine. It was a perfect time for philosophy, a lush evening that could have been in Rome — traffic sounds, the air smelling of strong food and summer.

The stock market had been boring all month unless you were in high technology, emerging growth, or new issues. The prices in those areas collapsed, making you think that if, for instance, you owned a computer stock, the Dow Jones was more like 600 than 1200. Fear of rising interest rates brought the Dow under 1200 for the first time since early June, although my energy stocks were firm and El Paso had stabilized between 16 and 17. I had added to my position steadily since the spring. In for a penny, in for a pound. It still looked cheap to me. Jokes about homosexuals and AIDS had replaced ethnic stories as the days got warmer. Too much communication panics us all. A client of mine in New York walked out of an art gallery opening when his wife insisted that the gay crowd in attendance made them too vulnerable to disease.

"What do women want?" I asked Seymour, who is a no-nonsense psychiatrist, a rare breed. Seymour was a professor at one of America's leading medical schools. He never subscribed to fads in treatment. He always knew what he wanted to buy in the stock market. And he understood human nature, a trait remarkable in his profession. He was a man of clean lines who did not hedge his bets.

"When all the crap is stripped away," he said, "and all the posturing and catch phrases are eliminated, women want someone across the table from them, or across the couch or the bed, someone who reaches out a hand and says, 'I'm here. I understand, I sympathize, I care about you.' Above all, they want someone there who lets them know that they are not alone. In short, they want someone to take care of them."

I have over seven hundred female clients of all ages and conditions in life, and I agree with Seymour. Of the seven hundred female clients, over 80 percent are unmarried, widowed, or divorced. One of their major problems in all cases is certainly financial. But beyond this their main problem is dealing with isolation and loneliness.

Betty Friedan, author of *The Feminine Mystique*, and generally regarded as one of the founders of the women's movement, recently spent some months in our city. One of my friends dated her several times. He told me the stories of those evenings the way high school buddies told stories to each other of evenings at drive-ins in the back seats of Daddy's car. The next week, my wife and I were at a party. Betty Friedan was one of the guests. Coincidentally, I was seated next to her at dinner. Wanting to break the ice, I mentioned to Ms. Friedan that my friend Mr. X had enjoyed his evenings with her. She blushed and said, "Did he *really*; what did he say?"

We have the same conversations millions of times, repeating

patterns of adolescence. I said, "What he particularly liked was the way you rubbed your thumb over the back of his hand."

She couldn't believe what I had said. Not knowing me, she stared, looking for signs of sarcasm; seeing none, she blushed even deeper than before. Then she flowed on about my friend, about the city, about her life, as if we were on a date as college students, with no lies, no scars, no ghosts from the past. "All the struggles are empty struggles," she said, "unless someone is there to hear about them. We all want a sounding board; we all want someone to hold, even if it's only symbolic."

Dinner continued and conversation changed to other subjects. As we were getting up to adjourn to the living room, Betty Friedan turned to me. "One more thing," she said. "Were you serious about me rubbing my thumb along Mr. X's hand?" She looked at me intently.

"Of course," I answered her. "You don't lie about something like that." She blushed again happily and moved on to brandy.

It is the sad fact of American life in the 1980s that millions of men and women are reaching out their hands and that no one is there to take them, much less have someone rub his or her thumb across. But as Americans are becoming more isolated, they are also paying more attention to their money. Women particularly are paying closer attention. A recent (1983) study by the New York Stock Exchange shows that a record 42.4 million Americans now own common stock or equity-oriented mutual funds. This figure is up over ten million from just two years previous, and almost 75 percent of these newcomers never owned stock in the past. Over 18 percent of the population is now in the stock market, compared with under 12 percent less than ten years ago. Fifty-seven percent of all these new owners of securities are female. The average new buyer of stock is a woman of thirty-four with securities worth slightly more than $2000.

I told this figure to Norma the Duchess, who sat watching the tape in the front of our board room in a summer dress made of silk. She snorted. "They all walk away from the market in seven months with a check for six hundred dollars, licking their wounds and using it as one more evidence of how they're screwed by the system."

"What have you done, Norma, to avoid that?" I asked. Norma reminded me of Ethel Merman. She rolled over you; she was Gypsy's mother and Annie Oakley and the hostess with the mostess on the ball.

"Most of us have not been brought up to have original minds," she said. "We have to depend on others to make a lot of decisions for us: doctors, lawyers, plumbers. When it comes to money, there are very few people of either sex who have any brains at all. So if we have to depend on others in the money arena, we have to set up some ground rules for ourselves.

"I'm a woman alone, a widow. Most widows in our society never had to make a single decision for many years other than what bag was going to go with what shoes. These women, all my friends, are terrified and alone. Even sadder is that a lot of them have daughters, divorced, depending on them all over again. There is bitterness and resentment."

The Duchess has a portion of money with which she will fool around. This figure was somewhere near $50,000, and she knew she was expected to trade if she was to keep her seat in the board room. Fooling around in the market was like paying the rent on her chair. She paid her dues that way and understood how the game was played: no free rides. "You can go to the mall, honey," she once told me, "or kill yourself slowly watching TV. I like the numbers going by, and the cigar smoke that reminds me of my two husbands. And another important thing that can keep older people going; *younger* people to whom they can teach a lesson." Norma the Duchess was not my client. She had done business for years with a broker named Abe, an old-timer who chain-smoked Camels and whose feet barely touched the floor.

Norma's first rule for widows is: always do business wherever possible with someone from your past. Don't be shy. No one can deny old-time relationships. At best he will want to take care of you. At worst, he will think twice before trying to screw you financially. Everyone clings to the past and will respond to your needs.

Abe had money of his own. He came into the office after a long investment career to keep himself alive. He believed that the moment he retired, he would die. Abe was famous for going to annual meetings of various corporations and saying: "I can put money into IBM or I can buy shares in your company. Why should I buy *your* company?" He made corporate presidents work hard for his money. But the presidents who gave good answers usually made profits for Abe.

"Abe loved me lifetimes ago," the Duchess said. "He was in business deals with my first husband, and a woman can tell when a man is gaga over her. He has made me a lot of money, mostly because I come into the office and rub his head. I keep promising and I never deliver. That's the secret. A woman should almost never deliver. Let Abe deliver. That's Norma's secret for rule number two: Rubbing a head is a very cheap incentive. And I make no more noise than a barracuda."

It is a treat to have Norma in our office. There are people you meet, if you are lucky, who teach you how to live a life that is full. But there's a fine line between getting people to pay attention to you and being a pain in the butt. Norma always offers something in return. She offers her wit, her observations.

The same afternoon in the summer a widow who *is* my client, and who plays it badly, walked in unannounced. "This is my last chance," she announced, "and I feel neglected. I parked illegally because I won't pay these prices to the parking lots and I know you can get my ticket fixed if I get one. Then, I brought in my daughter Jelene's account statement for some advice. She's with Merrill Lynch, but I knew you'd be happy to take a look. But what I really want is for you to pay more attention; I know that I need much more income."

Immediately I wanted to transfer *her* account to Merrill

Lynch. Anyone resents a relationship that is take, take, take. And no joy, either, in the taking. I spent almost an hour with the widow and set up an income program that would give her better than a 12 percent return on a combination of bonds, U.S. Treasuries, and utility stocks. As she was leaving, she looked at me with a sour face and said, "I know you must do this for *other* people, and I would like something with a little glamour, something that can triple. I'm not too old for some fun, so keep me in mind." What she wanted actually was something that would pay a dividend of 10 percent and never go down even an eighth of a point and would double in six months. That's what I want too, along with world peace, the perfect martini, and a pennant for the Red Sox.

I advise another woman, the Black Widow, who has an unusual investment philosophy. She buys only stocks that she has assembled on her so-called death list. Her husband, Lewis, had died, leaving his estate in total disorder; no will, his company's books in a shambles. Lewis' widow felt cheated and confused.

Eventually she developed her strategy to seek out public companies where one man controlled a majority of the stock and was close to retirement age. She figured that such a man would be pushed by his family and lawyers to sell the company at a good price and get his affairs in order. She had hit three takeovers in the last five years with this formula, twice tripling and once up 60 percent for her research efforts. She had eight companies currently on her list, and I knew eventually she'd be right on all of them. But she made me uncomfortable. "I'm just going with the odds, the actuarial tables," Lewis' widow told me. "I'm not the only one who's going to be alone."

Recently she had been branching out. Last year she bought Pneumo Corporation, which makes landing gear for aircraft, among other things, and she began praying for war and the B-1 bomber. She bought some energy stocks from me also, six months ago, and hopes each day for turmoil in the Middle East. "Everybody else should feel my pain," the Black Widow would say. "And when they do, I'll be there to profit from it." She holds a strange fascination for me, like the urge to stick one's finger into light sockets.

Here are *my* rules for widows who want to be smart about their money.

1. First of all, choose a stockbroker, adviser, or money manager who has a large, successful business, rather than a young person relatively new to the trade. Ask to speak with or see the biggest producer of business specializing in the stock market, *not* in commodities or tax shelters. A big producer is less likely to trade your account for commissions. He can afford to allow you to stay with your positions and, because he undoubtedly cares for his widowed mother, is ready to be sympathetic and helpful. Don't scoff at sympathy, either. Anything that gets someone to pay attention to your money is worthwhile.

2. Establish on your own, or with your adviser, your approximate annual income requirements. Include in your figuring all outside income from Social Security, rents, pension funds, and so on. Pile everything you *spend* into your needs, and do not skimp. Include utilities, clothing, entertainment, travel, mortgage, and taxes. Take these expenses and divide by twelve to give a monthly need figure. Be realistic and even give a little margin for generosity to yourself.

When you arrive at your need figure, bring it and the figure of your total available funds to your adviser. Tell him to put together, *before he does anything else for you*, a portfolio that will produce your *needed income*. After you get your income locked, you can breathe a sigh of relief. It will make your life a lot simpler and reduce the anxiety of asking, "Do I have enough money coming in?"

A. An adjunct to this strategy is this advice, which will make your life even easier. Bonds and stocks pay at many different times of the year. It is possible that your income plan, with various securities as part of it, will pay you erratically; that is, you may get $1400 in January, $1800 in February, but only $325 in March. I suggest that you sign a *margin agreement,* allowing you to borrow from your account. Take the annual income figure your portfolio will pay you, divide it by twelve, and once a month have your financial consultant, or broker, send you a check for that exact figure, one twelfth of your annual need. Life will be much easier for you, because every month you will receive $800 or $700 or $1250 or whatever. Yes, you'll pay interest on what you borrow. But the dividends and interest coming into your account will quickly pay off the loan. And any small amount of interest left over, which you'll pay at year's end, is deductible. Most widows I know can use deductions. Very often their homes or apartments are completely without mortgages, and this system of regular payments is worth the small interest charge.

One last refinement of this plan: open an all-inclusive account, like Shearson Lehman/American Express's Financial Management Account. It gives you check-writing privileges and a large insurance policy (up to $10 million on every account). Why not write your own check once a month rather than wait for the mail? Much more efficient. The annual fee is relatively small, and, again, it's deductible.

3. Always try to separate yourself from the crowd. This should be true when you deal with anyone — lawyer, banker, garage mechanic. Stockbrokers are particularly subject to guilt. So play on it. Find out the day of your broker's birthday. Send him or her a card. At Christmas, bring a bottle of wine or a bunch of flowers, something inexpensive but memorable. I promise that you will get attention in a very positive way. We all feel neglected, and a simple expression of thoughtfulness will get you to the top of the list. Why? Because no one else will make it, and you will be remembered.

4. Once your income needs are satisfied first, then use your own intuition, common sense, in dealing with any excess funds. Don't let stocks be a mystery. You are as capable as anyone at picking companies that can make money for you. You must

overcome your fears of doing so and make sure that the ideas are your own, not the ideas of your neighbor's husband, who used to manufacture linings for ladies' shoes.

A widow client of mine two years ago was very impressed with the merchandising abilities of the Limited, a chain of discount clothing stores. She liked its merchandise, its employees, and its methods. She bought the stock at 15 and set a limit for herself. The limit was ambitious. "When I double my money I'm going to sell. Make sure you force me to stick to my guns." A year and a half later she sold her stock for 31.

Pay attention to services and products you enjoy or appreciate. In most cases they are associated with public companies whose prices may be cheap. You can be your own securities analyst, and by getting involved, you will find your money less threatening and more fun. With a broadening of your investment interest, your own life will also become more interesting. Subscribe to periodicals that deal with business. I particularly recommend *Forbes* because of its light touch and comprehensive coverage, and for the aggressive investor and those of you interested in seeing what is possible for the entrepreneur in America, *Inc.*, the magazine of small growing businesses.

* * *

Summer is my favorite season in the stock market. Many of my clients are away, their minds on subjects other than their money. I am free during the day to pursue research and productivity rather than field phone calls about liquidating money market funds, transferring cash to a son's checking account, and sending out duplicate statements to accountants who have misplaced the original set. I am much more effective for my clients during the summer because I am free to think.

July was a quiet month in our markets, with the Dow Jones average in a trading range and high-technology stocks starting a slow death movement down. The beginning of August saw cracks in the year-long bull market. Clients talked to me of the collapse of "Whoops," that is, the Washington Public Power System's default on payments of interest on its bonds; of Brazil's potential default on her debts. On August 8 the prime rate was raised to 11 percent, and the Dow Jones dropped over 20 points, to 1163.05.

*　*　*

The Myth: There are good times and bad times to buy and sell stocks. You hear, "Never buy a stock on a Friday; weekend news can ruin you." Or "Stocks never do anything on Rosh Hashanah or Yom Kippur; the traders are all in temple."

The Truth: There are no seasons in the stock market. The ticker, like justice, is blind. The market can be strong or weak on any day, any hour, any season. Never hold off your decision to act because of the time of the week or year. Act only because of your decision on price.

*　*　*

I can feel that we are in for some tough sledding. The biggest clue to this is the rush to go public by people who sense that making money is easy and there's a sucker born every minute. The latter is true; the former true only for a few weeks every couple of years.

Watch financial pages for names of companies going public that make you smile or make you say, "Wait a minute." I've seen companies in registration for public offerings named Stuff Yer Face, Inc., JoAnn's Chili Bordello, Fabulous Fakes of America, and Muhammed Ali Arcades. Jerry Lewis drive-in theater franchises were available in the end of the 1960s just before Wall Street fell apart. When absurdity is rampant, common sense says sell short or get out.

There are several lessons to be learned from greedy markets that seem *too* greedy. One lesson is not to be in a hurry to replace that great sale. It is August 19. I'm selling a position I took six months earlier in Inexco Oil, a Big Board energy stock. I

213

bought the stock, over 100,000 shares, at between 8 and 9. I am selling it today at between 13½ and 13¾, a gain of better than 40 percent. This is a decision based not so much on the price of the stock, which I think will be higher in time, but on the action of the market, which seems to me fraught with danger.

What is the definition of a greedy market? It is when I cannot find bargains and when there is the temptation to spend money for the sake of merely spending money, of being in the game. Why do people always lose money in a casino? Because they are incapable of leaving the tables while they're ahead. Whenever you make money in a stock, there will be enormous pressure to roll it over into something else — pressure from your broker, pressure from yourself to double up and do it again. ("If it's this easy why not buy twice as much next time?") Walk away from the game unless you are convinced that the next story, the next stock, is a bargain. Remember, we never run out of inventory. I'm going to put the Inexco proceeds into money market funds and wait for something I cannot ignore.

The second lesson to be learned from greedy markets is that when it comes to money, men are just as emotional as women. What I call Yesterday's Heroes illustrates this point.

Yesterday's Heroes are stocks that were favorites for a while and then plummeted because the fads went out of style, or the earnings were disappointing, or the dream faded. Names like National Student Marketing, Equity Funding, Four Seasons Nursing Homes, or even Polaroid illustrate the point. Trying to buy a bargain, to catch these fallen heroes on the way down, almost always leads to further losses. Most of Yesterday's Heroes stay permanently destroyed.

I have a client who is a cool man. He manufactures sportswear, running gear, sweat outfits, tennis warm-ups. He does business all over the world and negotiates tough deals in Taiwan, Korea, mainland China, and India. He has had a fixation on Wang Labs for several years, always wanting to own it, always just missing it as it ran away from him. "What is this, a woman, for Christ's sake?" he would rant at me. "Every time I want her, she's just out of reach. The dogs I catch, like Warner Communications, like Coleco, are like I caught my wife. Wang is the beautiful mistress I never can catch."

"Wait," I told him, "you'll catch her, I mean it. You'll catch Wang if you're patient." One day several months ago the stock was selling at 41, and he couldn't stand it any longer. "Buy it for me!" he screamed. "Just buy it."

"Do me a favor," I said. "Do *yourself* a favor. It's near the high. When — not if, but when — there's a dip back to the thirty range, we'll buy it then."

Smoke came out of the phone. "It'll never be thirty again!" he screamed, and I bought it for him at 41½. On August 23 Wang sold at 28¾. Yesterday's Hero.

The same day, MCI, the long-distance phone system company, broke down 4¾ points to 15, on disappointing news from the United States government about rate charges. The stock had sold at 30 only short months before and had been a star performer, with two splits in a year. I knew I would hear from Detached Olivia that evening. She never disappoints me, and she always plays Yesterday's Heroes the way they should be played, *quickly and for short bounces.*

Detached Olivia has a formula for dealing with this situation; and the formula almost inevitably makes her money. She lives in Chicago and lends money to one of the biggest banks in Illinois. "No one can teach us anything that sticks," she once told me. "We have to experience life to have the principles sink in. Unfortunately, we have to make the mistakes personally to have any lessons be effective: like marriage and childbirth and divorce and making bad loans.

"The key to success is to benefit by these mistakes and not make them again. When I was a teen-ager I bought my first stock, Brunswick, ten shares at sixty-two. This was part of a course in high school. But I got hooked and I actually bought the stock with my savings from baby-sitting. I loved to bowl at the time with friends. I saw bowling alleys on practically every corner and Brunswick was one of the premier manufacturers of bowling equipment. How can this not go up forever? I reasoned. I finally sold it at twenty-eight, and subsequently it dropped below fifteen. Of course, with bowling alleys on every corner, the business, the fad, had peaked. Saturation of the marketplace.

"I learned a lesson early: Yesterday's Heroes are tomorrow's bums. So I track each year's heroes. When they eventually break down, and they all do, I watch the big break first, then I hold off until a subsequent break, which always occurs when the first selling wave subsides. When the stock finally stabilizes around the same price for a week, I buy it. Almost always there is at least a fifteen percent bounce, and that's where I sell. For trading, this has been foolproof for the last ten years. For making a fortune, it's no good. But I'd rather be right a dozen times in a row than make a fortune; a string of small victories is much more important to me than the war. I compare my method to multiple orgasms, which I'll trade any day for a twenty-year relationship with diminishing returns and two bangs a year whether you have to or not."

Several other of my women clients are people I make sure to check with every month, because of their original ideas and because they're money-makers. J. D. Baker lives in Dallas and looks like your image of a Texas woman: six feet one in boots, lives to ride horses, dance the Texas two step, and listen to blue grass. She travels all over the world as a management consultant and specializes, she says, "in cutting through the bullshit."

At thirty-six, she is unmarried. "Most people you will ever meet," she told me, "are very uncomfortable being alone. They have nothing they love to do that is solitary, like painting or reading or fishing. Women must be prepared to have their act be a single today. No matter what their profession, they must have a hobby that they love to pursue and that they have to pursue alone, something that gives psychic and emotional pleasure."

J. D. Baker is a purist. When she researches a subject, she leaves no sloppy edges; she goes to the heart. Her hobby is investigating companies with an eye to buying the stock. She buys only one company at a time and she goes into it with size and on margin for the leverage. Two years ago she bought Cities Service at 26. "I can count on two domestic energy companies to be bought out in the next three to five years," she said. "One is Cities Service; the other is Phillips Petroleum. They can each be had; the values of their reserves way exceed the current value of the stock. Also, aggressive companies can buy assets [other companies] a hell of a lot cheaper than it will cost them to drill and explore for themselves."

Three months later she sold Cities Service at 46½, after Occidental had announced its bid for the entire company. She put the entire proceeds into Phillips at between 29 and 31¼. I followed suit. This is a business where you try to pick the best brains and tag along for the ride. In my investment philosophy it is important to get something while you wait, a dividend, because you never know when a stock will pay off. Taking in some money while you wait helps your patience. In this case, Phillips at 30 yielded approximately 7 percent.

"Now I figure," J. D. Baker said, "that I've got a few years before Phillips pays off. I can relax and research what's going to be next. Never leave a man or a job until you pin down the next one. It will save you a lot of heartache, because that down time, full of anxiety, is the worst time of life. I can go on the hunt, knowing that probably Phillips will take a while to come through. If I'm out of the country and you can ever get fifty-three or fifty-five for Phillips, sell me out; a twenty-five-point ride is plenty for any Texas girl." Phillips is now my largest dollar holding, and I'll be happy with $50 a share. Twenty points is plenty for any Eastern boy.

My most successful investor in high technology is a divorced woman of thirty-four who, as she said, succeeds "because I'm willing to go the extra hundred yards, willing to cross the line that most people never cross." Daring Dora is her name, and she goes the hundred yards because she has a plan. "Most women never have a plan," she said to me. "They have aimless desires: a good job, a man, a mink. Let's face it, most women don't have a clue as to how to go about getting what they want. I want to retire with money at a relatively early age and to travel and enjoy myself. And I can't count on a man to provide this. I have to count on moi."

Daring Dora's husband remarried a woman who kept close tabs on him. One Sunday afternoon, after a visit, he returned the two boys he had had with Dora to Dora's house. Before he left, he took them for a walk up the street. Dora rushed out and placed a pair of her underpants in her former husband's glove compartment, hoping they would be discovered by the new wife. "We all drive each other crazy sooner or later," she said. "Let's at least be inventive about it."

A priest drove her home from a party one night and talked with her about spiritual love. They both had been drinking stingers, and Dora invited him in for a cup of coffee. He was seated in her living room when she emerged from the kitchen with the coffee. Dora had taken off all of her clothes. "Stingers do you absolutely no good," she told the priest, "if you want to hide behind spiritual love."

Dora came out of her marriage with "no money, only the monthly dole. When I say no money, I mean no chunk of money. There was maybe ten thousand dollars, and I was determined it was not going into earrings or a Volvo station wagon. I met a wonderful man once at a dinner party. He was in town on a book tour and he told me how terrible he was in school in science and math, but how he forced himself as an adult to master those subjects. He told me you can learn anything if you concentrate — medicine, auto repair, anything. He taught me that aptitude was bullshit and concentration was everything."

Daring Dora concentrated on computer programming and understanding software, and she put her $10,000 eventually into Prime Computer. "That was the tricky part," she said. "I understand the language and I had no fear. But knowing a subject and putting your money on it are two very different things. I lived near Boston then and I could do research. What I did was, I haunted the parking lots of the high-tech companies along Route 128. I spent a week in each of ten parking lots of technology companies at the five o'clock closing time. I would pick three kinds of people, a woman, a male engineer, an executive. The engineer wore jeans, the executive wore ties; easy to distinguish. I told everyone that I had inherited a lot of money and that my family was very eccentric and I was trying hard to be smart about investing my money and should I put it into their company? Everyone took me very seriously, because they were all intrigued."

Daring Dora told me that the people most excited about their company were the people from Prime. One woman told her, "We're bouncing off the walls here because we know we're all going to get rich." The woman was a secretary, Dora said, and secretaries are always the biggest cynics, but this one was holding out a little of every paycheck to buy Prime stock.

"I put ten thousand dollars in and walked out with forty-five thousand. While I owned the stock I read everything I could get my hands on about technology. I also read the local Route 128 newspapers for articles about executive changes and for help-wanted ads in the industry. I saw the beginning of a leak in the dike: people leaving Prime. And I kept the name of the secretary and called her periodically. She would tell me what was happening, because no one can resist a nut; either they're amused or intimidated. She confirmed my suspicions that prosperity was spoiling the company."

Daring Dora spun the entire $45,000 into Cullinane Database, because it was a premier software company that designed something everyone needed and was easy to use. "Like the flush toilet," Dora said. It became the first software company admitted to the Big Board, and she sold when it announced a name change to Cullinet.

"You can do all the analytic work you want," she said. "But

when a company changes its name, a company that is doing well, you know it's listening to the wrong people and is starting to get fucked up."

The $45,000 was now $115,000. The next company she rolled into was Apollo Computer, the week after it went public in 1983. She bought stock at 29, went on margin for more at 39 ½, and sold it for 48 when markets got too frantic for her in July. Her stake was then $222,000, and she put it into a government daily interest fund that was state-tax free. "Apollo is the stock I want to buy back after the market is destroyed. In the meanwhile, I'll keep looking, just in case."

"What if you put the same energy into personal relationships, especially with men?" I asked her.

"I've given up on ever finding a man. All my friends and I have the same conversation with every date. 'What did *she* do to you?' And 'What did *he* do to me?' In other words, what are the scars from the previous people in our lives? The women I talk with depend more and more on networking among themselves. My life is less troubled, now that I'm alone. There's always anxiety in a relationship, all this tension. The minute we need someone, we lose control. And we're frightened of this dependence on men; we've all been so disappointed. The biggest fear of my friends is, I don't want to be alone; who's going to care for me when I'm old?

"That's why a woman must have her solitary passion, her hobby. One of my friends says, 'Do anything for a man. If he wants you to put the kneepads on in the elevator, go out and buy the kneepads.' I don't agree; don't do it unless it amuses you. My solitary passion can last all my life, and it's going to make me rich. The sad fact of liberation is that we can't count on anyone else making things all right for us. And the vast majority of women are totally unprepared for this fact."

A cross-section of my male clients agrees vehemently. "It was always war," said an attorney friend of mine, "but it's now totally out in the open. I am a gentleman, I like to think. I give up seats on the subway to women; I stand when a woman enters the room. But six months ago I was coming down the elevator in my building. The elevator was crowded with people and I was in the front. In the lobby I stood aside and let three women exit before me, holding the door open. One of them looked at me as if I were beneath contempt.

" 'Don't hold the door for us,' she said. 'Just give us equal pay.'

" 'Well, holy shit,' I said to myself, 'if that's the way it's going to be, then the gloves are off. No special treatment and let 'em eat cake as far as I'm concerned.' "

Another friend of mine, in St. Louis, works in financial public relations. He arranges for public companies to tell their corporate stories at luncheons and dinners to institutions that may want to buy stock in the storytellers. For months he had been trying to get a certain lady portfolio manager to come to his lunches. She was responsible for over $100 million in growth assets, and she swung considerable weight in St. Louis financial circles.

"I was throwing a luncheon for a heavyweight client," my friend told me, "and I was trying to show how many bodies I could bring in that could take heavy positions. The lady portfolio manager was listed as a 'maybe' on my guest list. Halfway through the shrimp cocktail she walked in. I was honestly so grateful to see her that I jumped up, ran over, squeezed her shoulders, and kissed her on the cheek. Can you believe that she turned on her heel, walked out, and later called my boss to get me fired for 'attitude'? If this is the state of male-female relationships in this country, it's pretty sad."

I told these stories to one of my experts on the subject, Mildred the Marriage Minder. Mildred is a lawyer, a psychologist, a wife. Successful at being all three, she specializes in personal problems of all sorts. She is also that rare attorney, a practical one. "What do you think, kid?" she asked me. "This is new? The Indians used to give their *prisoners* to the women. The reason so many women are miserable today is that they've forgotten their nature, which is to be mysterious.

"You see, all men are basically dumb and are terrified of women. This, by the way, is exactly why there are so many fags today. They can't handle the way women treat them. But women have forgotten how to play on their sense of mystery. Think about it. Just our rituals alone: our nails, our hair, our hygiene. Women have much more interesting lives than men. And we can have everything we want if we play on our strengths.

"When I went to college in the fifties, the structure was easy. It was expected that we would get pinned in junior year, get a diamond senior year, and all that time accumulate china and glassware. Then in the alumnae notes everyone would write in, 'We just bought this house in Connecticut.' Tell me that women are happier today than they were in those days. I was on a panel with Gloria Steinem some time ago, and she admitted to me that she had difficulty getting dates because men felt intimidated by her. They feel intimidated by all hard-driving women. Again, because they're frightened of them. So the successful career woman cooks a casserole for herself and smuggles *Playgirl* into her apartment. We've got to go back into combat in the smart way and use our mystery.

"Let me give you an idea of what I mean. I have a male partner who thought he was happily married. Everything on the surface looked wonderful. But a woman for whom he obtained a divorce set her cap for him." Mildred the Minder has a brassy voice that gets very personal and makes you smile. Her manner is aggressive; she always gives the impression that most people are idiots but that she includes you in her club of smart people. She makes you want to be in her club.

"This woman," she continued, "made fudge for my partner. He was a sucker for fudge. Simple things from their childhood make men pushovers. Anyway, he and his wife went on a trip to France last summer. His birthday was to take place during the trip and they were staying at an inn outside of Arles that had a four-star restaurant. When they arrived at the inn there was a big sign outside, saying, 'Welcome Willy Farnsworth.' That's my partner's name, and he was knocked out by this. His wife was amazed also, because she hadn't planned the greeting.

"Before dinner, menus were slipped under everyone's door, and printed on top of the day's fare was 'Trentième Anniversaire dîner pour Willy Farnsworth Esq.' My partner could not believe it. But especially he couldn't believe when the divorcée who made the fudge emerged at dessert, wearing a chef's hat and carrying a Grand Marnier soufflé, which he also loved and which she had made.

"Within three months of coming home, Willy had left his wife and moved in with the fudge-maker. No honest woman can compete with a dishonest woman, especially one who does her research. If women truly want to throw off the disaster of the last ten years' so-called liberation movement, they'll find out what a man wants and do it. Make him think he's number one. As for men, they should do the traditional things: flowers, hold out chairs, get up when women enter a room. Don't kid yourself; women love it. Long ago we won the battle of the sexes. The feminists almost gave it all back. But the nice thing about that battle, it's never too late."

For these liberated times, it appears that Mildred's philosophy is radical; in other times it is obvious. But the line that is drawn between friend and enemy is much clearer today. One of my clients went to work years ago for Mary Wells at Wells, Rich, Greene, one of the hottest creative advertising agencies in the country. "I was nervous there at first," my friend said. "But once I realized that Mary Wells was in it for the money, and not to get laid, I could relax and do my job."

We want the most from the professional people who serve us: the lawyers, doctors, and carpenters we all need. What *you* all need is the ability to make your case somehow different, to make sure you get the quality and service for which you are paying. Here are some rules for women to get the most from their stockbroker or investment adviser.

1. Above all else, do not set up an adversary relationship. A

woman came to see me a year ago and said, "I've been referred to you but come with reluctance. As far as I'm concerned, all men are pond scum." Preconceived notions doom a decent business (or personal) situation from the start.

2. Ask him whether he has had a good relationship with his mother. I find that men who have this positive relationship can deal more successfully with women; more successfully in a human sense. And asking this question will separate you from the other clients. Making yourself unique always helps when you deal in any professional or service area.

3. Go in with a goal in mind. Do you want growth of capital? Do you want an income-oriented plan? Do you need primarily tax assistance or retirement planning? The more specific you can be about your financial problems, the more specific can be his advice.

4. Ask your prospective broker a couple of key questions and be sure the answers make common sense to you. The first question is "What is your philosophy of the market?" Unless your expert has a firm fix on what he believes will work over a period of time, you'd be trusting your money to the wrong person. He must have a consistent philosophy that can establish a plan for you. "Buy low, sell high" is not a philosophy.

The next question to ask is "Are you afraid to admit a mistake?" There is a great deal of ego tied up in the management of money. We want to be right all the time, which is impossible. You want to do business with someone who is a realist, who knows that he needs a good dose of cynicism to be successful at the game. I repeat that buying is easy. It's *selling* a stock that is the hard part of the equation — selling a stock and not looking back. He who looks back at the market dies of remorse.

* * *

August finished on a fearful note. Four stocks went down for every three that went up on the Big Board, and the American

224

Exchange and over-the-counter issues, particularly in computer and medical technology, looked as if they had all split three for one.

But it doesn't matter what the market does as a whole; it's what *your* stocks do that counts. Burlington Northern agreed near the end of the month to acquire the rest of El Paso Natural Gas Company, partly in cash for $24 a share, partly in shares of a new preferred to be issued by Burlington. Rule of thumb on takeovers: Let the other guy have the last buck. If I buy a stock at an average or 17 and I can net 23 for it in the open market, that's 26 percent. Staying for 24, I run the risk of the deal falling through. I will always sell a stock happily (if I catch a takeover) within 10 percent of the takeover price. Remember, we never run out of inventory. There's always another bargain to buy.

El Paso finished the month as the number twelve percentage leader on the Big Board, opening in August at 18⅞, closing before Labor Day at 23¼. I sold over 100,000 shares and put half the money into Phillips Petroleum under 33, half into money markets. Mad Mark the Institutional Salesman was bitter. None of us in the business want anyone to be righter than we. He sang his familiar song. "Once in a while," he said to me, "the blind hog gets the acorn." Let him eat cake and wait for MCI to recover.

"Nice month," Up-Your-Gross Smith said to me before I went off for Labor Day. His smile said, "Okay, you can keep your couch and your bookshelves a little longer. But I could probably fit four brokers in your office if you start to slip. A bit tight, but we could fit them in."

The first piece of mail I read after the weekend was a change-of-address card from a friend in San Francisco. My friend was a woman who traded corporate bonds for an investment banking firm. She loved her job, was very good at it, and made $90,000 a year. In the past, she'd often sent me postcards. They always said the same thing. "I'm here; wish you were beautiful." I met the bond trader years ago on a company trip to Boca Raton, where she gave the brokers a lecture on corporate bond trading. We became friends, and there remained that tension between us which promised something beyond friendship. But she moved west and I pressed on. Her career was more important to her, I thought, than anything else. She came to town a year or so ago, visiting clients: banks and insurance companies. We had a drink. "I'm a lesbian," she told me, virtually with the first sip. "I'm living with a woman who loves me. She's a magazine editor."

"I'm surprised you're gay," I told her. I *was* surprised.

"Women, you'll *not* be surprised to hear," she said, "have some lousy choices today. I'm a hard-nosed businessperson. Millions of dollars in profit or losses ride on many of my decisions. I want companionship; I want to tell someone about my day. Every man I dated from Wall Street wanted to be taken care of himself, to tell me about *his* day; his successes, his aches. Hard-driving men have no time for women like me. Being gay is a compromise the way most honest people compromise their personal lives one way or another. I want to be a success and I want to be cared for. This is a method to have most of it."

I took her hand. "I know that we've always been close," I said.

She laughed quietly. "Isn't it pretty to think so?"

9

Married Money: The Joint Account

Late Fall. The residents of our board room didn't care that the leaves were turning. Clients were beginning to grumble about the value of their portfolios. The Dow Jones average was holding firm, but this represented only thirty industrial stocks. The rest of the stock market was heading south, almost on a daily basis. Paul the Bachelor was making his rounds, trying to get a consensus, as usual, on his personal life. "I'm thinking of getting married," he said. "I'm really curious about what a Paul *Junior* would look like, especially if I marry a blonde with long, silky hair."

I got up to shake his hand. "Is this imminent?" I asked.

"God, no. I'm just gathering impressions. Plus, besides the fact that I'm not dating a blonde right now, I could never get married in a falling market. I need to feel *up* all over for something like marriage. U.S. Steel has to be at least thirty-five for me to even consider it."

"Then why all the speculation?"

Paul looked serious. "Fall always makes me wonder whether I was meant to marry."

Hope is still triumphing over experience in America. In 1983, better than two and a half million Americans married, more than in any single year in our history. Concurrently, the divorce rate declined by 3 percent, the first time it has done so in over twenty years. I asked Seymour the Shrink how he felt about this trend.

"People are realizing that there have been terrible mistakes made in our personal relationships. I guarantee you that these figures are strongest in the South, Southwest, and Midwest, where they didn't lose their heads because *Cosmopolitan* magazine told the women to throw off their chains. Daniel Yankelovich did a survey recently that reported that American men judge manhood primarily by the ability to support a family.

"One thing we have to recognize is that money is to the twentieth century what sex was to the nineteenth. Sex in the nineteenth century was embarrassing. There was a difference between what you *did* feel about it and what you *should* have felt about it. Money serves this role in our society today. Sex is legitimated now; it's understandable. Sex is very much involved in what we should feel. It's okay. This is now bedrock. Today what we want is an advantage over our neighbor in a monetary sense. It's much meaner, this concept that it's all right to fuck your neighbor's wife but coveting his money is the true anxiety-provoking subject. This is the modern dilemma: sex we can accept as fun, but money is deadly serious. Our modern taboos all surround our ability to create or accumulate wealth."

"Can you be that unusual person," I said to him, "who can follow the advice he gives to others?"

"You mean, how do I stand in relation to modern anxiety about money?"

"I mean, how can you get rich when you charge by the hour

228

and you can see patients for only so many hours a day, one at a time?"

"I *do* covet my neighbor's riches," Seymour said, "and I do count them. That's why I'm going to use the only method open to people who earn ordinary income: I'm going to put it all on black."

How can you get rich in the stock market? Bet your pile on one company, buy it, and keep buying, in the hope that if you are right, you can be right in a big way. Seymour the Shrink reasoned that, like most people in the market, with a diversified portfolio of stocks and bonds, one year he'd make a little money; the next year, most likely, he'd give it back. Seymour knew that the only way to accumulate wealth would be the long-term capital gains route where the maximum tax on any gain is currently 20 percent. If he was taking a risk by putting his money on black, he should have understood that; after all, he was a psychiatrist.

"But I feel I have a unique opportunity in the next several years," Seymour said, "while the risk is relatively small and the reward potentially enormous. I am going to put all my available and excess cash in the foreseeable future into the new A T and T. I believe that the new Telephone, if I can buy it at seventeen or lower, will produce an extraordinary return *if I can wait it out.* I say wait because it will take time, perhaps years, for it to realize its potential as a high-technology stock.

"While I wait, it will pay me seven percent or so in dividends, a reasonable return as I accumulate more shares at, I hope, prices lower than today. Telephone's Bell Labs is the greatest research facility in the world. I can't believe I can own Bell Labs in the teens and collect a dividend on it, to boot. I can't put a price tag on this asset, Bell Labs, and my gut tells me that the institutions that today shun Telephone as having too many problems, too much competition, will be clammering for the stock in the thirties some time later."

Everyone I try this theory on who is relatively sophisticated

— trust officers, institutional salesmen, securities analysts —
scoffs at the reasoning. Everyone with an IRA investment to
make, $2000 to put into a retirement fund, thinks it's a great
idea. In this case I go with the small investor. I certainly go with
Seymour, who's sick of people saying to him, "If you're so
smart, how come you're not rich?" He is going to be rich.

Stockbrokers look at retirement accounts when business is
lousy, and the autumn had not produced any upturn, particularly in the over-the-counter market, which had turned so sour
in July. As examples, such formerly high-flying stocks as Altos
Computer, Eagle Computer, Fortune Systems, and Victor Technology showed declines from their highs that averaged over
70 percent. At the end of September the Dow Jones average
was at new high ground, around 1253, and IBM traded at a
peak of 124½. But the ordinary investor never owned IBM,
and his portfolio looked like a scene from *Apocalypse Now*. ("I
love the smell of Baldwin-United in the morning.") So the calls
went out from board rooms across the land to investors to
consider zero-coupon bonds or certificates of deposit or electric
utility stocks with high yields for IRAs and Keoghs, and the
larger portfolio-holders licked their wounds and worried about
possible higher interest rates, the deficit, collapse of third world
countries, and a return of inflation.

"I just borrowed the money for this year's IRA," said my
client Junior Dierks, a divorce lawyer. "Actually, I borrowed
only two thousand. I've *got* the $250 to put into my wife's IRA.
[A nonworking spouse's contribution to a retirement account is
an allowable $250.] You know that half the lawyers on Wall
Street end up borrowing money in April to pay their taxes?
It's because we're paid so erratically and nothing is ever with-
held and none of us puts anything aside. We can make three
hundred thousand a year, and if you tip us upside down you'll
never find more than five bucks and change."

Junior Dierks is probably the number one divorce lawyer in
our city. "I know the secrets," he says, "of probably fifty thou-

sand lives, if you consider all I'm told about in-laws, siblings, cousins, and aunts."

I asked him whether he'd noticed any changing of patterns in divorce during the last several years.

"Not yet, thank God. I say thank God for the business aspect of it. Because everything in history is cyclical. Sooner or later we'll return to the way things were when we were growing up, when you felt like a freak if your parents were divorced. My parents had a lousy marriage, as it turned out, but they stayed together because it was unthinkable to be split. There was a real stigma attached to it. For the last ten or fifteen years the pendulum has swung the other way. It's become too easy to divorce; the first disagreement, and everyone wants to take a walk. Most of my cases today hinge on trivia: Who would get the pink plastic vase in the bathroom? But in twenty-five years in the divorce business I have boiled down my experience into three principles for long and successful marriages.

"Number one: Respect the individuality of your spouse. Recognize and appreciate the qualities that attracted you in the first place. This often means stepping back to recall these qualities. But it's worth it. There is nothing so satisfying as having companionship, as you move on in age, with someone with whom you have solved many problems, been through many struggles.

"Number two: Take time alone with your spouse. Vacations are necessary, or an occasional weekend, even if it's in a hotel down the block. Every relationship needs renewal, and this can be accomplished only by periodically being alone together, away from your house, your children, your jobs.

"Number three: Sex. A long-term sexual relationship is difficult, but certainly not impossible. What it requires is patience and giving, by both partners. The woman must realize that a man requires more time to become aroused. Not just because he's older, but, quite frankly, because he's been with the same woman for so many years. The man must be patient also, with

231

his wife and with himself. Vacations will help. The key is staying with it, not becoming exasperated, guilty, or impatient. Sex will work for many years but requires careful tending, loving touches, and mutual affection."

I bought Junior Dierks $2000 worth of zero-coupon bonds. The $2000 investment would mature in 1991 at $5000, an effective yield of over 11½ percent. There has been a lot written about zeros in the last several years. But the concept bears repeating, particularly in regard to retirement plans and planning for children's education.

When the prime rate was between 16 and 20 percent and the cost to borrow from corporations was staggering, some smart treasurers and investment bankers invented the zero-coupon bond. Most bonds pay interest twice a year and mature (pay off the principal) at a certain date in the future. Most bonds are issued at par, $1000, paying their interest at a fixed rate until that maturity. Zero-coupon bonds pay no interest, but are issued at a discount so that you can plan for a certain need — retirement, a child's college education — with the certainty that the money you want will be there.

Here is a typical schedule of zero-coupon bonds, backed by U.S. treasury obligations. I list various maturities, varying amounts of money, and what the amounts become merely by the passage of time. These are perfect vehicles for people who find it difficult to save, who dislike the fluctuations of the stock market, and who need the reassurance of an established plan for established goals. Remember that bonds trade in thousand-dolllar denominations, but listings in newspapers omit a zero. A bond price quoted as 85 is actually $850; a price quoted as 28½ is actually $285.

Schedule:
Here are examples of U.S. government zero-coupon bonds, showing the discounted price and maturities. Prices are as of spring 1984.

MATURITY	PRICE	YIELD TO MATURITY
11/15/90	45 ⅞	12.21
11/15/92	35 ⅞	12.32
11/15/94*	28 ½	12.23

*In this last example, for instance,
$2850   becomes $10,000 in 1994,
$7125   becomes $25,000 in 1994,
$14,250 becomes $50,000 in 1994.

In marriage, we all have our formulae for getting along. A client of mine who broadcasts sports for NBC says, "The most successful marriages are the ones where one of the partners is a great actor or actress. One member of the couple is the key to its success. It's all compromise, of course, but it's that one actor who backs off, fakes it, swallows pride, gives a little more, who provides the glue and the secret. Look at any so-called happy marriage, and you'll always find one of the pair who deserves the Emmy for making it work."

I was reminded of this one day early in November, when I knew that the year had become totally schizophrenic, the way of most lives, nothing pure. The stockbrokers in our board room had fallen into a bunker mentality. Every customer who called had the same complaint. "The market is in the biggest bull rally in history and I'd be doing better with my dough in a savings bank at five percent."

I was at a luncheon being sponsored by a company on the American Stock Exchange in which I had a large position. It was a company heavily dependent on the capital goods industry, selling at around 10 with a lot of cash and little long-term debt. Its business was picking up dramatically with the upturn in the economy, and I was sure the stock was undervalued. Sometimes hearing a company tell its story is dangerous. You can fall in love with the story and the management and lose perspective on what is really happening. The ideal situation calls for not becoming emotionally involved with your stocks. Easy to say, tough to do. But whenever possible, I always urged my corporations to present their corporate tale at analysts' meetings and professional gatherings. I wanted others to buy the stocks I did, preferably at higher prices than I had paid.

Therefore I was annoyed to see a famous couple at this particular luncheon. It was Phoebe the Freebie and her husband, Mr. Lurch. They were both stockbrokers. Mr. Lurch had a curious gait; he seemed to scuttle along sideways and always looked as if he were sneaking into a room rather than entering it. Phoebe the Freebie led her husband around, moving from firm to firm, from stock to stock, from town to town. They did a lot of cold-calling and sold a lot of annuities, and they made presentations together, proving to potential investors (always husbands and wives) how to invest as couples, working together, making joint decisions.

It was a good marketing idea, and together they netted better than $100,000 a year. But they were famous in the investment community for being the cheapest couple in the city. "We are going to go for an entire year without having to buy one single lunch or dinner." Virtually every day of the year in the money business there are public companies presenting themselves to stockbrokers at luncheons, cocktails, or dinner meetings. Stockbrokers are invited as guests in the hope that ultimately they will buy shares in the companies. The gatherings can be for promoting new issues, bond offerings, for introducing products, or even for generating good will. Aside from such investment world activities, there are receptions nightly in almost every major American city for charities, for cultural events, for neighborhood causes.

Phoebe the Freebie and Mr. Lurch would typically go to luncheon at a hotel's private dining room for a municipal bond fund. They would have cocktails for fifteen minutes, a sit-down meal, hear the pitch for half an hour, and go back to the office. At five-thirty they would go to a cocktail reception for an over-the-counter company, pig out on hors d'oeuvres, listen to the story, and leave. Most of the time dinner was not necessary. But if they were still hungry, they could walk into a gathering of Polish Americans, nibble on homemade goodies, and include a few samples of different desserts. Usually, Phoebe the Freebie would scoop a dozen shrimp or a bunch of Swedish meatballs and eat them later at their apartment. On weekends there were loads of free events if one watched calendar sections of the local newspapers. No one ever questioned Phoebe's snitching food. They lived in a town where it would have been considered bad form. In addition, there was so much room in the canvas tote bag she always carried that most of the time no one ever noticed.

"This is how we beat the system," Mr. Lurch told me. "This is much more adventurous than most travel, although I'm sure we could work the same routines anywhere. Some of the speeches are boring, and sometimes the meals are not all they could be. But it proves that you can't starve in America; that if you have a clean suit and a black dress you can live by your wits. And you can make marriage a wonderful game if you do things together. With the money we saved on food and liquor alone last year, we bought a twenty-thousand-dollar annuity, guaranteed at eleven percent for the first three years. That's not chopped liver."

"Aren't you embarrassed to be known as freeloaders?"

"I'm proud that Phoebe and I are frugal and creative. The only thing that annoys me is the people who are jealous of our unique relationship. Once we even brought pecan muffins, dozens of them, to the office from a breakfast meeting on Cattle Tax Shelters. We passed out the muffins to the brokers, and one of them called the hotel where the meeting was held to blow the whistle."

"Well, you must have learned a moral from that story, Mr. Lurch," I said.

He began to slide away from me. "Yes, there's a moral," he said. "No good deed goes unpunished."

Most joint accounts are between husband and wife and read as follows: "Joint account with rights of survivorship." This means that on the death of one party, the survivor inherits the entire contents of the portfolio. Supposedly, both people control the account and jointly make decisions to buy and sell. Actually, in almost every case I know, the husband makes all the decisions and, to boot, often signs his wife's name whenever both signatures are needed. I suggest that every woman who reads this book and who owns a joint brokerage account with her husband check the monthly statement from the broker. Read your statement together to make sure both of you understand what is happening with your money. Take nothing for granted. Both of you should have something to say about the management of the funds, and both of you should be aware of all the range of financial products available to meet your goals: government issues, certificates of deposit, zero coupons, convertible bonds — the entire array of possible investments.

Above all, in any joint account, meet your broker or adviser in person. Make sure you both understand what he or she is talking about, including the risks. In any professional or service situation, be it with doctor or lawyer or financial adviser, it is a must to look across a desk or table and like what you hear and see. The explanations should be in language you both understand. The more jargon and catch phrases you hear (like "interface" or "synchronicity"), the less likely it is that you will be successful.

One of my clients called me recently about his joint account with his wife. "Quickly," he said, "remove Grace's name from our account. She caught me with matches from the Sheraton and they had a room number written inside the cover."

"So," I said, "you could have been out of town on business."

"The Sheraton is two blocks from our house."

Naturally, running a very psychiatric business, I hear many tales of infidelity, from both sides. There seem to be two definable ways in which partners deal with it. One camp says, "Never admit anything, no matter what the circumstance." The other camps says, "I can do it, she can do it, as long as we're discreet. We're adults, right? We can approach this subject as adults. I'm not saying this is an open marriage, but we kind of come and go as we please."

Let me tell you, no American is adult about infidelity. In every marriage I have witnessed — and remember that I have thirty-five hundred clients — the couple that "comes and goes as we please" eventually comes and goes to divorce court. I have customers who are experts on this subject, Jake and Jean, the King and Queen. They are the king and queen of pornography; they publish eleven magazines and manufacture video cassettes and audio cassettes that specialize in the titillation of America. Their products are sold on most newsstands and in every adult bookstore in the land. They privately love to invest in gold, silver, precious metals, and natural resources, because they believe the world is coming to an end.

"Look," Jake said to me, "this stuff is bred into me. If your ancestors came from Eastern Europe, they expected every day to be moved out of their village or to have the Cossacks set upon them. Every European always hoarded gold to bribe his way across borders or out of trouble."

"The bomb isn't going to take bribes," I reminded him.

"It isn't the bomb; it's what's happening to our society," Jake said. "Jean and I don't kid ourselves. With the crap that we produce, and with what's allowed under the First Amendment and the values that are rampant today, it's Greece and Rome all over again. Tell me you couldn't bribe the Visigoths in Greece and Rome with gold coins? Christ was sold out for, what, thirty pieces of silver? Our nation's spool is unraveling, and Jean and I are going to be prepared."

"I didn't know you were a student of history, Jake," I said.

"Well, you know we do these photo layouts, Caesar getting laid, Buffalo Bill in an orgy with Indian maidens, George Washington giving head at the Battle of Yorktown. You realize we have to research our scenes." Jake and Jean, the King and Queen, always seemed to be detached in their lives, because what they did for a living demanded detachment. They were not evil people; like most of us who are not doctors or lawyers, they backed into their professions. It was an accident.

"I was basically selling insurance," Jake told me, "and a

client couldn't pay the premiums. Nor could he pay me the rent on a storefront I rented him in Newark, New Jersey. He was publishing an early skin mag where you were lucky if you saw a tit. He scooted and left me an entire monthly run of his magazine. I sold the lot to a news dealer customer of mine and learned that I could make money if I sold only half the print order.

"Jean and I were married at the time and she had been an English major. So I said, 'What do you think? You think you can write a story that can get my pecker up?' Turns out she's a natural; been imagining those things for years. Now she can put them on paper, get the rocks off for thousands of poor bastards. You've got to understand that each business is like every other business; all with headaches. And when you strip all the crap away, you are left with one question. *Not* is what you do socially redeeming, but *does it make a profit?* So we started with a little magazine, and suddenly pornography comes into its own.

"The sixties made everything but murder permissible, and it even seemed for a while that murder was okay as long as it resulted in the death of your parents. Guccione at *Penthouse* went with pubic hair and Larry Flynt at *Hustler* went pink. But what really made Flynt was Jackie Kennedy. When he published the nude pictures of Jackie Kennedy, you knew that every month he had to be more and more outrageous, and since we all are voyeurs, Flynt could go wild, and the public loved it. It became chic to have *Hustler* passed around your office. That way, everyone could pretend to be disgusted. It was the logical extension of people saying they bought *Playboy* for the interview or for the story, for Christ's sake, by Bernard Malamud. Jean and I had better fiction in our mags because we gave people what they wanted — honest fantasy."

I had dinner not long ago with Jake and Jean. They wanted my advice about going public or staying a private corporation.

"The big question," I said to them, "is if you go public, with all the inherent new responsibilities, with all that new money and need to find uses for it, won't this spoil your personal relationship?"

"You don't violate what works for you in a marriage," Jake said. "What works for us is that we feel a need; we understand what the isolated American wants. Understanding that, we love each other and feel closer to each other than most other couples can ever feel."

Jake kissed Jean's neck. He nibbled her ear.

"The first thing you learn in this business," Jean said, "is that the biggest problem in the country is loneliness. For years I wrote the letters-to-the-editor column in all our magazines. Ninety-five percent of our readers are poor, harmless, lonely people who will take affection from a blow-up rubber doll because they have never had successful human contact. We did a poll. Forty percent of our readers are virgins. Remember one thing about life." Jean dropped her voice an octave. "All of us have a dark side that we mostly keep under wraps. If the President of the United States dresses up in women's clothing in the privacy of his bedroom, whom does it harm? But if the Washington *Post* had a creepy-peepy camera in there and published the pictures, which they would, the market would drop five hundred points and the Russians could walk in without firing a shot." She nuzzled Jake's cheek and ran a hand through what was left of his hair.

"I have hundreds of women clients," I said, "and all of them, I have to tell you, would probably be offended that I manage the money of pornographers. They see what you do as total exploitation of women, degrading and destructive."

Jake and Jean, the King and Queen, laughed at me. "The dream of the Carter administration," Jake said, "was to make everyone believe that not only did God create us equal; he *kept* us that way. This view of history has destroyed more civilizations than I have pubic hairs in my magazines. Our publications are loaded with women employees. They work with us because they have families to support."

Jean interrupted him. "A black girl, just out of college," she said, "interviewed us in the early seventies for an editorial job. She had grown up in Watts, in Los Angeles. Her résumé was terrific — Cornell, English major with honors. She had a good sense of humor and sense of herself. "Were you on the barricades in the sixties?" I asked her, merely conversationally. She looked at me. "I couldn't *afford* to be a hippie," she said, which really, I think, said it all about the sixties, the rebellion of spoiled white liberals from the middle class. Women who have to support their families and have to live with reality are not feminists."

"What about the women who pose for the pictures? Are they exploited?" I asked.

"We have to fight off the applicants for porno stills and for the films," Jake said. "They think they're going to be stars. At worst, they are incredibly narcissistic. They feel the whole experience is uplifting, not degrading at all. After you understand that, it's a struggle just like any other racket. Although I'll admit you perhaps meet more sleazy people in our business than, say, in investments."

"I'm not so sure of that, Jake," the Queen said. "It's only that they dress better on Wall Street."

"We went to a party at Larry Flynt's house in Los Angeles," said Jake. "The house, of course, was weird. Since Flynt was shot and converted by Ruth Carter Stapleton, all sense of reality had been lost. His bedroom had a huge bank vault in it. The room was all dark brown and greens with a giant oil painting of Jesus over the bed. The entire bookcase, as far as I could tell, was filled with books on death and dying.

"But the people at the party were like any other set of conventioneers. One magazine had just put a woman on the masthead as publisher, and her sole job was to go out and fuck the wholesalers. I know an awful lot of supposedly straight businesses that use entertainment the exact same way. Everyone there was buzzing about the hotline phone numbers for a sex message. One magazine at its peak was getting *eight hundred thousand* calls a day on their number. The phone company would get seven cents a call; the magazine, two cents. That's sixteen thousand dollars a day. Tell me that our countrymen are not obsessed. This is why we keep on buying gold and silver."

"You really want to talk about obscenity," Jean said, "let's talk about leveraged buyouts. Tell me that William Simon walking away with over sixty million dollars on a risk-free investment of as little as a hundred thousand of his own dough is not the most obscene thing you've ever heard. What's going on in leveraged buyouts makes us look like Goldilocks and the Three Bears."

The public paid $27.50 for 3½ million shares of Gibson Greeting Cards in May. Gibson Greetings had been a subsidiary of RCA. William E. Simon, former secretary of the treasury, and a partner owned 65.6 percent of the company acquired in a technique called the leverage buyout. Essentially the technique involved buying a company with loans collateralized by the company's own assets. *In other words, you and I decide we want to buy a division of WXY Corporation. We determine what the division may be worth, go to some friendly banks eager to lend money, and say, "Lend us the funds to buy this division from WXY."*

We pledge the assets of the division against the loans. And we ourselves put a value on the company when we approach the lenders. After we buy the division, we'll bring it public as a separate entity and at a premium price. Then we can deal with the bank debt and make ourselves rich in the process. No risk, except to the new stockholders, who sink or swim with our management ability. These leveraged buyouts occur daily on Wall Street, with debt replacing equity and the banks holding billions of dollars' worth of paper that may or may not someday leave them holding empty bags.

"There are always bigger thieves around," Jake said. "Another reason to buy gold. But we're lucky. Who would ever think that Jackie Kennedy's snatch could cause a revolution and allow us to live like a king and a queen?" He raised his glass in a toast to his wife. They were respectively seventy-two and sixty-eight years old.

* * *

A recent Census Bureau study said that six million wives now earn more than their husbands. The number of women workers has jumped from seventeen to forty-three million since 1950, an increase to a current 42.7 percent of the total workforce. I always wonder, when I make a decision, "What is my down side? How badly can I get hurt if I do the following?" This planning also includes wondering about the future of my business. Who will be my clients in the next five, ten years? Obviously I am going to be dealing with many more women, who will be making more money decisions than ever before. I also have to consider what areas in which to invest for the future. Where is the growth going to be in the next decade?

What is the ultimate in combining sex and money? It is the business of the future, the hype for the eighties and nineties: biogenetics, the science that can produce the superrace, the science that can make us immortal. There is a man I know who *knows*. Like the Leprechaun, he is nervous about what he tells you. He hates to stand still, because there are too many things in the world to discover; too many people from Washington wanting the word; too much money to be made without wasting time with fools. This man is the Professor, and he reminds me of M, James Bond's chief of the British Secret Service.

I see the Professor every summer when he rents a house in the seaside community where we live for three months a year. There are legends about this place, so it attracts people who care about history. General Philip H. Sheridan of the Union Army summered here. Wild Bill Donovan, the founder of the OSS, lived here and recruited heavily among its residents. The daughter of F. Scott Fitzgerald sits here in her house looking over a marsh out to sea. The lights that flash in the distance are not green, but there is magic here, and that magic attracts the Professor.

242

At an August cocktail party, I waited for a moment when the Professor stood alone, carefully tasting a martini as if in his mind he were breaking the gin down into its component parts. I couldn't waste his time, so I was prepared to pounce quickly, take my lesson, and get out.

"Professor," I started, "do you recall in the movie *The Graduate* when the man at his parents' party tells Dustin Hoffman, 'Plastics'?"

"Certainly," said the Professor.

"I want to know the word for the eighties," I told him. "Just one word, like 'plastics.' "

He savored another sip of his drink, looked at me, and said, "Imaging."

"I was hoping you'd say 'biogenetics.' "

"You want to hear only what *you* want to hear," said the Professor. "This is typical of your generation. If I were going to stress that area, I would not use the term biogenetics. I would rather use bio*hype*. That is what has characterized that world so far."

"If I can really be selfish, Professor, where can I start to find out what's going on with biohype?"

"You're transparent." He smiled. "But I do know a man you can call. He is a malevolent sort, antisocial in quite a destructive way. He is a biologist as Werner von Braun was a physicist. One gets the impression that this man would work for anyone who would build him a laboratory and provide unlimited bodies on which he could work.

"Now," he said, "I keep hooking the ball off the tee. I think perhaps it's too much right hand. What do you think?" I think that golfers should always ask advice of people with twenty-seven handicaps.

The next week I called the Professor's biologist. Why did I reject imaging and insist on biogenetics? Again, my inquiry involved common sense. The two areas that seemed to summon up the most speculation, the most hype, if you will, involving the next twenty years of investment opportunity are robotics and genetic engineering. So far there are very few ways to make a pure play in robotics. Most of the companies involved in the field are small divisions of corporate giants. To buy stock in the giant because of a tiny robotics division makes no sense. A pure play involves just that: buying a company involved only in the area you seek. On the other hand there are dozens of companies participating solely in biogenetics.

When you invest in future technology, in pie in the sky as opposed to basic industries, you must do it in an area surrounded by *emotion*. It may be years before any biogenetics company makes any money at all. But the emotion of finding a company that makes a breakthrough in cancer research or in solving the food problems of the world or in manufacturing artificial blood can send that stock through the roof. I always want to have a small amount of money in areas that collective emotion can push through the roof. Genentech was the first of the biohype companies to go public. The first day it offered its shares, in 1982, the stock jumped from 35 to 80. A great rush if you owned it at 35; a little different perspective if you got sucked in at 79¾.

Investing in emotional fields requires the guidance of an expert. It is no different if you need help with a ruptured disc or a problem in labor relations. Who is your expert in the field? Who can tell you what companies to watch? The Professor's name got me to my expert. He was prepared to give me thirty seconds as a courtesy and go back to his work.

"I'm going to call you Dr. Mendel. Okay with you?" I said. "I give all my heroes nicknames." (Gregor Mendel was the person who gave us the principles of heredity, Mendelian law. You know, two blue-eyed parents will have a blue-eyed child, but if one parent has brown eyes and one parent blue, then . . . Well, you remember from sex linked traits in high school.)

My Mendel liked that. His sandy hair grew in clumps from his head like a scarecrow's. "I'm a perverse bastard," he said, smiling, and offered me a hard, dry handshake. Many stockbrokers had contacted him in the past, but they always seemed to call at dinnertime and they always wanted to sell him annuities. He wanted to talk about biology and about making gobs of money. Dr. Mendel looked very much like the actor Donald Sutherland. He had the ability to throw a wicked grin at you from right field, and it left you with no doubt that he was up to no good. "You probably think that all scientists are alike," he told me. "And you probably went almost up to trigonometry and struggled with accounting and all you remember from biology was dissecting a crayfish and putting it down a girl's sweater."

I told him that was a reasonable summation.

"Well," he said, "let me tell you one of the differences between computer scientists and us stars of the world of biology." Dr. Mendel told me that of prime importance was the ego of the biologists. "We are out to win Nobel Prizes and we believe we walk on water. Most of us are Jewish, because Catholics don't want to do this research; too much conflict with their faith."

"Gregor Mendel was a Catholic monk," I pointed out.

"True, but Mendel experimented only with peas," my doctor said. "Faith was a lot simpler in the nineteenth century.

"Now," he went on, "computer types don't know how to speak to humans. They fear germs. They talk with their heads down, and their hobbies all seem to include playing the clarinet. But there are several major differences between us. One to remember is that computer scientists manipulate to send us a more efficient American Express bill. *We* manipulate to cure cancer. That's why we deserve our egos.

"My favorite difference," he said, "is sexual. The computer boys are locked into their terminals. This is sex to them. Especially since *they get a response*. Playing the games on the keyboard replaces any human activity; they don't want it and they don't really need it. But I and my fellows love women. Don't get me wrong. I can also spend seven days in a lab. But when I emerge, I want a strange piece of ass." He leered at me and gave that work-of-the-devil grin.

Enormous monies are needed to develop and implement research in the field of biogenetics. For instance, Genentech raised almost $87 million for the clinical testing of only three compounds. Many of the new companies for this reason have affiliated with major drug corporations. This gives them not only financial clout, but the ability (and the necessary huge staffs) to deal with domestic and foreign regulatory authorities, like the Food and Drug Administration.

The basic area of all this research by all the genetic companies is recombinant DNA technology, essentially, messing around with the stuff of life. The concentration has been on two major applications: human health care and agricultural research. Blood fractions are involved in much of the research, laboratory-engineered fractions to make blood purer, free from adulterations like hepatitis and AIDS, and much less expensive than ordinary plasma. Immunology is another large area of research, the campaign to increase the body's resistance to disease. Artificially produced lymphokines, regulatory proteins, are in early stages of production; they are the proteins that can attack and regulate disease and build up the body's immune systems. In agricultural applications, this research would lead to increased production of plants and plant foods, the growth of soil-enriching ingredients, and the biological control of harmful organisms and insects.

Dr. Mendel was married and had three children. He paid little attention to any of them. After we started to do business I came one night for a drink to his house. Mendel's wife looked older than he. Her hair was gray and unbrushed. She was dressed for comfort, not style, in unpressed slacks and a tan cashmere sweater that she must have owned in college. She was in her early forties but looked as if she had given up on a lot of things for a long time. She was eating dinner alone in the kitchen, and she was trying to pour salt out of the kind of salt cellar that grinds its contents. "It has to be ground, Alice," Dr. Mendel said. "She's a physicist," he added, as if that explained everything.

He always dressed impeccably — neatly pressed three-piece suits, highly polished shoes, shirts with French cuffs. Mendel loved to trade stocks and he loved to talk. "Can you fix me up with women?" he said one day. "I'm high as a kite, all charged up. I need the release that Alice cannot provide."

"I'd fix you up with either my sister or my mother, but not until you've won a Nobel."

"Why, you son-of-a-bitch . . . ." he started, then saw that I was joking. "Never mind. I never have problems getting women. I have a technique."

I asked him about it.

"My technique is in two parts," he said. "And I use it on graduate students who idolize me, at receptions where I am well known, or on trips where I have never before met the person. The first part of the technique is that I say unusual things. When asked what I do, I say, 'I spin flax into gold,' or 'I have perfected a technique to grow a potato the size of a watermelon or corn that reaches five stories.' That gets them interested.

"Then I don't waste time; then I state the obvious in un-usual terms. For instance, I say, 'I would like to eat Jell-o out of your belly button,' or 'I would like to start dinner by kissing between every one of your toes.' To some, this sounds ridicu-lous. Those women think I'm kidding. Others, and there are many, know I'm deadly serious. If I tell them this at lunch, I take them to a public place where no one would suspect and I kiss them and touch them and take their hands and put them on me." His voice rose. "I take them to a church or to an empty wing of a museum or to the back stairs in an office building where no one would ever think of going. It is romantic and exciting, so much more than a motel. And if friends see you going into a church or a museum, who would guess? None of them have the imagination of a biologist. You have to under-stand that I am in a field that creates miracles; there are no other fields that create *miracles*."

Suddenly Dr. Mendel began being recruited by Wall Street

as heavily as a first-round draft choice. A venture capitalist told me, "We're combing the corridors of all the major universities for biologists. We go in, target the right guy, the biggie, and say, 'Do you want to be a millionaire?' One thing about these academics, they see the kids in jeans in Silicon Valley and it kills them to see *them* or you making a fortune. You wait long enough, everything happens. And they figure now is their time.

"At Harvard, none of them invested in Otto Eckstein's Data Resources, and he sold out for millions. That panicked the academics; they're nervous that they'll miss out again. So we've got all America's scientists signing up for ten or fifteen percent of the action; the only ones who say they'll stay above it all are the ones who are lucky enough to have married money."

Half a dozen companies chased Dr. Mendel, but he was chasing two things: women of all ages, and factors in the blood that could be trained to wipe out cholesterol. He finally signed with a company that gave him 12½ percent of the deal, and he was left totally alone to conduct his research.

"What is their business plan?" I asked Dr. Mendel.

"They tell me that they go after a pitcher and a catcher and we make our first breakthrough in November. That's the plan. That, and I've got two hundred and fifty thousand shares. Comes the next window of greed and we go public."

When financial types talk about "looking for a window," it means just that, an opening. If a private company wants to go public and the investment climate is decidedly fearful (that is, the market is lousy), then they will wait for a more receptive moment, those times when greed suddenly reappears. In other words, a greedy window in a wall of fear.

Mendel would escape from the laboratory quite often and come to my office to trade. One day he said to me, "I took one of the secretaries in this building between floors down the fire exit, had her naked from the waist up."

"You are one sick scientist," I told him.

"Not sick at all." He smiled. "I just do the things people

dream about. I find a building full of lawyers and bankers and stockbrokers very conducive to sex. It goes with the ambience."

Many times he would stop to chat with different brokers; he would ask people at random what scientific breakthroughs they thought the most significant. He seemed quite interested in the comments of Jane the Impaler. Big Jimmy Minot commented to me, "What's he looking for, a model for the Bride of Frankenstein?"

What I was looking for was a system to acquire the biogenetic companies. There were so many stocks from which to choose and there was so much guesswork about which would prosper, it was difficult to make a selection.

"Here's how you play biohype," Dr. Mendel told me. "You buy *five* companies in small amounts, one hundred shares each." He bought a hundred each of Genentech, Biogen, Molecular Genetics, Collaborative Research, and Genetics Institute. I will do the same. Using these vehicles as I would use a savings account, every time the stock market or the Dow Jones average declines 25 points, I'll buy another hundred shares of each, regardless of price. These are representative companies in the field, all with strong cast positions. Except for Genentech, they are numerically cheap; none sells for over $20 a share. I predict that within four years one of the companies will be out of business, one about the same price as today, one lower, and two of the companies up over ten times. It is almost impossible to pick one. But if you buy a package and *keep* buying, you will have a bonanza, because today's biohype will be tomorrow's riches. This is an excellent way and a relatively safe way to buy any industry that you think has an extraordinary investment potential for the future.

After I had known Dr. Mendel for some time I became used to his tales of lust in hotel ladies' rooms or in movie theaters deserted in the afternoon. One day I left the office to play a four-thirty squash match, intending to return for some quiet work without the interruption of phones. The board room was still at six-thirty, the desk quote machines frozen on the closing prices, the news tickers asleep for the night, as if everything important ended with the last trade on the New York Stock Exchange.

The door to my office was closed, but I thought nothing of it. The cleaning crew often shut the doors to the private offices when they had finished vacuuming. I barged right in and flipped on the overhead light, and there was Dr. Mendel, his head buried between the legs of Jane the Impaler Kaplan, who lay full length on my couch. Her pantyhose were draped over my Quotron; her shoes sat on my desk. The two people jumped to their feet, Jane talking a blue streak and Mendel just grinning his bad-boy smile. I didn't excuse myself. It was my office.

"I think we can all sit down and talk about it," Jane said. "We're adults."

"There's nothing to talk about," I said. "Feel free. I just object to the place you chose."

"You're not going to tell Up-Your-Gross Smith," she said, looking wistfully at her pantyhose.

"This is absurd," said Dr. Mendel to me. "Why don't you just take yourself out to dinner for an hour or so? There's nothing to talk about; find a logical solution. I just offered one."

"I have a better idea. Why don't *you* two go out for dinner." By God, they left. Jane put her shoes on over her bare feet, they straightened themselves out, and they left. The next day I was in the office early. Jane the Impaler had usually made a dozen phone calls by the time I arrived. She did not show up the entire morning. At two o'clock I heard from Dr. Mendel. "You're not mad at me, are you?" he asked.

"Of course not," I said. "I'm thrilled to have my clients bird-dogged on my couch."

"*You're* my stockbroker," he promised. "Don't you know that the biologist's theme song is 'I'm Always True to You Darling in My Fashion?'"

"I'm relieved to hear that," I said.

He paused. "But I know you'll understand. You don't really

do anything with tax shelters. I thought it would be fair if I threw Jane a little something in that department . . ."

The next morning, Jane the Impaler was at her desk when I walked in. She was, naturally, on the phone. Cradling the receiver under her chin, she handed me an envelope and gave me her biggest smile. I worried when Jane Kaplan smiled at me. Sitting at my desk, I ripped open the envelope. Inside was a handwritten note from Jane. It said, "The businessman saw a prostitute in a hotel lobby. He asked her how business was. 'Terrific,' the prostitute answered. 'Every prick's a prospect . . .' " But I took solace in the happy marriages among my customers, even in the relationships reported in the press.

Mary Cunningham recently resigned from Seagram to work full time with her husband, William Agee, in his venture capital business. The *New York Times* said, "She decided she couldn't serve two bosses."

At the end of the first week in December, the White House could say, "The recovery is on track and the leading indicators show substantial economic improvement is still ahead. Full steam ahead." Unemployment in the nation had fallen to 8.4 percent in November, the lowest in two years. At the same time, the Dow Jones Industrial Average was off 12 points, to 1265.24, with stockbrokers and their clients continuing to suffer as secondary issues, *not* the Dow Jones thirty stocks, continued to be clobbered. But greed is always just beneath the surface.

Remember, fear and greed are the emotions that control the stock market. Greed will dominate in the remainder of this decade as the volume of trading continues to reach record levels, and investors perceive that more money can be made in shares of companies than in real estate, old masters, antiques, or precious metals. Greed makes everyone want to participate. It is chic to be involved in trading the market, the way it became chic to buy Pop art or Eames chairs. The pressure to become part of the crowd is intense. We are a nation of faddists, and no one is going to want to be left out of the action.

It is beginning already. A lawyer client of mine brought me a client of his, a woman newly divorced who needed guidance in handling her settlement. I was just into my explanation that bonds pay interest twice a year, when a man dressed in a black Chesterfield coat jumped into my office and slammed the door behind him. "You spend one nickel of my money," he yelled at everyone, "and you're finished in this town, *finished*."

The woman was on her feet in an instant, her face contorted like a sprinter's. She grabbed a letter opener from the top of my desk. "Don't follow me, Simon!" she screamed, and went for the man in the Chesterfield.

It happened so fast that neither the lawyer nor I had time to react. Man and woman grappled and fell onto my couch and from there onto the floor. The lawyer and I got them separated, each still straining to get to the other. The former husband and wife were still screaming, but murder no longer seemed likely.

"There is a restraining order on you, Simon," the lawyer said to the man. "You are not supposed to appear within a mile of my client."

"That's no client, that was my *wife*," the ex-husband raged. "I don't want IBM sold to buy *bonds*."

"I'll do what I want!" the wife exclaimed.

The lawyer looked at me and took his client by the arm. "We can't talk now," he said. "She's in a state. I'll call tomorrow and make an appointment."

"This will cost you, Simon," she added to her ex as the lawyer swept her out the door.

The man in the Chesterfield was bruised, rumpled, and out of breath. "I don't feel so well," he said. I indicated the couch, and he flopped down on it. I went to my desk and dialed a client with whom I wanted to discuss a new computer-software company he had just bought. The ex-husband lay on the couch, massaging his neck. When I hung up he said, "The line between love and hate is very thin."

"I've heard that," I said.

He stared at me. "I was attached to that IBM."

252

"I could see that."

He stared at me silently, embarrassed. "That software company," he finally said. "I couldn't help overhearing . . ."

"Yes?"

Still rubbing his neck, he grinned hesitantly. "It sounded awfully good. I feel like a fool but . . . do you think I could buy a few hundred shares?"

When the blood is up, the action in the stock market is irresistible. And the blood is going to be up through the rest of the decade. Simon may not have his IBM. But the software company won't come after him with a letter opener, either.

With the first snows beginning to fall, the sad stirrings of Christmases past began to show up in the customer phone calls. A divorced lady client called me. "I need a fix," she said. "You've got to buy me something volatile; something I can watch go up and down so I have something to look forward to every day."

"What's wrong?" I asked her. She was attractive, in her mid-thirties, and had a good job helping to run the state's department of tourism. She had two pre-teen-age children.

"It's so damned depressing to have limits," she said. "I'm driving to work this morning at seven-fifteen and I'm stuck at a traffic light. Since it's so early, I haven't had time to do *anything*, so I'm putting my make-up on while the light is red. I look up and there's this guy alongside in the next car. He's looking good, especially for seven-fifteen in the morning, and he's shaving. He's got an electric razor plugged into his cigarette lighter. Well, we both looked at each other and we instantly *know*: there's no time, it's too much effort, we've both got so much baggage to drag with us. So we shrugged and laughed at each other and both thought that that traffic light meeting probably would have been the best moment we could have had.

"Do me a favor. Find me something volatile I can watch. Something that's going to move quickly, up and down."

Epilogue

December is for children and stockbrokers. Children because of Christmas, stockbrokers because it is the season of tax-loss selling, a yearly exercise that creates losses in portfolios against profits taken earlier in the year. It also creates the biggest month for commissions.

"It's wonderful," says Paul the Bachelor. "You spend eleven months of the year trying to make a score, and four weeks trying your damnedest to give it all back." Customers and stockbrokers alike almost never sell a stock for a loss until December. For eleven months a year we are all optimists. On the twelfth month we face reality because it is painless. It is the month of Christmas and Chanukah. It is the month of office parties. No one points fingers or calls names in December. No one fires his money manager or investment adviser. Everyone leaves that for the new year, and tax-loss selling is something joyful you do after a luncheon that includes two drinks and perhaps even some wine.

Up-Your-Gross Smith held a mandatory sales meeting on December 14. After the usual pitch for products he wanted us to push, he clapped his hands three times and three women walked out of his office. Each wore a dark suit, dark stockings, and had on her lapel a pin in the form of a green dollar sign.

"These are the women from Cold Calling Corps," Smith said proudly. "They are going to lead us to the end of the eighties and into the nineteen nineties, because they are going to bring us unprecedented new business. These ladies are hired on for the first quarter of next year. They will circulate among you, making a hundred and fifty to two hundred calls per day to bring you leads. These leads will bring you orders; these orders will make you commissions. It is proven that women callers are fifty percent more effective, that they get through to their objective sixty percent of the time more than men, and that men pay *seventy percent* more attention to what a woman says on the phone. Use them, gentlemen, use them and prosper."

Jane the Impaler raised her hand. "What are they going to cost me?" she asked. "If they're my Christmas present, I'd rather have the cash."

Big Jimmy Minot blew his whistle, and a minute later we heard the cowbell of Mad Mark the Institutional Salesman, who was buried in his department under research reports; he never deigned to come to meetings. But the rest of us stayed and learned what miracles would be wrought by the new system.

Later, as I was leaving after finishing some paperwork, Peter the Bargain King stopped me in front of the Reuters news ticker. "It's all over," he said; "our whole way of life down the toilet."

"You mean the cold-callers?" I asked. "Don't worry; they'll be gone in two weeks."

"First the trickle, then the torrent," he said. "We're no longer in the business we love of buying and selling stocks. We're in the insurance game, the tax shelter, option, commodity games. Cradle-to-grave financial planning isn't why I came into the investment world. I came in to buy and sell Occidental Pete, to push and pull General Motors and Texaco. I came in it to buy something for one dollar and sell it for two.

"Now they're telling me I've got to take a legal pad, go to my best client's home, sit down with him and his wife, and say, 'Have you considered an individual retirement fund?' I mean, do I look like a pisher, or what?"

At the elevator, Paul the Bachelor was waiting for me. "Got a lot of plans for the holidays?" I asked him.

"I liked the looks of those cold-callers," he said. "Smart

merchandising. Well dressed; well groomed. The blonde I liked especially. Nice touch, with the dollar-sign pins."

"Any office gossip these days, Paul?"

"Would you believe that broker who sits in back of me and has been seeing my secretary has broken her heart? He gives her excuses and only three nights a week, between six o'clock and eight, when he's supposedly seeing clients. I wouldn't care; it's his life. But she comes in crying and she's good for nothing the whole day. The latest? She's breaking up with him because he won't buy her a Cuisinart. He told her his wife's got a Cuisinart and she never uses it, so why should he make the same mistake twice? Can you love more than one woman at one time?"

"I don't know, Paul, can you?"

"I thought I was in love last week, but her children kept coming into the room and I thought, 'You buy anything today, you've got to buy the whole package.' " He looked at me and sighed a sigh as old as sighs. "It isn't easy," he said, and he pushed the button for the lobby.

As I entered my garage I spied the Leprechaun, his coattails disappearing into the elevator as the doors shut. I watched until the light stopped at 4, then ran up the back stairs to head him off. As he was unlocking the front door of his Mercedes, I grabbed him by the belt of his tweed coat.

"Aha!" I said.

The Leprechaun jumped as if he were going to be mugged. "Haven't I helped you enough this year?" he pleaded. "Aren't I entitled to a holiday?" He tried to pry me loose from his belt, but, having run up three flights, I was not going to let go.

"Someday you'll need me," I said.

He snorted. "I've already got an IRA."

Then I realized that the Leprechaun was drunk. "You went to a Christmas party, Leprechaun?" I was incredulous. The Leprechaun, like Mad Mark, joined nothing. He was drunk and defensive.

"We all do things that make us uncomfortable," he said.

256

"Like letting myself be assaulted in my parking garage by people looking for handouts. But if that's what it takes to allow me on my way, buy Digital. It's going to double its sales in nineteen eighty-four, and the idiots that sold the stock at seventy will be clamoring to get back in at ninety." I loosened my hold on the Leprechaun's coat. He smoothed himself down and got into his car. I knocked on his window and he lowered it about six inches. "I do promise to return the favor sometime," I said. "Merry Christmas."

"Fool's names and fool's faces," he replied, and the window slid up with a *snick*.

It was an exciting finish to a record-breaking year. The Dow Jones Industrial Average finished up over 20 percent; the Standard and Poor's 500 Average was up over 17 percent; inflation and the prime rate were lower; and gold was down 15 percent for the last twelve months, to $380.75. But a *new idea* to start the year, a buy signal on Digital. This was the kind of news that sends stockbrokers skipping home, never minding snow, ice, traffic jams, or being caught in the correct-change toll booth line a nickel short.

Next week it would be back to the action that never stops, back to the characters and the adventures, the "almosts" and the "if onlys." Every new year was the same in this sense: prices change, the names change, but fear and greed are immutable. If we can learn to recognize these emotions when they smack us in the face, we can all grab a Leprechaun and begin to make ourselves some money.

I stopped for gas at my local station, half a mile from my house. Snow was falling, and the two sons of the station's owner were stringing Christmas lights around the windows of the garage. Herbert the Big Hitter was supervising the filling of his Eldorado's tank. To his credit, Herbert would not own anything that was not made in America. "Sea Island cotton, Jack Daniels, and Detroit City," he would trumpet to his clients who drove Jaguars and Mercedeses and BMWs. He waved to me:

"It's going to be a great fucking year in 'eighty-four. I can feel it," he said. "I'm gearing up for the biggest production, the biggest markets in history."

"That's not what George Orwell said," I responded.

"Who the hell is he with?" Herbert asked. "Prudential-Bache? I bet he doesn't even do half a million gross a year." He spun away in his Cadillac, having tipped the owner $10 for checking the air in his tires.

As I took back my gas credit card, the owner chuckled to me. "I see another satisfied customer dressed as Santa Claus kidnaped his broker and tortured him for twelve days. The broker was chained and handcuffed to a bed and his nose was broken. Anybody ever threaten you like that?" Everyone in the office had joked about the incident, reported by all the news services, but everyone had his own horror stories, and if you looked carefully enough, you'd see we all had crossed our fingers, grateful that some strange dissatisfied Santa hadn't yet found a set of handcuffs in our size.

My wife, Susan, had the fire going and the cork out of a bottle of wine. The children were all away for the evening. We dined alone and later had port in the living room in front of the fire. "This is the greatest," I said. "Some pasta, some wine, a good port, and, most important, an idea for next week. It's Digital at seventy, near the bottom. What an idea!"

"I've got a better idea," she said, and we went upstairs. Susan shut off the phone "so that some client can't call on his way to Palm Beach to remind you to take a loss on some municipal bond."

"It's a business that never stops," I said. We could hear the howling of the wind and the creaking of our old house.

"Everything stops sometime," she said. And she was right.